Reconstructing the Civic

Reconstructing the Civic

Palestinian Civil Activism in Israel

AMAL JAMAL

SUNY PRESS

Published by State University of New York Press, Albany

For information, contact State University of New York Press, Albany, NY
www.sunypress.edu

Library of Congress Cataloging-in-Publication Data

Name: Amal Jamal.
Title: Reconstructing the Civic: Palestinian Civil Activism in Israel / Amal Jamal.
Description: Albany : State University of New York Press, [2020] | Includes
    bibliographical references and index.
Identifiers: ISBN 9781438478715 (hardcover : alk. paper) | ISBN 9781438478722
    (pbk. : alk. paper) | ISBN 9781438478739 (ebook)
Further information is available at the Library of Congress.

Library of Congress Control Number: 2020940102

10 9 8 7 6 5 4 3 2 1

For Randa

and

for all those free spirits that aspire to make our life better

Contents

Graphs and Tables

Prologue

This study took a number of years to complete for many reasons—some related to its nature and some not. One reason I delayed publication relates to the sensitivity of the issue at hand. Much of this study was based on a public opinion survey regarding civil society organizations (CSOs). The public's attitudes toward these associations had to be handled cautiously, as I did not want them to be misused for other purposes. This fear was born out of my past experiences conducting research on the culture of media consumption, in which I, fully committed to scientific values, published data that were critical, received poorly, and conceived as highly detrimental to these media institutions. While the data were published to serve the scientific community and the public good of society, these institutions summarily ran a campaign against the research and ultimately called into question its value. In this research, I expose the extent of the community's familiarity, acceptance, support, or rejection of specific CSOs; and its findings again gave me pause. To escape the implications of the "rating culture" that is gradually taking hold of our lives, including in the field of civil society, I hesitated to release this information, despite society's expectation that this community is more civil and tolerant.

The objective of this study is to explore the general processes and trends of civic engagement and organizational networking in the Palestinian community in Israel (PCI). The PCI's vibrant community of CSOs serves as an ideal case study for exploring patterns of civic struggle and resistance vis-à-vis policies of compliance and subordination in ethnic states. Therefore, these statistics are not meant to identify the public's attitudes at a specific moment in time, but rather to reflect the development of its consciousness and its patterns of collective action, which might either reflect or contradict the organizational and institutional processes taking place in the broader social and political environment of civil society.

A second reason is personal and has to do with the positions to which I was appointed immediately after securing the funds to conduct the first phase of this research. First, I was elected as head of the Political Science Department at Tel Aviv University in 2006. I served in this position for three years, during which my days were packed with tasks and plans that left little time for reflection or writing. When my tenure was over in 2009, I was offered a position as the director of I'lam—Arab Center for Media Freedom, Development and Research in Nazareth. I'lam's importance and its central position in Palestinian civil society led me to accept the position, which was far more demanding than I initially imagined. These two management positions involved heavy responsibilities and were time-consuming. Managing a civic association and simultaneously exploring its role in society is not an easy task. It is a sensitive combination, which entails a careful, ethical balance. Therefore, I decided to wait to regain the distance necessary to sensitively judge this phenomenon. I left my position in I'lam at the end of 2017. This step enabled me not only to devote more time to finish this research, but also to reflect on the findings of the research and reveal new insights based on the combination between my personal experience and professional capacities.

Leading a civic association helped me to understand many issues that were not immediately clear to me in the beginning as a scholar with no practical experience in the field. While I initially feared such a delay would prove a disadvantage, it revealed itself to be the opposite. Many of my personal insights followed a long period of contemplation, analysis, and evaluation. In this time, I managed to develop a deeper, anthropological perspective on the field of civil society. This perspective enabled me to strengthen my capacity to make sense of the tremendous amount of data I had gathered over the last 10 years. While the age of these data risked rendering the research outdated, the passage of time offered many benefits. For example, the process of gathering data never stopped. I was constantly conducting interviews and focus groups. I participated in many meetings of civil society activists and even initiated several new projects that have found a central place in the civil sphere, such as the Freedom Protection Council and the Strategic Thinking Project—two initiates I led and aimed at empowering civil society activism in Israel in general and in the PCI in particular. I also conducted surveys that enabled me to compare data along the 10 years of research and was able to identify many similarities and differences in this span of time. As civil society is an ever evolving field, it cannot be understood through rigid or stable constraints; this time was therefore necessary to provide an accurate depiction of the field and to be understood through open, varied, and dynamic concepts and methodologies.

Before moving ahead, I would like to thank many people who helped me complete this research. First, special thanks to Aaron Back, who was kind enough to support some of this research through the Ford Foundation ten years ago.

Umayma Diab was the first to assist in executing the first survey of the research. She also helped to build the initial questionnaire, collect materials, and partially analyze the statistical data. I would like to thank her for her generous help in every step of this research and for adding many insightful notes, which I found to greatly improve this research. I also wish to thank Liron Lavi, who assisted in analyzing some of the statistical data and whose explanations thereon were very valuable. Her assistance was vital to the study's completion. I would like also to thank Victoria Koukvin for helping with the statistical data analysis of the second survey and Camellia Darawsheh and Rasha Kinaan for helping to finalize the bibliography and streamline the spelling of the Arabic names.

Kholod Massalha and Widad Helo from I'lam assisted in conducting the second survey and organized the focus groups with leaders of many central Palestinian CSOs. They put great effort into making these challenging tasks possible, and I deeply thank them for their fantastic work. Also at I'lam, Samah Basoul provided many notes on the book, which helped to improve its quality. She also assisted in embedding much of the data into the text.

Also, Ali Haider's work on an early draft of the manuscript was particularly enlightening and helped to identify some missing parts of my analysis, while also contributing his own vast knowledge in these areas. Ali was the manager of Sikkuy, an Arab-Jewish CSO at the time, and his experience was a very important factor in reflecting on the manuscript.

My dear friend Amal Abu Zidan provided very valuable comments on this study. He read the manuscript and provided many insights based on his experience as a civic activist.

I owe a special thanks to Professor Yael Yishai and her willingness to read the manuscript and meet me personally to discuss some ideas and suggestions for improving the analysis. Her vast experience and extensive knowledge contributed a great deal to the book's organization and helped to highlight its contribution to the complexities of this field.

I would like to thank Anna Kensicki for her tremendous help in preparing this manuscript for publication. Anna's edits and insights helped improve the flow of the book and clarified many of its arguments for readers.

I would also like to thank the two anonymous reviewers of the manuscript for their valuable comments and suggestions, which helped to improve the flow of the arguments made in this book.

I also wish to thank the many surveyors who interviewed people in the PCI far and wide. Without their efforts, the data collected for this book would not have been possible. In this vein, I also want to thank the people who participated in the focus groups' sessions and enriched my understanding of civil society. All those who agreed to be interviewed in person and who contributed their knowledge and experience to the book were integral to the research's success.

My thanks go also to Michael Rinella from the State University of New York Press for his generous support in the entire production process.

And finally, I would like to thank my dear family, especially my life partner, Randa, for allowing me to dedicate many hours to complete this manuscript.

Chapter 1

Introduction

This book is about the causes, patterns, and goals of civic activism among subaltern, homeland minorities and how and why they seek to reconstruct the meaning of the civic in ethnic states. It is also an effort to enhance our understanding of how and for what purpose intellectual elites mobilize national minorities and institutionalize their political visions and interests in civic and human rights organizations. Why and when do homeland minorities mobilize and activate civil society organizations to achieve collective goals? What types of groups and individuals carry out this venture, and to what extent does their civic activism reflect the emergence of a new type of social capital that assists them to achieve their common goals? To what extent and why do homeland minorities conceive the civic sphere as a necessary avenue through which they promote their interests and represent their identity in ethnic states? To what extent can reconstructing the meaning of the civic in ethnic states assist homeland minorities in overcoming their subordination to the exclusive power of ethnic majorities in ethnic states? To what extent does decolonizing the public sphere from ethno-national underpinnings form a strategy of struggle for homeland minorities in their search for freedom and equality? The answers to these questions are governed by three environmental conditions.

The first concerns the power structures in which civic activism takes place. These structures can vary greatly. One of the major variations relates to the nature of the political regime, which can include both democratic and nondemocratic regimes with liberal, pluralistic, and egalitarian values and ethnic, illiberal, and nationalistic regimes. Another major variation in power structures relates to the positions of the social agents therein. In asymmetric power structures, the spaces to maneuver and resources afforded to different agents is a major factor in explaining their behavior. In this regard, one has to differentiate between power structures that result from a colonization process that renders indigenous peoples minorities in their own homeland and other national experiences in which the difference between indigenous and immigrants does not exist.

The second condition influencing patterns of civic activism among subaltern homeland minorities is the state's policy toward this type of activism. In this regard, one can differentiate between instances in which the state is open for change in order to represent all its citizens and acts to protect the spaces afforded to certain groups to promote their worldviews, interests, and values and the other contexts in which the state has an exclusive hegemonic national ideology serving a dominant majority and excluding other social groups that are transformed into "immigrants" in their own homeland. In this vein, one could also differentiate between two types of states. The first prioritizes a universal national identity that is inclusive of all citizens, based on equal citizenship. The second type of state does not yet possess a fully developed national identity, despite the domination and privilege it affords to certain social groups (Brubaker, 1996). Whereas the first of each differentiation is characterized as civic-republican, the second is seen as ethnic and could be either ethno-republican or ethnocratic.

The third condition dictating patterns of civic activism is the cultural and normative environment in which civic activism takes place. Here, one can differentiate between two contexts. The first is an open and inclusive environment based on prioritizing individual liberty, autonomy, and equality. The second is traditionalist and based on an exclusivist common good that is often associated with a patriarchal social structure, a theologically committed culture, or both; these factors limit the values of the former and instead promote a belief system that can violate basic civic values.

The first contribution of this book is conceptual. It demonstrates that the conceptualization of social mobilization, especially of subaltern homeland minorities based on an epistemology of compliance, or groups' adherence to legal, political, and social norms, is not only misleading, but also empirically and normatively inaccurate. An epistemology of compliance views power relations from the perspective of the dominant institutional order and therefore focuses on exploring existing gaps between norms and behavior (Brosig, 2012). Such an epistemology, which is very dominant in institutionalist and functionalist traditions, including state-centered approaches, is not only empirically misleading, but also normatively problematic. It takes the dominant normative system and power structure for granted and thereby justifies the prevalent control mechanisms (Parsons & Harding, 2011; Jorgensen, 2010; Harding, 1993). It also views any behavior not compliant with the system as deviant and therefore illegitimate. This approach gives priority to obedience and conformity and decontextualizes political behavior, thereby missing one of the most central dimensions of non-consent, namely *dissensus* (Ranciere, 2010).

This book presents an alternative approach to the understanding of subaltern homeland minorities' political behavior. It argues that by focusing on the politics of minorities' civic mobilization, we can better understand the complexities of the field of power, especially in societies characterized by ethnic conflict and asymmetric power relations. It is argued that in such contexts, it is disagreement and contention that truly reveal the dynamics of power, manifested in the struggle of homeland minorities to transform the power structure in which they act from an exclusive nationalist one that submits them to a colonizing project into a civic political structure in which they enjoy full, equal access to decision-making mechanisms and share the values of the common good.

In broader terms, this study demonstrates that by not committing to rigid, pre-given conceptualizations of something that is ultimately dynamic, we can better understand the collective behavior of subaltern social groups (Higgs, 2001). This approach allows us to examine the ideas, motivations, and concerns behind groups' social behavior, especially when it comes to their challenge of unjust political structures. It also allows us to examine the extent to which the civic activism of members of subaltern homeland minorities leads to the rise of a counter-public based on *philia* (civic friendship), as depicted by Aristotle in the *Nicomachean Ethics* (1906), developed by Arendt in *Men in Dark Times* (1968), and turned into a necessary condition for achieving genuine justice by Schwarzenbach (1996) and Leontsini (2013).

For the purpose of illustrating this alternative approach, the following pages explore why and how subaltern homeland minorities mobilize, and demonstrates that such occurrences happen when the terrain of power relations does not grant them spaces to influence their environment, become part of the sovereign civic community, express their identity, promote their interests, and translate their expectations into policy through the active participation in the conventional political system. It is assumed that when these spaces are blocked, social groups would mobilize to overcome the structural constraints that limit their sense of being part of the civic community and constrain their political efficacy. They would use any opportunities given to them to assert their will to engage, represent their identity, and empower themselves as legitimate agents in the states in which they live. This book demonstrates that this pattern of behavior is particularly salient in states characterized by asymmetric power relations, ethnical structures, and the promotion of policies of internal colonization vis-à-vis subaltern homeland minorities. In other words, these subaltern groups are motivated by a sense of inherent unfairness that instigates patterns of collective dissent and behavior that go beyond the dominant party's conceptualization of normative political behavior.

In the following pages, we argue that the mobilization of subaltern homeland minorities is motivated in particular by these groups' elites, particularly their grievances and political aspirations (Gurr, 2015). The emerging elites of subaltern homeland minorities are not satisfied with individual rights. They aspire to transform unjust power structures and promote the integration of their identity, interests, and worldviews in the face of policies that set limits on their ability to translate resources and social capital into political power. When the political elites of subaltern homeland minorities conceive of formal political structures as limiting their maneuvering spaces, they seek alternative channels to materialize their social capital and promote their group's aspirations. Civil society activism becomes a central avenue of collective conduct to overcome the constraints imposed by the formal political structures. The civic realm, which is not completely autonomous from the state, still allows subaltern homeland minorities the avenues necessary to assert their identity and promote their interests. Such patterns of collective action and the relationship between civic activism and the state become an interesting avenue to explore.

The study of civil society—or, as Etienne Balibar calls it, "civility"—is a well-established area of the literature in which elites are portrayed as transformers of the power structure in which they maneuver to maintain spaces for contention. These spaces allow them to have a say in institutionalizing power relations (Balibar, 2002) and enable them to achieve relative autonomy from the state, especially illiberal states, which view homeland minorities as a threat to their identity. Elites of subaltern homeland minorities not only use the opportunities made available by the state's inability to control all avenues of life, but they also seek to prevent the institutionalization of power structures that eliminate their groups' ability to take part in defining the main concepts and structures of power. In other words, these elites not only challenge power relations and transform states' values to protect their own interests, but they also do so to enable a new civil, rather than ethnic, political language, as the language of the state.

The following analysis demonstrates that to conceptualize civic mobilization of subaltern homeland minorities as an articulation of civility, it must not be considered a homogenous phenomenon. Conceptualizations of challenges to the hegemonic power and politics of control is legitimate only when it takes into consideration the internal differences of the subaltern groups' own diverse belief systems.

By voicing their discontent with structures of domination, subaltern homeland minorities promote not only their own identity and interests, but also their right to internal disagreement. This disagreement could be manifested through different modes of social capital. In the following pages, we explore a case study that delves into the specific types of social capital that lead to these disagreements, namely religious patriarchal connectivity and civil professional networks. These two characteristics cause group members to be divided among themselves and compete for social loyalty in order to transform the dominant power structure.

Although these cleavages could become a burden on subaltern homeland minorities' abilities to achieve their goals, they also represent the plurality and measures of mutual recognition and tolerance that legitimate their struggle for justice. Whether these subgroups are granted a legitimate place by others or whether they plant seeds of distrust among the different factions reveals the extent to which their efforts against the dominant power structure is ultimately effective. Considering the treatment of these differences, especially between those relying on traditional modes of social capital and new civil initiatives that challenge the basic values and social structure of society, is an interesting analytical perspective that promotes a genuine understanding of subaltern homeland minorities' mobilization.

Any analytical venture of subaltern homeland minorities should be aware that the level of availability of social capital could become an opportunity for the dominant power structure to maintain the status quo. Groups' treatment of their internal differences have a direct impact on their ability to address the asymmetric, valuational, and political order. Sustained disagreement and competition for these resources enable the hegemony to demonstrate its liberal and pluralistic character, while delegitimizing or at least belittling the struggle against it. In the following pages, we examine how limitations to groups' social capital impacts subaltern groups' efficacy.

The following analysis uses Palestinian civic activism in Israel to verify its theoretical arguments and thereby provides empirical evidence about subaltern homeland minorities' civil activism in postcolonial contexts. As we explore each of the analytical frameworks of civil society and its modes of activism, we highlight its prevailing causes and patterns of mobilization. Further, this book introduces new observations on civic activism in ethnic states in a unique and infrequently examined context.

Civic activism in ethnic states with postcolonial settings is not sufficiently addressed in the literature. Exploring its causes and pattern in this context sheds new light on aspects of civic activism that go beyond the liberal settings that dominate the literature. This context enables us to explore the characteristics of civic activism more deeply than their mere functional efficacy and provides us a deeper examination into their meanings and implications on asymmetric power. Such an endeavor enables us to overcome current limitations in the civil society literature, especially those that blur activism's particularities, and reveals that civil society does not always take place in a welcoming and receptive environment.

Civic activism that seeks to transform power structures and reconstruct the meaning of the civic so that it represents the expectations of all citizens equally faces unique conditions in illiberal postcolonial settings. Exploring such a reality enables us to examine the nature and genuineness of states' commitments to democratic values and civic ideals and how their policies toward civic activism, especially of subaltern homeland minorities, relate to the discourse on democracy and liberal equity.

Further, the present context also enhances our understanding of the salience of traditional norms and patterns of social organization in subaltern movements. The civic activism of subaltern homeland minorities, which are not necessarily homogenous, is an interesting phenomenon through which we can explore the diversity of the struggle against unjust power structures. In this context, the civic activism we explore promotes a culture that not only challenges the illiberal state, but also values of the civic activists, who on their part seek to transform their own society as well. In the following pages, we explore these important differences between affirmative and transformative perceptions of the civic in traditional societies.

In this regard, we examine the patterns of civic practices that emerged in the last several decades among Palestinian citizens of Israel (PCI). The following pages explore the relationship between the social and economic changes taking place in the PCI and the emerging civil society networks engaged in the struggle not only for collective rights on the political, cultural, and economic levels, but also for the transformation of the entire exclusively ethnic power structure into an inclusive civil one. There has been a substantial growth in civil society organizations (CSOs), popular committees, and youth movements that implement this undertaking and mobilize the broader public to construct an oppositional consciousness that resists the marginalizing, repressive, and silencing policies of the state. Not only does this case represent a new approach to conceptualizing Israeli politics, but it also provides a rich empirical example for challenging well-known assertions in the literature on civic activism.

This examination reveals that emerging Palestinian elites' political desires to harness their power in the reconstruction of Israel's civic sphere uses external and internal economic resources; this, we argue, is the primary factor responsible for the PCI's unique pattern of civic activism. For the purpose of making this argument, the following pages provide new data on the PCI's emerging middle class, demonstrating that its sociopolitical elites are continually opening autonomous avenues for subaltern segments of their society to reconstruct the civil environment in Israel. One of the central avenues they are pursuing is the institutionalization of civic activism to use the legal and political opportunities given by the state to contest its policies of repression and marginalization.

This case study provides evidence as to the self-constitution of a subaltern homeland minority group in a political context characterized by conflict, domination, and colonization. It also enables us to delve deeply into the efforts of the emerging sociopolitical elite to translate its assets into social capital.

Any discussion of Palestinian civic activism in Israel must begin with a discussion of its background and its relationship with the state. When exploring the history of the Palestinian minority and the state's attitude toward it, we refer to two significant variables and compare them with other cases that appear in the literature. The first variable is the role of the PCI's indigeneity in its identity and history. This element, as the author has illustrated in a previous book (Jamal, 2011), is a significant factor governing the behavior of the Palestinian minority, its self-perceptions, and its environment. The other variable is the state's evolving, exclusivist identification as Jewish and its prioritization of this aspect of its identity over its functioning as a democracy, as manifested in the Nation-State Law, legislated in July 2018 (Abramovitch, 2018). The ramifications of the state's Jewishness on the status and rights of the PCI plays an integral role in the formation and utility of non-Jewish civil society. These two variables, which are complementary and dialectically interrelated, render this case study an interesting example through which we can explore the meanings and ramifications of civic activism in a context that could be defined as a "state of exception" (Agamben, 2005).

The PCI are part of a nation that is in conflict with the state in which they practice their citizenship. Based on this conflict, the PCI, as a homeland minority, demands an inclusive and civil, rather than ethnic and exclusivist, public and political sphere in which it has the opportunity to be taking part in determining the public good and its practices. That said, one must note that both parties' engagement in the broader Palestinian-Israeli conflict, with all that entails—historical injustices, physical and symbolic violence, and mutual mistrust—is an integral part of the PCI's identity. The centrality of these factors in the PCI's identity creates a constant and intrinsic ideological, political, and civil tension between themselves and the state. This tension is the impetus for the civic activism explored in this book, which covers Israel's policies toward land, housing, health, education, welfare, and other civil realms.

Israel's policies toward the PCI have been characterized by the continuous passage of legislation that empties Palestinian citizenship from any substantial meaning. By contrast, Palestinian politics in Israel demonstrates the insistence of Palestinian citizens on protecting their national Palestinian identity and demanding full citizenship rights in the state. The tension between these two characterizations and the role played by CSOs in managing their manifestations and repercussions are central topics to be explored. The story and characteristics of the emerging CSOs' networks are told through the discussion of the unique combination of theories and empirical data amassed over the last decade. The perspective of the author and his experience as an academic and civic activist render the following study unique. It is both an academic and practical endeavor, comprising a rich analysis of the history, data, and reflections of more than 10 years of personal engagement in the field.

The meaning of the civic is usually determined by the state through its legal and political mechanisms. Therefore, civic meaning is often characterized as statist, which in turn is perceived to be not only normative and natural, but also neutral and universal (Connolly, 1973; Mitchell, 1991). This ontological bias renders mere participation in civic activism as something that strengthens the given political order. Any alternative conception of civic activism—for example, one that does not support the pregiven political conditions—is viewed as an illegitimate form of mobilization. However, such a perspective abolishes the political aspect of civic activism, emptying it of its humanity and its intent to reconstruct the conditions and values under which one lives (Arendt, 1958). This is especially true in illiberal ethnic states, such as Israel.

The State of Israel is legally defined as Jewish, despite the fact that more that 20% of its population are not Jews. The hegemonic power structure in Israel, especially in the last several decades, has demonstrated the extent to which the dominant ideology of the state and the majority of the Jewish public are characterized by an epistemology of loyalty and compliance. Despite the structural pluralism reflected in the Israeli public sphere, it seems that a very strict spirit of procedural majoritarianism guides participation therein. Therefore, the civic in such cases submits to conditions set by majority rule, regardless of the values and perceptions it promotes. Disputing these values or perceptions and their manner of determination therefore is not considered by the state and the Jewish majority to be civic, but rather a betrayal of it.

This study demonstrates that Israel's conception of the civic stands in complete opposition to the genuine meaning of what Hannah Arendt called the *vita activa* (Arendt, 1958, 1968). Arendt's conceptualization of the civic is open not only to debating the values and patterns of collective and personal conduct with an a priori determined political community, but also to challenge the guiding political community itself. This community's boundaries are not fixed, and the transformation of its embedded power relations are encouraged to be transformed (Ranciere, 2010). Arendt's conceptualization of the *vita activa* promotes civic disagreement and communication to shape the conditions in which groups live together. Therefore, civil society is based on the continuous search for emancipation and the transformation of entire systems under which one lives. The civic is therefore an everchanging pattern of civility that not only overcomes the hegemony's political biases, but also serves an avenue through which one is liberated (Balibar, 2014, 2002). In this context, the concept of praxis, as explicated in the Aristotelian tradition, reviewed by Arendt in her theorization of the human condition, becomes very central. This concept of praxis is based on the plurality of the human condition, the necessity of communication in order to constitute the civic community and the eternal renewal of society by the continuous regeneration of society by new beginnings (Habermas, 1973).

Moreover, much of the literature on civic activism entails a liberal bias, which is committed to individualism, egalitarianism, rationalism, voluntarism, and pluralism (Smith, 1997). It assumes a given culture and a common good as condition of civility. However, these assumptions should be conceived as a result of the civic process itself. The patterns and complexities of subaltern minority groups, especially indigenous national groups that seek to reconstruct the avenues of civility in which they counter discriminatory and repressive power structures, particularly in ethnic states, is an important avenue of research that has not been addressed in the literature on collective action or on civil society.

The following analysis differentiates theoretically between the legal-procedural and the substantive dimensions of the civic. It demonstrates that this differentiation is political and a product of political power relations rather than existing a priori to them. Specifically, this study explores the conditions, both inside and outside Israel's Palestinian CSOs, that determine their aims and approach to reshaping the public sphere. This case study aids in our exploration of this theoretical argument in the context of a conflict between a hegemonic, ethno-national majority and an indigenous, subaltern national minority.

Our examination of the PCI entails not only exploring the boundaries of the civic, but also verifying its substance. Civic activism that counters a non-egalitarian political order cannot be viewed in exclusively ethnic terms, as it not only serves the interests of the minority group, but it also defends civic values that are applicable to all citizens, regardless of their origin or identity. The PCI's civic activism therefore is examined not only based on the extent to which it counters state policies to uproot Palestinian history, remold Palestinian identity, and repress efforts to integrate its view of the common good into that of the state. It also examines the extent to which this activism promotes egalitarianism, tolerance, freedom, and equality as common values that define the state and society in which it lives.

Any examination of civic activism must relate to the "civil society argument" embedded in the third wave of democratization, which posits a direct link between the growth of CSOs and the establishment of a democratic culture (Huntington, 1991; Walzer, 1992). Although one may agree with the importance of CSOs to democracy, it is doubtful that there is a unidirectional causal relationship between the two (Berman, 1997; Alexander, 2006; Edwards, 2011). The critique of this Tocquevillian tradition creates a need for a more open and pluralistic view of civic activism that incorporates subaltern experiences (Kilnani, 2001). These critiques make it clear that there is no one type of relationship between civil activism and civic values (Cohen & Arato, 1992).

Our analysis of the PCI's activism establishes that it is not the mere emergence of CSOs that determines a state's chances for democratic development. Rather, it is the dialectics between the values promoted by these CSOs and the broader encompassing political culture of the state, which enable mutual tolerance, effective plural representation, and participation of the various social and political worldviews in determining the nature of the political regime.

The following pages demonstrate that CSOs are not essentially democratic or liberal. There are forms of civic activism that use the open civil and political spaces to promote an illiberal reality and poor democracy (Berman, 1997). By contrast, the civility of the state is determined by the ability of liberal and human rights CSOs to facilitate constructive social change and promote democratic values, such as mutual tolerance, liberty, equality, and social justice.

One of the avenues addressed in the following pages relates to the well-established constructive relationship between civil society and social capital (Putnam, 2000). This relationship, which assumes that social capital enriches civility and thereby democracy, as conceived in the pluralist tradition is questioned. This questioning is even more relevant in conflict situations such as the one examined and in traditional patriarchal society. We examine this relationship in the backdrop of a newly emerging body of literature that challenges liberal bias and demonstrates that there is not an imperative relationship between social capital and democracy. Social capital is not a trait that carries inherent effects. Its political importance originates in its ability to mobilize and transform the political conditions to promote change in the mechanisms and patterns of distribution in society (Anthias, 2007).

Examining Palestinian civic activism in the Israeli context enables us to explore new theoretical avenues such as the meaning of the civic, but not according to preconceived, liberal presumptions. It challenges the context in which most treatments of civil society are examined, demonstrating the relevance of colonialism and therefore the sensitivities of postcolonial theory for the examination of civic activism. Applying postcolonial theory to the civil society and social capital literature is not new (Chatterjee, 2001). Nevertheless, exploring its treatment through a case study that does not meet the criteria set by previous scholars of the topic could be intriguing and may add new insights that are missing from the current literature on these topics.

On the empirical level, this book provides a comprehensive picture of the civic associations that were established in the last few decades and analyzes their increasingly important role in protecting the political and cultural rights of Palestinian society. These associations also provide various services that were rendered necessary as a result of the state's policies of neglect, repression, and surveillance. Our analysis traces the major social and political transformation in Palestinian civil society in Israel, especially the rising of the educated Palestinian middle class. It explores the way in which the latter seeks opportunities to institutionalize its impact on its political, social, and cultural environment.

The following study is conducted in the context of the social sciences and provides us with a deeper and unique exploration of the dynamic relationship between civil society and the state (Flyvbjerg, 2001; Ragin & Becker, 1992; Platt, 1992; Campbell, 1975). Examining the emergence of a homeland minority's civil society, its patterns of conduct, and its relationship with an illiberal, ethnic state helps to overcome three theoretical and two empirical shortcomings in the literature.

The first theoretical and empirical disadvantage is that very little research has been conducted on the civil society of minorities in conflict situations. A cursory examination of the professional literature on civil society and its relations with the state demonstrates that most literature assumes the existence of political and cultural homogeneity in the state and society (Cohen & Arato, 1992; Seligman, 1992, Edwards, 2004; Keane, 1998; Walzer, 1995; O'Connell, 1999; Ehrenberg, 1999). Most of the same literature also ignores the existence of national, cultural, and ethnic differences in civil society, which creates unique constraints for organizations advocating for social change. Despite the existence of common goals, many of these types of organizations find themselves operating within national or ethnic frameworks that the literature generally fails to recognize. Although in recent years there has been some reference to national, ethnic, and cultural diversity, this literature is still in its infancy and requires further analysis to demonstrate minority civil societies' unique range of activities and the challenges they face, especially indigenous civil societies, which struggle against illiberal and antidemocratic forces with limited funding (Alvarez et al., 2017; Jacobson & Korolczuk, 2017; Bodo, 2016).

By exploring a case study in which a subaltern group seeks to voice the injustice it faces in a reality in which a hegemonic majority asserts its own narrative and perceptions of justice, it is possible to expand on the literature on civic activism into new philosophical avenues. The struggle of CSOs to voice injustices in a system in which the dominant discursive regime does not allow others spaces of utterance and instead promotes a politics of silencing enables us provide an alternative theoretical framework to understanding and examining of civic activism.

The second theoretical and second empirical obstacle is an almost complete absence of foundational knowledge concerning the link between civic activism and the reconstruction of the civic among subaltern homeland communities. This is especially true when relating to the disposition of the minority toward services provided by the state. There is some literature that examines the role of CSOs in socially and politically empowering their society and their impact on advancing its economic well-being through the provision of basic services. However, this literature does not refer to dilemmas that arise in conflictual, postcolonial contexts, especially for minority CSOs who must cooperate with a state that simultaneously promotes policies of repression, surveillance, and neglect against them. In such cases, minority CSOs provide services to their population that indirectly facilitate these policies. The withdrawal of the state from service provision renders the civic sphere shallow; such a phenomenon leads to abolishing social rights that form a fundamental dimension of citizenship (Marshall, 1950).

Additionally, this book addresses the tensions between the minority's desire for autonomy from the state; its demand that the state shall not discriminate against it in various policy areas, such as land allocation and education; and the protection of vulnerable groups' rights against the patriarchal structure of the minority society itself. Specific dilemmas such as the involvement of the state in protecting women's rights are perceived by certain minority CSOs as a violation of the minority's cultural autonomy. Another dilemma that arises in this context is in the field of education, where some Palestinian organizations require equitable allocation of resources for Palestinian educational institutions, but at the same time strive to maintain minimal state involvement in determining the school curricula.

It is worth noting the distinction made by Foley and Edwards (1996) between civil society operating in states that limit the civil sphere, and states with an autonomous civil society. In the former, the activities of civil society challenge the regime, its institutions, and its policies, and strive to change the regime's nature. In the latter, the civil sphere is open, and therefore CSOs freely apply their resources to support a wide array of civil activities. This case study comes to critique Foley and Edwards's distinction and demonstrates that one ought not accept dichotomous and static differentiations of this field.

Palestinian civic activism demonstrates that the relationship between the state and civil society is not unidimensional and can assume a variety of shapes. These shapes vary across all aspects of life, such as state service provisions including health, education, and welfare; to the legal framework that defines the scope of civil society's freedom of assembly and expression. In states lacking a universal civic culture, the relationship between the state and civil society is impacted by their respective values (Smith, 1997; Verba

& Almond, 1963; Dahl, 1998). CSOs that seek to empower and develop the minority society and democratize the state could be viewed by the latter as a threat and thereby be labeled illegitimate, as we shall see later.

It follows that the existence of a free civic space does not necessarily equate with a reality in which civic organizations are able to influence state policy and promote equal treatment. Nominally enabling civic associations to challenge the state and its institutions could be employed as a means of promoting the democratic image of the state without being substantially democratic. The existence of free "civic space" in which society can operate and promote its various missions does not preclude the state from promoting inequitable policies that conflict with the concept of universal citizenship.

This book also challenges the dominant perceptions of social capital that prevail in the literature on civil society. It demonstrates that, despite the attention paid to social capital in various theoretical traditions, including critical Marxism, its treatment has been mostly limited to liberal and pluralistic democratic philosophy (Putnam, 2000). This literature assumes an ontological reality in which the dominant political culture is civil; however, this is not always the case. The pluralistic philosophy assumes that voluntarism, rationalism, individualism, and autonomy are given features of the social fabric. Although in many cases this is true, it cannot be assumed that they uniformly govern political processes. As we shall see, they are constructed through the political process rather than being a precondition of it, and their manifestations are a result of society's struggle over its identity and the character of the political order.

Exploring Palestinian civic activism in Israel's illiberal, postcolonial context demonstrates that social capital, as it is defined in the theoretical literature, does not aid our understanding of the complex Israeli reality in which Palestinian civic activism takes place. Examining political contexts that do not meet the existing standards in the pluralistic tradition can promote a broader understanding of the concept of social capital and its centrality in examining civic activism.

One question that arises in this context relates to the degree of cooperation between organizations and civic activists, based on their values and interests and the nature of their relationships vis-à-vis their environment. By examining patterns of civic activism, one can begin to understand how well the dominant elite succeeds in fostering organizations' connections with their environment as a means of strengthening its social capital. This is explored by examining institutionalized networks of friendship, mutual recognition, and communication channels that strive to strengthen mutual ties in an effort to influence state policy toward the needs of the society that it represents (Bourdieu, 1985).

In other words, this case illustrates how the lines of controversy surrounding the concept of social capital translate into the asymmetrical power dynamic between the Palestinian minority and the Jewish majority in Israel. It causes us to reflect on the assumptions of the common, pluralistic perception of social capital, especially its emphasis on the universality of social ties, trust, and reciprocity. The fact that the subaltern Palestinian minority in Israel is not part of the common conception of citizenship in Israel and therefore is not a partner in determining the state's civic virtues and political and legal cultures is an important factor to consider in examining the relationship between social capital, civil society, and the state.

The following pages demonstrate that the Israeli context is characterized by a "civic gap" between different types of citizens in accordance with their ties to the state's dominant national identity. The Palestinian struggle for the transformation of Israeli citizenship from an unequal, differential control mechanism into an equal framework of civic rights marks an important avenue for examining and expanding on the current theoretical model of social capital. This expansion takes into consideration postcolonial insights that may be of great importance to the development of this subject, which until now has fallen into the traps of the elitist discourse. By integrating the subaltern tradition into the discussion of social capital, as have Partha Chatterjee and Bhiko Parekh, the Palestinian-Israeli context brings great theoretical value to the discussion (Cahtterjee, 2001; Parekh, 1995).

One of the major contributions of this book is an exploration of the extent to which Palestinian civic activism has developed elitist tendencies as a result of the birth and growth of an educated elite class over the last few decades. It explores the extent to which the emerging educated class initiates and controls various social networks and whether it manages to overcome the burdens of internal, mutually competitive dynamics and avoids segregating the resources of social power and wealth and stimulating mutual suspicion. By exploring the class origins of Palestinian CSOs, we also examine the qualities of the Palestinian civil elite, shedding light on significant ideological developments of the PCI. Because the PCI is a subaltern homeland minority, one can assume that fighting against the state's discriminatory and alienating policies would strengthen and bond civic activists for the sake of promoting the common good of the entire society.

To explore this point, the following pages examine the competitive relationships between CSOs, focusing on the levels of trust and mistrust between the civic elite and their social environment, as well as within the elite themselves. Our empirical data help to explore these types of "gaps" between the different types of CSOs, especially the secular and the religious ones. It also aids in their social engagement and the gap in Palestinians' levels of voluntarism in the general public and in CSOs.

If we agree with most of the literature on the state's policies toward the PCI, arguing that the former seeks to render Palestinian citizens subtenants and second-class citizens, relegating them to segregated enclaves through a sophisticated infrastructure of exclusion, control, and supervision and intentionally neglecting their social, cultural, and financial needs, the PCI's civic activism could be framed as a sophisticated form of resistance against these state policies. Efforts made by CSOs to promote the interests of the PCI are, from their own perspective, an opposition to the state's policies of "hollowing out" Palestinian citizenship by robbing it of any agency. Palestinian citizenship in this context cannot mean only expressing Palestinian history and culture and challenging the state's attempts to dismantle them, but also playing an active role in determining the meaning and contents of the Israeli common good and transforming the hegemonic power structure to recognize the basic rights and aspirations of all Israeli citizens, including its Palestinian community.

The Methodological Framework

It is difficult to determine which method is the best for studying civic activism, as different methods will impact the type of evidence we collect. Therefore, in this research we used a range of methods; together, they comprise a unique and multifaceted contribution to the literature, which helps us to further explore various aspects of Palestinian civil society.

Many questions come to mind when tackling the subject of the PCI's civic activism. Not all could be addressed in a single volume. The following analysis is limited to few central questions that address the main causes and motivations behind the emergence of Israel's complicated network of Palestinian CSOs over the last few decades. The extent to which the process of establishing CSOs is related to internal sociological developments in the PCI, such as the rise of a new middle class, is another question that is addressed. Another set of questions we address reveals the similarities and differences in the meaning of civic activism for different activists and CSOs. Finally, we examine the major dilemmas that subaltern homeland minority CSOs face in ethnic states and the extent to which one could view the process of establishing CSOs as a form of resistance against the state's discriminatory policies.

Obviously, these questions produce many subquestions, which are presented and answered throughout the text. The answers are based on empirical findings, gathered through a variety of means, including public opinion surveys, focus groups, participatory observation, and personal interviews, all conducted over the course of the last ten years. We conducted two different surveys, which included questions on civic organizations, political parties, and volunteering. The first survey was conducted in late 2006 and early 2007 among a representative sample of 807 Palestinian citizens. The second survey was conducted between September 2016 and February 2017, based on a random, representative sample of 586 Palestinian citizens. In both surveys, each participant was interviewed personally for 90 minutes. The surveys' purpose was to depict the general public's attitudes toward volunteering, the activities of Palestinian CSOs, and their contribution to the strength and well-being of the PCI. It should be noted that the surveys were not meant to measure the CSOs' representability. Instead, the surveys questions were meant to define the nature of relationship between the CSOs and the general population: the CSOs' image in the eyes of the general public; the extent to which they fulfill the public's expectations; and their ability to provide for the public's needs and promote its interests under difficult political circumstances. Respondents were asked about their ideology, religiosity, satisfaction, and expectations of and by CSOs. They were also asked questions that compared their attitudes toward CSOs and political parties. This comparison has two main purposes: first, to examine the opinions of some that Arab political parties are an integral part of civil society, mainly because they are opposition parties rather than governing ones; and second, to examine the links, as perceived by the public, between civil and partisan activity, not just structurally, but also with regard to CSOs' and parties' behavior.

The surveys reflect widespread public opinion (Shamir & Shamir, 2001). Of course, these opinions are not necessarily based on objective facts or detailed observations of CSOs' activity. They may be based on notions or ill-based impressions. Nonetheless, even uninformed public opinions reflect the general atmosphere, or the common view of the public, which carries significant social, political, and organizational implications (Dalton, 2019). The public's view of CSOs' activity can help us better explore the relationship between these organizations and the general population, and the level of public awareness of their activities and challenges. Furthermore, public opinion may indicate the public's willingness to support or even defend these CSOs in times of need (Lax & Phillips, 2009).

Our second methodology is the focus group. Two forms of focus groups were used. The first type was a standard focus group that was organized in four different locations and at different times. The second was conducted three times through observations of meetings between CSOs leaders in three different locations.

The four regular focus groups had 46 participants in total, including 31 men and 15 women from the north, center, and south of Israel. We used snowball sampling to recruit participants. Well-known civic activists were contacted and asked about people they knew who were engaged in CSO work. Each new person led to another. The focus groups were conducted in various locations to enable a diverse group of participants to attend. The first one took place at Tel Aviv University, the second in Nazareth, and the third and fourth in the city of Baqa Al-Garbiyye. The focus groups' purpose was to clarify and discuss the general issues that preoccupy leaders and activists of CSOs. The focus group is an ideal approach to define the main issues and controversies at the center of the work of leaders and activists in specific social fields. While focus groups cannot provide wide-scale empirical data, they do enable a deeper exploration of specific relevant issues that cannot be achieved through an inclusive opinion survey, as we explain more thoroughly later.

The second type of focus group took place through three meetings of CSOs leaders in Haifa on January 29, 2016; in Nazareth on March, 18 2016; and in Shefa'amr on March 16, 2018. In each meeting, 10 to 12 leaders of various CSOs participated. The participants of the three meetings were not identical, although seven of them were the same in all three meetings. The observations of the author enable us to reflect on the common attitudes and differences in Palestinian CSOs' strategies of struggle and resistance in the face of Israel's nationalization policies and its efforts to target its international financial resources. The data collected and analyzed in these three meetings are presented in various parts of the book rather than in one separate chapter to add depth to each discussion (Boyatzis, 1998).

The third methodology we employed is the personal, semi-structured interview. We sampled 70 Palestinian CSOs' leaders and activists from across Israel. The interviews were performed throughout the research, and the outcomes are presented throughout the book in aiding our analysis of other findings. The interviews' purpose was to expand our knowledge of various findings; thus, the information gathered during these interviews is narratively analyzed and helps to answer research questions that cannot be answered solely through the empirical data gathered from the surveys (Murray, 2003; Riessman, 1993). The semi-structured personal interviews also help to define underlying trends among various leaders originating from different backgrounds, especially secular and religious (Potter, 1997; Seale, 1999; Willig, 2003). Through this method, we were able to transform the findings into theoretical insights extracted from the situation on the ground according to the rules of grounded theory, instead of enforcing abstract theoretical frameworks on reality (Glaser, 1992; Charmaz, 2002).

The fourth methodology we use is the questionnaire, which was completed by 97 intermediate-level activists in CSOs, in an attempt to explore their views regarding CSOs' activity. We compare these responses with the public's opinions and with those of their directors and supervisors. The activists' point of view is methodologically important, as it provides an intermediate position between the public and their leadership, thus enabling us to address any unexplained gaps in their attitudes that may be explained through the activists' views. In addition to general questions about CSOs, activists' questionnaires included questions regarding their involvement in various policy and decision-making processes in their associations. The purpose of these questions is to examine the compliance between CSOs' inside dynamics and their formally declared policies to the public. It also reveals any gaps between elite leadership and intermediate-level civic activists.

Chapter 2

The Theoretical Framing of Civic Activism

A Critical Appraisal

The purpose of this chapter is to lay out the theoretical and conceptual foundations for the study of subaltern civic activism in ethnic states. The impetus for this study is the deep disagreement between the main schools of thought and the theories governing the study of civil society and civic activism. We have no intention of reconciling these different positions. However, it is important to present the debates taking place in the literature, first, to provide context for the rest of the book. Second, a central aim of the book is to demonstrate that civic activism is better understood when conceptualized in postcolonial terms, as essentially counter-hegemonic. This conceptualization reconstructs civility and establishes a form of social agency that resists the exclusivist hegemonic power structure, seeking to promote a more comprehensive concept of the common good that is committed to genuine justice. In this regard, we draw attention to the mobilization of resources to address the consequences of the state's withdrawal from society and its institutionalization of the politics of neglect. Further to that, our discussion draws attention to the implications of the normative order that legitimates the self-perception of the hegemonic political order. Finally, we promote an analytical conceptualization of civil society that overcomes the institutional bias characterizing much of the literature. The book presents a dynamic, constructivist, and agent-based understanding of civic activism, which is defined by its efforts to reconstruct the civic sphere and simultaneously reconstruct its own identity for the sake of establishing a more open civic community based on an alternative common good and in which all members take part.

This section illustrates the axes of the theoretical discussions in the literature of civic activism. We differentiate between the dominant discourses on civil society and civic activism, which are characterized by a liberal pluralistic tradition and perceptions grounded in the subaltern, constructivist philosophical tradition. A theoretical point explored in this chapter explores the ideal framework to better understand the roots, characteristics, patterns of activity, and effects of a homeland minority's civil society in a conflictual reality.

The liberal-pluralistic tradition, which assumes universality and technologies of compliance, seems to miss the point when dealing with subaltern civic activism. The shortcomings of the liberal-pluralistic tradition illustrate a need for an alternative theoretical and philosophical framework that is loyal to the struggle of marginalized agents who not only resist the dominant power structure, but also advocate for integrating their rights, needs, and values in the definition of the common good of the state. While subaltern groups seek emancipation from hegemonic power structures and value systems, they also express willingness to reconstruct their own identity and self-perceptions. This understanding of civic activism is indispensable to the introduction of a new framework of the civic that is free of hegemonic bias, especially in ethnic contexts. Such a framing avoids falling into the traps of pregiven conceptualizations that assume civic activism is by nature liberal or positive (Balibar, 2002).

This understanding of civic activism must also be examined in the postcolonial context not only to provide evidence of these theoretical presumptions, but also to broaden and deepen our understanding of the complexities of civic struggle against hegemonies. This is especially true when CSOs seek to challenge a hegemonic ethnic power structure and simultaneously struggle against traditional forces in their own social and political environment. In the latter, CSOs use civic spaces to promote social values that do not match civic ideals such as equality, liberty, friendship, and autonomy.

Civil society, as a theoretical concept and an empirical reality, has been the focus of many scholarly works over the last few decades. Therefore, it is legitimate to question the need to revisit this topic and whether such a visit could add to our knowledge on the phenomenon. In answering these questions, we must explore the existing literature on the topic of civil society and argue that there is a separation between the literature on the liberal tradition, which we find very telling but biased, and the literature on subaltern politics in postcolonial settings, which hides very important insights that this book seeks to make apparent.

Most of the literature on civil society does not address sociopolitical settings that are not civic. Furthermore, most of the writing on the topic misses recent developments in the literature on democratic politics and civil liberty, equality, and justice. This literature therefore also fails to engage with the literature on conflict and domination, in which identity politics and political coercion impact the struggle for civil rights, as well as national emancipation. In such settings, the meaning of the civic introduced by the hegemony entails discriminatory features, as they demand subaltern groups accept the predominant ethical and ideological order that marginalizes them and precludes their "right to have rights." In such settings, hegemonic "civic" values are "uncivil," rendering the meaning of subaltern activism incompatible with the prevailing political order. Therefore if one frames subaltern activism as "compatible," it affirms institutionalized inequality and its submission to a sophisticated form of domination. This form of domination and power meets a Foucauldian understanding of power relations (Foucault, 1980). Understanding subaltern civic activism in postcolonial settings therefore must recognize the efforts made, resources mobilized, and the strategies used to transform the entire political system and its values so that it emancipates all citizens and reconstructs the common good, so it becomes universally civic. In the postcolonial context, these dynamics are rooted in their antagonistic underpinnings, and civility is conceived either as an alternative value system based on the right of all to have equal rights, or it is limited to the conceptualization and means made available from within the system of domination.

It is commonly accepted that the civil sphere comprises voluntary associations and un-institutionalized popular initiatives and movements representing the struggle for civic values. According to such a view, the agents of the civil sphere are pregiven, rational agents that seek to promote their worldviews and interests in a given political environment. Notwithstanding the importance of such an understanding, such an approach presumes that the identity of civic activists are static, rather than something which is constructed as a result of and during the struggle against their exclusion.

Civic agents strive to be heard and legitimated and remold both the civic sphere as well as their own self-perceptions through their advocacy. This means that they act politically and struggle against the established social and political order as a part of a society that has no part for them, as posited by Jacques Ranciere (2004). Civic activism is a struggle for civility, namely rendering civic values into that which determines the distribution of the "sensible" (Balibar, 2002; Ranciere, 2004). This struggle raises many questions regarding its origins, meaning, and implications; the nature of the relationships between its various elements; and the nature of its relationship with the state, especially in a postcolonial setting where the state views itself in exclusively ethnic terms and promotes a colonization process that marginalizes and represses a substantial part of its population.

Much of the literature on this subject bears witness to its complexity and varied manifestations. There is no single or widely accepted definition of civil society and its social and political role, meaning, and ramifications on its immediate and broader environment. It is widely accepted in the literature that different conceptual and philosophical paradigms highlight different aspects of civic activism and its various functions.

Despite these differences, no one disputes its importance and influence. Liberals, libertarians, conservatives, elitists, Marxists, neo-Marxists, and post-colonialists all agree that the civil sphere found between the state and the individual is socially, culturally, and politically important. They also agree it reflects transformations in the understanding of human collective existence in common political entities. The civil sphere is an original form of human action in which the crystallizing of human agency and the patterns and norms of advocating the self takes place.

The civil sphere comprises various grassroots agents—CSOs, movements, and ad hoc gatherings—operating vis-à-vis the hegemonic order, both on the institutional and disciplinary levels. It is about collective efforts based on solidarity to free the self from the oppressive hands of the dominant political structure by engaging with it and seeking not only to transform it in ways that enable the realization of rights and the fulfilment of needs, but also to reconstruct the civic by promoting an alternative comprehensive common good. Therefore, civic activism is assumed to be empowering and to aid in society's development, as it is not only vital to the provision of services that the state chooses not to provide, but also central to discussions on public policy and the promotion of civic discourse, which carry practical ramifications for the state's decision makers. This kind of activism is also essential to defending citizens against arbitrary decisions made by the authorities, especially in political structures that are dominated by exclusive ethnic groups.

Many conceive of the civil sphere as universal (Habermas, 1989). Or, in other words, the civil sphere is seen to be a manifestation of the citizens' will (assuming all citizens are equal) to control certain aspects of their lives, detaching these aspects from political, economic, or familial influences. Thus, civil society is a dynamic phenomenon with ever changing organizational, ethical, and procedural manifestations; combined, these manifestations render citizens as agents who seek to express their sovereignty over large parts of their lives. This means that active civil spheres, replete with voluntary activism, institutionalized civic associations, un-institutionalized popular movements, popular initiatives, and media campaigns that promote CSOs' unique visions of reality, all indicate the existence of social forces that counter the market's increasing control over citizens' lives, and stand against the state's authority, which strives to expand both its disciplinary and authoritative sovereignty. This conceptualization means that civic activism is inherently political. It also means that it cannot be understood without paying attention to the ways it is influenced by market-driven forces. Civic activism is essentially political for the mere fact that it strives to transform the consciousness of society and the institutional structures in its environment. Despite its politicality, civic activism does not include those agents that strive to become part of the state or its regime. Furthermore, such activism cannot be driven only by profit.

Civic activism cannot be reduced to the mere manifestation of the action that takes place in the civil sphere, as the liberal-pluralistic tradition does. Expressing the collective aspirations, desires, ideas, and interests of citizens who choose to act autonomously, according to rules that are not based on financial calculations, in the promotion of structurally common goals is central for our understanding of civic activism. It is true that autonomy must be viewed as an essential trait of civic activism. However, it cannot and should not be perceived as given. Civic autonomy is the aim of excluded citizens' struggle to express their aspirations and to define their existence outside or even against the state, rather than as an integral part of its order. This distinction is made not only in light of the perception that the state is expansive in nature and seeks compliance and order, but also because it is imperative that we do not assume that the state's order and the identity of civic agents struggling against it are a given. The entire political order in which civil struggle takes place is a result, rather than the cause of, civic struggle. Civic agency is shaped by the nature of civil society's struggle to define the political field. Therefore, it is important that we examine this process and how it transforms not only the external reality, but also the self-perception of its agents.

Therefore, civic activism is essentially political, as it strives to extract certain social realms from the state's or markets' direct control and create a sphere that reflects civic ideas that aspire to influence the public, shape the state, and protect human dignity in face of the harsh, neoliberal, and economic market. In doing so, civic activism attempts to influence decision-making processes and policy making in the formal political system without becoming a part of it and seeks to promote certain lifestyles, paradigms, and normative beliefs while still defying social stability and hegemonic perceptions of human security.

Therefore, any understanding of civic activism must address its subversion against hegemony and its control. Civic activists, whether individuals or associations, are better explored as leaders of social and political change who are also shaped by the field that they seek to transform. In this respect, they seek to denounce the status quo or any attempts to perpetuate it by interested political forces. Civic agents are better examined as an expression of society's freedom and its members' struggle for autonomy. Therefore, civic institutions should not be understood as an integral components of a government system. They are better analyzed as agents seeking to reconstruct the political field in ways that keep it as open and as inclusive as possible (Ranciere, 2004). Accordingly, the current treatment of CSOs blurs the boundaries between civic activism and policy making and become deeply engaged in the latter, cannot be applied unilaterally, particularly in understanding counter-hegemonic groups. Blurring the lines between civic activism and governmentality renders civic activism a tool of the government, rather than an autonomous force that seeks to promote an agenda determined by civic ideals.

One also cannot but point out the importance of avoiding any reification or essentialization of the homogenization of the civic sphere. Civic activism is essentially multifaceted. The diversity of the civic sphere is a result of the social struggle that makes civic activism what it is. Observing the competitive interactions between various perceptions of the civic and the values and norms that shape the existence of various groups in society becomes important to the study of civic activism. Therefore, it is the patterns of competition and conflict, rather than consensus and agreement, that characterize civic activism (Coffe & Bolzendahl, 2011). In other words, it is resistance rather than compliance that we ought to examine in our explorations of the unique practices of civic activism (Richmond, 2011; Randle, 1994).

From a historic perspective, civil society's development was conceived as a part of modernity and the development of mass society (Habermas, 1992). According to this perception, voluntary CSOs replaced traditional social institutions and blocked the expansion of the state's control over every aspect of social existence. Thus, many perceive civil society as an important element in the development of modern democracy (Keane, 1998a). In modern societies, the development of civil society is also integral to economic development. Many have identified similarities between civil society and market forces, painting civic associations in the free market's colors (Marx, 1906–1909; Offe, 1999; Jessop, 2007; Douzinas & Zizek, 2010).

Civil society is still described by many in terms of its class and thus is considered to be a part of the bourgeois order, which perpetuated power gaps between the various social classes (Cohen, 1982; Gramsci, 1994). This theory captured an important aspect of civil society, which is also common to bourgeois democracy: both perpetuate the distinction between socioeconomic and legal-political equality.

According to this paradigm, civil society, despite being voluntary, promotes a liberal worldview and therefore acts as a major power mechanism in capitalist democratic regimes. Changes in fundraising policy and the growing dependency of CSOs on market mechanisms—especially the need of these associations to adapt to managerial, practical, and commercial ways of thinking—clearly reflect the structural link between civil society and free market economy. One of the purposes of this study is to challenge the bourgeois perception of civil society in order to liberate it from the epistemological and ontological underpinnings that trap us in partial and selective manifestations of the phenomenon.

Civic Engagement and the Theorization of Collective Action

One of the distinct qualities of civil society is that it is facilitated by voluntary collective action. This phenomenon was addressed by many important thinkers in the history of political thought, one of whom was Alexis de Tocqueville (1961). Tocqueville established a large-scale tradition based on the relationship between voluntary collective action, limitations on the government's ability to impose its will and overstep the limits of its authority, and the development of a liberal and pluralistic democratic tradition (ibid.). The engagement of citizens in collective activity, reflecting not only their rights, but also their responsibility for their environment, has been a central element in the emergence of participatory democracy (Ekman & Amna, 2012; Adler & Goggin, 2005).

Civic engagement and its many forms have been a central strand in political theory and practice for more than 100 years, starting with its theorization by John Stuart Mill (2001; Ekman & Amna, 2012). It remains vital to democratic societies and has been normatively raised to the status of a virtue and a duty; analytically it has emerged as its own field of research, with scholars seeking to understand the patterns, motivations, drives, and consequences of civic engagement and participation (Van Deth, 2014; Ekman & Amna, 2012; Fishkin, 2009; Barber, 2003; Barry & Hardin, 1982; Kaase & Marsh, 1979; Pateman, 1970; Verba, 1967).

The disagreements between scholars on the topic is tremendous and cannot be fully examined in this context. Nonetheless, the continuation of these debates mirrors the importance of civic engagement in defining the meaning of the political, the rules by which it takes place, how these rules are set, who takes part in them, and how they are institutionalized into dominant regimes about the community in our age (Ranciere, 2010; Conge, 1988). Given the many facets that it entails, it becomes clear that civic engagement is not merely a procedural issue, but rather an essential component of the modern human condition (Schwartzberg, 2015).

Hannah Arendt conceptualizes this aspect of humanity in her concept of *vita activa*, which means that by virtue of humans' participation in deliberating and deciding the nature of the public good, humans express their humanity and distinguish themselves from the animal world (Arendt, 1958). Determining who takes part in orchestrating interactions between humans and their social, economic, cultural, and natural environments engages them in continuous debate. The processes that lead to certain patterns of communication, coordination, and institutionalization of disagreement become an interesting avenue to explore. This is especially true, as these processes are what defines the political order and not the other way around. Therefore, how and with whom human engagement and participation occur must be analytically and normatively valued before they lead to particular goals and decisions. If for Arendt human action enables humans to escape the "ceaseless cycle of nature," providing them with a sense of history, remembrance, and freedom of contemplation, it is necessary to ask which humans take part and how the consequences thereof become routinized into existing power structures (Tsao, 2002).

That said, engagement and participation do not solve the problems of public wisdom and reasoning in democratic settings. Therefore, political participation and the changing modes of collective action lead scholars to discuss issues of public wisdom and reasoning and their relationship with the epistemic and ethical aspects of democracy (Schwartzberg, 2015; Feuerstein, 2008; Cohen, 1988; Riker, 1982). The assumed reasonableness of the public and its ability to act based on its best interests instigated heavy debates regarding the assumption of reasonableness and the many factors that influence the ability of the public to choose the best option possible for its general good. The differentiation between choosing the best option and choosing the best option among those available raises the importance of agenda setting and the ability of elites to manipulate the options available to the public (Feuerstein, 2008). Furthermore, it raises the meaning of the public and how it becomes conceptualized as part of the political process rather than preceding it. It is publics rather than public that ought to be explored, and how they deliberate is the challenge that must be addressed, as manifested in the works of many recent scholars of deliberative politics (Habermas, 2005; Neblo, 2005; Macedo, 1999). This urge becomes even more pressing in the Internet age, which is manifesting itself in ways that are much more complex than many of its early scholars could have anticipated (Sunstein, 2017; Dahlberg & Siapera, 2007).

Such debates lead us back to the challenge set by Mancur Olson when he challenged the basic assumptions common in the professional literature on collective action (1965). In the conventional literature on collective action, common wisdom dictated that one can conclude the rationale of a group based on those of its members in attempts to achieve common goals (Barry & Hardin, 1982). Olson was among the first scholars to tackle the incoherence of this common belief, pointing out the lack of coordination between the rationality of individual and group behavior, even in cases where there is consensus on the goals of the group and the means to achieve them (Olson, 1965; Barry & Hardin, 1982).

In spite of Olson's claim or maybe because of it, collective action has received a lot of attention in the literature. The emergence of behavioral theories and critical neo-Marxist trends began drawing attention not only to the epistemology of collective action, but also to its relations with institutions and its impact on the structure of the entire political field. Opposing traditions drew attention to different factors of collective action and necessitated going beyond individualistic-liberal analysis that focuses on voting and elections to shedding light on other forms of collective action manifested in social movements, civic associations, voluntarism, and philanthropy. These phenomena became central fields of study in sociology and political science. Questions such as how we can explain the growth of collective organizations, how voluntary groups of citizens behave, and according to what instrumental motivations and values they act, became fundamental to the study of collective action.

The development of social and political theory dealing with collective action gained a lot from the rise of social movements and civic associations that challenged existing theories on the topic (Bennett, 2003; McAdam, Tilly

& Tarrow, 2001). Not only did old conceptualizations require reconsideration, but also new circumstances, especially the rise of new information and communication technologies, made it impossible to theorize collective action without relating to new forms of gathering, mobilization, and protest (Bimber, Flaganin, & Stohl, 2005; Bennett, 2003; Castells, 2009).

Old forms of social organization have been transformed and began appearing in new forms, bypassing institutional rigidity, special limitations, and hierarchical leadership patterns (Bennett, 2003). Nonetheless, these new patterns of mobilization still sought to empower society, helping to not only develop certain social and cultural aspects of it, but also to provide for social forms of resistance to hegemonic power structures and to counter the dominant discourse and common social practices. These new-old forms of collective action sought to influence institutionalized politics and democratize government. The transformation of civic engagement opened the door to new ways to define the collective action, based on pertinent ideals of civil and human rights.

One product of collective action that has been institutionalized is civic organizations, which comprised loosely arranged, collective gatherings, and operated and continue to operate on the border between the legal and political power of the state, and society's basic cultural and political freedoms. CSOs in the form of social or professional associations, popular committees, and social movements were voluntarily established based on the understanding that citizens have insights and communication skills that enable them to come together and design their future according to their own will, versus hegemonic political forces, which strive to preserve a reality that serves their interests (Melucci, 1989; Tarrow, 1994). However, it is important to note that these forms of collective action have not resulted in a perfect match between their declared intentions and the result of their activities in all cases. Therefore, CSOs cannot be theorized as unified, rational entities in a neutral, social arena. They do not just exist alongside any political power structure. The wealth of literature in the field demonstrates that this form of collective action is vital to any society (Cohen & Arrato, 1992).

Accordingly, these social forms have been conceived as deriving from social, economic, and political interests and needs, and their goal is to impact their political sphere and transform it to fit their interests, needs, and ideals without or even despite the state's direct involvement (Seligman, 1992). Some have argued that CSOs enrich public life and provide society with some of the material and symbolic demands that result from the withdrawal of the neoliberal state. By doing so, they not only challenge the state's bias and its shortages, but also reconstruct the meaning of political engagement and participation. The state's bias and its inability or reluctance to participate in certain social and cultural activities lead some social groups to take initiative and establish civic associations or social movements to pursue their aspirations in the face of the dominant power structure (Keane, 1998; Touraine, 1983). Some civil society scholars stress that these collective forms are meant to limit the state's power over certain aspects of life that, according to them, should remain autonomous and untouched by the state (Burnell & Calvert, 2004).

This understanding motivates us to think about CSOs not only from an institutional perspective, but rather from a neo-institutional one (March & Olsen, 1983). Such an approach encourages us to take into consideration that CSOs are political agents that do not exist prior to their action, but rather are made such by what they do. CSOs are defined by their action, which in a way is related to their institutional structure, but goes beyond it. CSOs are forms of collective action that seek to mobilize and advance collective engagement in the political field (Barely & Tolbert, 1997). Such an understanding renders institutions dynamic processes that both structure and are structured by their environments (ibid.; Shepsle, 1989).

This perspective considers social power not only in behavioral or hierarchical terms, but rather as something more complex. As Lukes demonstrates, power is not and cannot be understood unless all forms and aspects of it are thoroughly examined (2005). This is especially true when considering resistance to power structures led by collective, voluntary activity. Bourdieu and Wacquant illuminate this further:

> The field of power is a field of forces defined by the structure of the existing balance of forces between forms of power, or between different species of capital. It is also simultaneously a field of struggles for power among the holders of different forms of power. It is a space of play and competition in which social agents and institutions which all possess the determinate quantity of specific capital (economic and cultural capital in particular) sufficient to occupy the dominant positions within their respective fields (the economic field, the field of higher civil service or the state, the university field, and the intellectual field) confront one another in strategies aimed at preserving or transforming tis balance of forces . . . This struggle for the imposition of the dominant principle leads, at every moment, to a balance in the sharing of power, that is, to what I call a division of the work

> domination. It is also a struggle over the legitimate principle of legitimation and the legitimate mode of reproduction. (Bourdieu & Wacquant 1996, 76)

These comments indicate a need to examine struggles between different patterns of social networks based on their diverging value systems, as a starting point, especially when examining civic activism in a power structure that is organized based on ethno-national stratifications.

The Civic and the Political in Collective Action

Most intellectual traditions dealing with civil society do not assume a single collective plan for it. Foley and Edwards (1996) distinguish between civil society that challenges the state and civil society that is not necessarily politically motivated. But this kind of distinction may be rather too dichotomized compared with the complexity of most CSOs, their diversity, and their activities, as we shall see later on.

While civic associations are not strictly a direct product of the power and capital structure, they should not be conceptualized as separate entities. A central aspect of civic action aspires to decrease the power of capital, which seeks to define the form of collective existence. As civic activism depends on economic forces, it seems logical to view it in light of its ambition to escape their influence and create autonomous social, cultural, and political spheres of action. Civic activism would therefore be about preserving an open space for social interaction, where identity and politics are discussed freely in an effort to seek leverage over the political domain. Accordingly, it cannot be theorized as bounded to any preestablished identity that impedes citizenship or transcendental beliefs calling for free, unlimited social communication.

In other words, civic activism institutionalized in civic organizations is best conceptualized as that which empowers citizens and limits the state and capital's power in order to insure political resistance, competition, debates, and deliberations—the basic manifestations of civil society itself. Within this definition, every social interaction is equally legitimate, because the ideal of equality is a basic and undeniable tenet of civic associationalism.

Most CSOs define their own goals and ideals and strive to impact their social and political surroundings autonomously and without coordination with other organizations. In fact, associations' freedom to act is one of the basic principles of civil society. This freedom, which is detached from the state-based power structure, is itself the political dimension of civil society.

Therefore, the distinction between civil and political society cannot be strictly defined. CSOs play a political role beyond the formal scope of state politics, even if they are not described as political organizations per se (Linz and Stepan, 1996). They seek to influence the state's politics and provide citizens with resources—symbolic, institutional, and material—thereby releasing many from their dependence on state resources (Chatterjee, 2001). Furthermore, voluntary CSOs, formally institutionalized or public interest organizations, are manifestations of civic activism, which reflect the desired autonomy of society, or parts of it, from the state's power structure and institutions, regardless of the nature of their activities (Khilnani, 2001).

A significant body of research argues that civil society should not be inherently linked to political society. And yet, if we want to understand civil society's significant contribution to modern political culture, we must define it in political terms (Linz and Stepan, 1996). This interpretation of civil society seems to be especially true in strong states with a clear and comprehensive social or cultural national project. The state's involvement in a project of this kind, often found in national ethno-cultural states, may manifest itself as an invasion into the potential realms of civic associationalism, and encourage bias, which defies legal and universal political ideals.

When reviewing civil society's theoretical background, we cannot be content with a significant a priori model, which includes several institutions either positioned against the state or detached from it. Civil society is a theoretical concept and an ethical paradigm as well as an institutional, social, and political reality, which has taken many twists and turns throughout history. There is no single definition for civil society. Different paradigms and different theoretical and ethical platforms describe civil society in different terms to the point that its limits are blurred.

In his contribution to understanding the conceptual history of civil society, Sunil Khilnani (2001) explains:

> In its original sense, [civil society] allowed no distinction between "state" and "society" or between political and civil society: it simply meant a community, a collection of human beings united within a legitimate political order, and variously rendered as "society" or "community." (p. 17)

Khilnani explains how the German tradition, inspired by Hegel, divided the concept and led to the understanding that the state and civil society are "redescriptions of one another" (ibid.). Contemporary descriptions of civil society, like that of Cohen and Arato (1992), suggest that the focus of civil society is "the socialization structure, associationalism and patterns of organized communication of the institutionalized life-world or in the way to be institutionalized" (p. x). The institutionalization of these civic organizations was initiated by the state, but also contributed to the establishment of the state's public sphere. Hence, the relationship between CSOs and the state is dialectic rather than dichotomous. Accordingly, civic associations must be theorized as operating within the state's boundaries and use legal tools and regulations created by the state; however, the latter is also shaped by CSOs' activism rather than a stable and rigid institution. This means that the relationship between the state and civil society is dynamic and transformative, according to which they shape each other's character and policies. CSOs are not part of the state's bureaucratic hierarchy, and their goals are set in an autonomous sphere, opened by the state itself, to make it more responsive to civic preferences and choices. Such an understanding invites us to pay more attention to the ways civic associations constantly strive to change or shape the state's policy and apply pressure on it to submit to their demands. The core of this relationship is the ability of CSOs to maintain their autonomy without losing their legitimacy and effectiveness in influencing state policies. Such efforts do not mean that CSOs, by lobbying the state, achieve all of their goals; such an understanding renders the state the mere arena on which civic actors play. As we have already clarified, the state, especially ethnic states, have ideological and valuational commitments that shrink the spaces for CSOs to influence their dynamics and policy making. The interaction between various CSOs and the state may lead the state to change, depending on the power relations between itself and the civic realm.

By conceptualizing the public sphere in such a way and focusing on the links between civil and political society, we are able to describe their limits without stumbling into the trap of merging them or creating a rift between them. Civil society relates to political society when it bases political order and citizenship on equal civil engagement as a common ground for all the state's citizens and communities (Vertovec, 1999; Delanty, 2000; Enjolras, 2008).

Accordingly, the civic aspects of civil society come to highlight its universalism and its central ideals, such as equality, without ignoring the variance and the ideological and organizational competition within it. Civil society is assumed to be pluralist, tolerant, equal, democratic, and liberal in essence. However, it is important to note that these ideals are not always realized de facto; they may be ethical aspirations that are not necessarily translated into a practical reality. Various civic associations may act differently vis-à-vis the state. Therefore, the autonomy from the state and the struggle against the latter's striving for closure, in the sense of stabilizing the dominant power structure, becomes a central dimension of civic activism. Accordingly, civil society is better conceptualized as countering the stabilization of the hegemonic power structure and the total submission of society to state dictates. It is a constant, subversive fight against the stabilization of this unequal power structure, which does not satisfy the expectations and the will of all citizens, despite the fact that part of society may be satisfied with its privilege.

Conceptualizing civil society in exclusive, autonomous terms could therefore be misleading. Civil society and the state need not be conceptualized as rivals. Nonetheless, attention must be given to the tensions between them. In contrast to the state's identification with coercion and compliance, civil society ought to be conceptualized based on the notion that the political sphere is open to free and competing activities, seeking to create contact with the other and structure common goals. One must not presume civil society is committed to a particular political stance vis-à-vis the other.

Civil society could be conceived as inviting many social interactions without the presumption of any one particular result. Thus, civic activism is a dynamic process of interactions between various—not necessarily equal—social players, whose balance of forces or functional division are flexible, and may lead to unforeseen results. This understanding of civil society assumes that one of the main elements in civic engagement and practice is the existence of spaces of relative *free will,* where civic associations may promote their ideals and goals while respecting the movement and space of similar organizations vis-à-vis the state, which consistently seeks to control and organize crucial social spheres. Hence, civil society cannot be built on a dogmatic ideological concept, which strives to achieve political and social predefined order. On the contrary, civil society is best conceptualized as open, flexible, and pragmatic. Other, less cautious conceptualizations would contradict the very essence of civil society, which has an infinite sphere of existing possibilities.

The concept of civil society is not oblivious to political players' tendency to identify the state as the one true model of collective existence (Dunn, 2001). Yet CSOs are unable to ignore politics and identify the social links with one specific model or result. The treatment of civil society must pay attention to the self-establishment of society through self-mobilization despite the state's efforts to dominate these aspects of sociality. Therefore, an examination of civil society in a specific context must pay attention to the way social mobilization occurs in the sphere of CSOs, civic movements, and other forms of social communication. Therefore, one must examine the organizing principles and conceptual schemes of civil associationalism and the extent to which these practices evade attempts to submit them to primordial, exclusivist social groups or predictated state models, as well as their search for social forms that avoid fatal conflicts, which could endanger the basic trust needed for their political existence.

Civil Society, the State, Religiosity, and Minoritarian Politics

The dynamic and nondelineated concept of civil society suggests that we cannot exclusively identify the emergence of CSOs and institutions with democratization and liberalization processes. Most of the literature on civil society would agree with the assertion that the mere existence of such associations does not necessitate the existence of a civil society. Civil societies are formed through their activities and their free competition over possible models of the state. The main index of civil society's existence is its associations' performances and their attempts to achieve goals based on equal civic ideals. This means that when such institutions are removed—willingly or not—from the debate regarding the dominant political order, and when they are bound to identify with a predetermined hegemonic political or ideological order that promotes a rigid set of beliefs or provides only basic needs, the concept of civil society is emptied of its essential meaning. This does not mean that civil society always achieves all of its goals and objectives. It is by challenging the dominant power structure in a way that enables change that civil society remains loyal to its internal logic.

The state is defined as a complex, modern institutional structure, whose logic's best expression is the dialectic connection between segregation—defining acceptable and unacceptable practices—and openness to accept conflicting forces and competition against its power (Ranciere, 2010; Balibar, 2014). This dialectic enables the state to manifest definitive or soft characteristics according to its discretion. These characteristics also assist the state in promoting its advantage over its human and physical surroundings, and reinforces its existing control over its environment. One of the essential mechanisms of state power is its monopoly over symbolic and material violence in an effort to secure the state and its order (Bourdieu, 1991). Unlike absolute traditional regimes, modern democratic states can be characterized through their own "opposing personality," namely by hiding their violent nature, which is the best way to understand the basic logic of the state. This camouflage is achieved through disciplining and governance mechanisms. The state's principles of generality and its natural presence are its best tools; they enable it to control and contain potential violence. But the need for more sophisticated camouflage is greater in democratic regimes, in which violence contradicts the spirit of the people's sovereignty and therefore appears as a guarantee for control over an exceptional situation in an effort to maintain order. Civil society makes it difficult for the state to hide its violent nature, as it challenges the state using the means provided by the state itself. The state, despite being a complex and intricate mechanism, opens spaces for CSOs' action and movement or tries to block them. By using these spaces, CSOs can expose the power structure reflected in its policy (Ophir, 2010).

Hence, a thorough examination of CSOs' contribution and influence must consider the environmental structural consequences, as well as the state institutions' intentions and policies toward them. In addition to CSOs' influence on the state's democratization process, we should explore their potential influence on development and empowerment. CSOs aspire to develop and empower society, and at the same time influence decision-making mechanisms in the public sphere. They seek to promote democratization processes in the state in an attempt to reinforce citizens' involvement in public policy making, especially to prevent capital from manipulating the state's directives and to dictate development and resource allocation policy based on equality, justice, and integrity. Comparative research thus often presents different and contradicting contributions and functions of CSOs.

The current research explores CSOs as a contingent phenomenon; their nature is decided not by their definition, but rather by their position within the balance of power and the political paradigm they promote. Some CSOs adopt a neoliberal paradigm and act accordingly. These organizations employ the free market paradigm and promote a compatible civil ideal. If, in those instances, CSOs are affiliated with the state's hegemonic worldview, they play an essential role in its control system. Other associations may adopt an alternative socioeconomic paradigm that challenges neoliberalism. These two models stand in clear and direct tension. This kind of tension increases in cases of ethno-national conflict, something that must be considered when exploring civil society's nature and roles. The affinity between ethno-national identity and socioeconomic status can potentially become a major cause of social conflict. The concept of "ethno-class" becomes relevant when a certain ethno-national group is perceived as an alienated, low socioeconomic class versus a hegemonic group of different ethno-nationalities and classes. In such cases, the low ethno-class' CSOs face a few layers of control and alienation, namely financial, ethno-national, and political.

These disagreements surrounding civil society reveal its complexity. Additionally, they also point to its different manifestations in various contexts. However, these concepts do not have to be diametrically opposed. They can illuminate different dialectical and complementary aspects of the phenomenon. Tension and conflict are in fact the essence of civil society. Diversity can add vital facets and characteristics to civil society, thereby strengthening its existence. They allow different social forces to prevail simultaneously, which can increase its autonomy and freedom. One might even say that the legitimation of civic organizations is based on their activities' variance and moral and ideological pluralism. In this way, diversity thus leads to the growth of contradiction and tension and is an integral part of civil society. This tension is one of the manifestations of power relations in state and society. Furthermore, contradictions and tensions in civil society can become a means of control that is based on legitimacy, something that is far more effective than the state's coercive or oppressive power.

This complexity also makes civil society a unique phenomenon to study. The phenomenon is even more complex in situations of conflict and struggle between society and the state. In such situations, the role, characteristics, and consequences of civil society become even more intricate. The nature of conflict and its foundations, especially when it comes to identity conflict based on nationality, ethnicity, or religion, affect relationships between CSOs, which may act in accordance with and within the boundaries of their affiliation. It is important to note that civic activity is usually theorized as striving by its very nature to serve universal goals. This raises the question of whether identitarian CSOs could be considered part of civil society or not. Therefore, the general debate on civil society must take into account the centrality of conflicts, their characteristics, and their implications on patterns of behavior and on the discourse of civic associations. It is highly agreed on that the loyalty of civic organizations to a value system of rights is an important criterion for evaluating their degree of affiliation to civil society, especially when promoting the rights of subaltern and marginalized groups.

Of particular note in this context are the differences inherent in civic organizations that promote religious worldviews and dictate a value system that is not necessarily based on or subject to the principles of equality or freedom, both of which are core values in civil society. This may affect the role of civic organizations and the characteristics of their contribution to citizens' freedom and welfare. In such cases, there may exist a clear tension between liberty and welfare, as religious organizations may promote conservative worldviews that are built on hierarchical authority, but at the same time provide essential services to a sizable segment of society. Such a situation requires us to distinguish between these types of organizations, as their behaviors and differences implicate their suitability and contributions to the broader vision of civil society.

In addition to what has been said so far, it is also important to note that minority civil society, whether based on national, ethnic, or cultural status, is a unique phenomenon that requires attention when addressing its nuances. The mere variance in CSOs operating in the name of a minority, especially in countries with an ethno-national character, raises many questions that require sensitive attention. In ethno-national states, this is especially true, as they contain a national or a cultural minority whose civic organizations oppose the ethno-national identity of the state (Toland, 2017). In such a reality, the interaction between CSOs and the state should take into account the distinct ethos of these agents. Perceptions of the state, its roles, its policies, its values, and its behaviors toward civic organizations that challenge its prevailing worldview make for an interesting and important arena that is ripe for greater study (Brown, 1989). Although there are studies of minority civil societies, they do not approach the depth needed to understand how civic activism and CSOs meet and conduct their activities within the framework of ethnic nation-states. This book comes to shed light on this unique situation.

Civil Society, Democratization, and Neoliberalization

The democratization waves in South Africa (Habib, 2005; O'Donnel & Schmitter, 1986; Schneider, 1995) and Eastern Europe (Linz & Stepan, 1996; Pelcynski, 1998; Havel, 1985) have led many researchers to conclude that there is a positive relationship between the rise of social associations empowerment and democratization processes. Many researchers believe that these democratization processes were strongly influenced by the emergence of civil society, which presented new challenges to authoritarian political regimes (Huntington, 1991; Cohen & Arato, 1992). Most of the studies in the field of democracy describe civil society's role as vital and necessary (Burnell & Calvert, 2004; Mendelson & Glenn, 2002).

These unequivocal views of civil society were common in the 1980s literature, but later scholars raised doubts regarding the causal relationship between the number of civil society institutions and their chances for affecting political and social development, empowerment, and democratization (Mercer, 2002; Clarke, 1998; Haynes, 1996; Hulme & Edwards, 1997; Edwards, 1999; Wiktorowicz, 2000). Some deduced that while the emergence of a civil society may be a prerequisite for development, empowerment, and democratization, it is not always a sufficient condition. It is unclear whether the rising number of civic institutions necessarily leads to significant changes in the basic principles of the dominant political order (Foley & Edwards, 1996). Clearly, we must distinguish between civil society's role in development and empowerment and its contribution to the democratization of state and society. While CSOs may provide basic and elementary needs that strengthen and empower various groups in society, this does not necessarily mean they can change the dominant social culture or political regime and bring democratization. History shows that the connection between the number of CSOs and democracy is associative rather than causal or binding. This argument could be best exemplified by countries with strong religious movements that establish broad networks of CSOs that empower society, but simultaneously lead to its religionization (Peled & Peled, 2018; Israel, 2015).

Therefore, discussions of the relationship between civil society and democracy have become very central in the professional literature. Historically, the most dominant camp, called the "civil society argument," asserts that voluntary participation in CSOs and the existence of many organizations necessarily contribute to the strengthening of democracy. However, this camp has been challenged in recent years by a number of opponents to the participation claim, among whom questions regarding solidarity and social capital have been raised (Walzer, 1992; Tamir, 1993; Gutmann, 1998).

Any study of civil society cannot take the tradition of the "civil society argument" for granted anymore. There is a need to raise doubt regarding the relationship between civic activism and democratic values without completely rejecting the importance of the existence of many CSOs as an active space in democratic settings. A space of civic action that forms a counter public in the face of governmental arbitrariness and social conservatism is indispensable for democracy. But not every civic activism serves democracy. There are CSOs that do not necessarily operate to promote democracy and the values of democratic citizenship. On the contrary, there are CSOs that promote values that counter not only liberal beliefs, but also democratic pluralism and seek to promote conservative worldviews that do not tolerate difference. Many religious or nationalist CSOs are known for supporting belief systems that are intolerant and do not promote individual autonomy, freedom, and collective rights; rather, they oppose them. This phenomenon has been depicted as "bad civil society" (Chambers & Kopstein, 2001) and draws attention to the notion that it is not only the growth of civil society that matters, but also the values CSOs promote and the patterns of political participation they facilitate. According to Chambers and Kopstein:

> In addition to looking at associations from the point of view of participation versus nonparticipation, we suggest that the political and moral significance of associations also requires that we look at associations from the point of view of the substantive values that are promoted within associations. From this perspective, the political value of civil society for democracy clearly becomes a contingent affair. As two critics of civil society literature put it, "if civil society is a beachhead secure enough to be of use in thwarting tyrannical regimes, what prevents it from being used to undermine democratic governments?" (Chambers and Kopstein, 2001, p. 842)

Accordingly, one cannot explore civic activism without addressing the existence of "bad civil society," as we do in the following pages. As Chambers and Kopstein suggest, it is important to examine the nature of civic organizations, even if they do not constitute a majority in one historic moment. They argue:

> First, even if it is the case that illiberal forces are small in number today, it is not waste of time to try to understand the phenomena of bad civil society. This might allow us to identify warning signs of the growth of bad civil society in the future. But second and more important, the danger contained in bad civil society is not exclusively about the ability to directly destabilize the state through the mobilization of large numbers of people. Illiberal forces need not set their cap on the state to undermine

> liberalism. Because illiberal forces cannot destabilize the state does not mean that they cannot contribute to an insidious erosion of values that leaves liberalism vulnerable to all sorts of threats . . . The most important of these threats is the potential spillover of extremist rhetoric into the mainstream of political discourse. (Chambers and Kopstein, 2001, p. 843)

This pattern of solidarity and values inherent in illiberal organizations reflects the vertical organization Robert Putnam warned against when he made the indispensable connection between civic organization and the strengthening of democracy (Putnam, 2000). However, this warning does not stop here. As Amy Gutmann illustrates, racial organizations that call for hatred are also organized based on solidarity between their friends, which enables them to develop a considerable degree of mutual trust. Therefore, the "test" for bad or good civil society isn't based on the extent of organizations' participation or social capital but on the kind of values they promote (Gutmann, 1998). In other words, the differentiation between CSOs must be based on the worldview they promote. However, such a differentiation is problematic, as ideological differences and competition between various worldviews in the public sphere is the essence of civil society. One of its central characteristics is its pluralism, specifically its exchange of ideas and diverse worldviews. Furthermore, it is only natural that CSOs representing different worldviews depict their opponents as illegitimate. Therefore, the test of "the kind of values" that civic organizations promote is a problematic test, especially in contexts characterized by "thick" valuational differences across society. According to Rosenblum and Post: "In segmented societies, groups are more inclined to see membership as mutually exclusive and to be hostile to the idea of plural identities and multiple, overlapping memberships" (2002, p. 5).

Nancy Rosenblum joins Gutmann in not being satisfied with participation as having a political and moral positive influence. Cooperation is a necessary condition, but not sufficient, when we examine the relationship between civil society, democracy, and civic values. As Rosenblum and Post argue, "many theorists conceive of civil society as the 'seedbed of virtue' and that cooperation and shared responsibility generated by associations produce 'social networks' and 'virtuous cycles'" (Rosenblum and Post, 2002, p. 18). This proposition cannot be taken for granted. Rosenblum posits that the contribution of associations to the moral development of society calls for cooperation at the expense of mutual empathy (Rosenblum, 1998). Despite the importance of cooperation and its conceptualization as a test for the strength of civil society, one must pose the question—based on whose values? The mere cooperation between civic associations does not guarantee that they cooperate on values that nourish human respect, equality, and freedom for all.

When answering his critics on cooperation and the relationship between civic associationalism, trust, social capital, and democracy, Putnam (2000) theorizes the concepts of bridging and bonding. Whereas bridging promotes crossing lines between different types of citizens, bringing them together on the basis of their common goals, bonding emphasizes the internal solidarity in the association. Chambers and Kopstein claim in this regard that Putnam's diagnosis is interesting but not substantial enough to explain the values and messages that the members of an association receive. They argue instead that the effect of social organizations on public morality and the promotion of democracy are related to ideological content and the messages propagated to its members. These messages determine the type of link between the act of association and the promotion of democracy and democratic citizenship (Chambers & Kopstein, 2001).

Chambers and Kopstein's critique renders the criteria necessary to draw the line between bad and good civil society indispensable. Such criteria cannot be only normatively rigid. They must have an analytical dimension to be of any theoretical value relevant in different political and historical contexts (Kopecky & Mudde, 2003). The criteria of differentiation also cannot be such that they favor liberal values over religious or national ones, for such bias is limiting. For such criteria to be helpful, they must incorporate difference and tolerate open competition over power in society. Such an understanding enables us to differentiate between CSOs that promote conservative social values with which we do not agree, and CSOs that target not the contents of opposing value systems, but rather the mere legitimacy of difference and pluralism. Delegitimizing difference, silencing critique, and shrinking the spaces available for associations to represent the spectrum of opinions and lifestyles is the line that helps us differentiate between good and bad civil society, even when such associations propagate social beliefs with which we do not necessarily agree. In other words, it is the legitimacy of pluralism, deliberation, and competition that draws the line between civil and uncivil (bad) civil society.

The ideas raised by critics of the "civil society argument" have us also draw our attention to other important aspects of this phenomenon. One of these aspects has to do with the way we conceive of civil society within a given context. Civil society, it is argued, is not a self-sustaining and autonomous phenomenon. The context in which it operates, especially the nature of the state and the political regime under which its CSOs operate, greatly impacts its characteristics and ability to shape its environment. Quintan Wiktorowicz (2000) suggests, "Rather than assume that civil society enables democracy or serves as a mechanism of empowerment, it is important to understand the political context that shapes and limits its potential as an engine of political change" (p. 46). The structural opportunities given to CSOs are vital for their contribution to empowerment, development, and political change (Tarrow, 1996). The state has a huge impact on the ability of CSOs to influence their social and political environment. Evidence from many states illustrates that civil society's role in challenging the state appeared most prominently during regime change (Wada, 2005). Yet the case of the Weimar Republic proves that civil society also has a disastrous potential when CSOs are the subordinates of radical political forces that try to weaken democracy (Berman, 1997). In severe political and ideological conflicts, CSOs may provide an easy organizational infrastructure for political forces with right-wing, chauvinist ideologies to attempt to limit or destroy organizational rivals; such acts stands in direct opposition to civic values. For example, the new right-wing CSOs in various states across Europe and in Israel provide the needed information and analysis to motivate hegemonic political forces to restrict the activities of rival CSOs. Another example is religious CSOs; many such associations support a worldview that limits the individual and the community's autonomy and movement spaces and enforces a fixed system of values and rituals. The leaders of these associations use the means given by the law to act against civic values, such as liberalism, freedom, and social autonomy.

Unlike the Tocquevillian analysis of 19th-century America, CSOs may have an exclusivist tendency and a sectarian nature, and may carry high internal tension and conflict (Whittington, 1998). A political-ideological competition, or competition over resources, may render CSOs an effective tool for fighting political or ideological adversaries. These associations can be seen as devolutions into sects or "tribes," fighting over power and influence, in contrast to the common opinion of them as representative of the liberal, democratic, and tolerance values of civil society.

Foley and Edwards (1996) raised concerns regarding the negative use of CSOs by radical and nondemocratic religious movements, which may use CSOs to promote undemocratic political change. This concern is not necessarily true for every religious organization, but there is no doubt that some religious CSOs promote ideals and behavioral norms that contradict civic and democratic ideals.

Despite the dangers of civil society, many researchers—mostly liberals—agree that civic institutions have positive potential. As illustrated by Linz and Stepan (1996), civic institutions may generate contra-hegemonic projects, which limit authoritarian regimes. These institutions create an autonomous space for social interactions, which help them to address the basic needs of the population, despite the fact that their existence does not necessitate democratization of state or society. CSOs may be wealthy and active without having the power to influence the state's policy-making process. On the other hand, we cannot ignore the structural role of CSOs when states retreat from their traditional commitments to citizens, or the business world faces new challenges that prevent corporations from providing jobs and fair wages. Van Til (2008) expounded on this when he summarized civil society's services and contributions to society's well-being. He pointed out that CSOs provide

> communitarian solutions that are more people friendly than those emerging from bureaucracies; pluralistic solutions to problems that must be shaped to different subcultures and groups within society; an appropriate balance between service and advocacy in the remedy of social ills; opportunities for deliberation and dialogue in the definition and resolution of social problems, and efficacy and efficiency in the delivery of subcontracted services. (Van Til, 2008, p. 1072)

Thus, we must consider the political sphere's intentions and policies when analyzing CSOs in their political context. Some regimes may present a facade of democracy and at the same time limit civil society's contribution to issues neglected by the state. One such example is when the welfare state is minimized. In such cases, CSOs may become a part of a neoliberal process, in which the state retreats from its welfare commitments and transfers responsibility to the hands of CSOs funded by the state or outside sources, which play their part, willingly or not (Foley & Edwards, 1996). While this kind of situation may empower CSOs and expand their influence over the political realm, they still perform duties that belong, traditionally, to the state. These processes lead to the neoliberalization of civil society itself by bringing it closer to competitive behavioral patterns that are common in the free market.

This process may seem to create an ostensibly strong and vital civil society, but in fact it more strongly symbolizes the state's retreat and the weakening of its welfare services, and it transfers responsibility into the hands of society itself. The challenge here stems not only from the state's retreat, but also from the success of the dominant political elite to shift a significant portion of its responsibilities over to society itself and to enforce a worldview that normalizes this division of labor (Harriss, 2006). Another related challenge is the penetration of competition and market values into the realm of civil society, which considers costs versus benefits and profits versus losses. Civil society's guiding principles thus become functional efficiency and organizational benefit, instead of service or the associations' original ideals.

Civil Society, Civic Engagement, and Social Capital

Any discussion of civil society and CSOs would not be complete without referring to the aspect of social capital and the issue of civic engagement. As discussed later, the definitions for social capital are based on civic engagement, while the latter is perceived as social capital, which promotes the society's welfare and democratization (Dalton, 2008; Berger, 2009). Reflecting on the social capital issue will help us to understand the meanings and implications of social networking and the accumulation of individual and social traits, which can help to explain civil society's contribution to the welfare of society within which this process occurs. Though social capital cannot be reduced to mere functional evidence because of its own value, its contribution to the existence and development of further social layers is also significant. The emergence of CSOs based on the growth of social capital, and as a result of this growth itself, becomes a kind of index that marks possible developments of society's relationships within itself and with its environment.

By focusing on civic engagement, we are better able to explicate the degree of society's engagement in civic activity, and the extent to which it assumes responsibility over its reality. This engagement reveals the traits, meanings, agents, and implications of civil society on other aspects of life, something that becomes important for understanding social, political, and cultural developments. Taking social responsibility through civic engagement reflects the society's self-understanding and is an indication of its relationship with its immediate surroundings, particularly with the state.

It is important to note that civic engagement does not necessarily mean an acceptance of the state's fundamental ideals or a manifestation of a state's conceptualization of citizenship. Civic engagement may also involve challenging the dominant power structure and challenging the status quo.

Therefore, while civic engagement may be a way of accommodating the status quo, it can also symbolize defiance and opposition. Hence, social capital and civic engagement are variables that can educate us as to the measure of civil society's growth, activities, and strength. They can both also be used as indicators for analyzing civil society's measure of activism and effectiveness in its social and political environment.

The concept of civic engagement has been interpreted in various ways. Some scholars widen its scope and perceive it to mean any civic activity, individual or collective, as a contribution to society. Others try to limit their definition to prevent what some scholars would call "conceptual stretching" (Sartori, 1970). Civic engagement is a social-moral engagement, motivated by a public spirit and aimed toward solving problems and overcoming general challenges (Berger, 2009). While this definition is widely political, it is very limited and intelligible. Not every activity based on the gathering of several people is considered civic; bowling, for example, is not. But this definition tends to emphasize the political aspect of civic engagement by saying its goals are collective and are achieved without the state's direct involvement. The more citizens are engaged in managing their communal life, the more their dependency on the state weakens and their desire is reflected in their public life. Some researchers have divided civic engagement into different levels. One level is individual activism, which includes ethical consumerism, charity, signing petitions, and lobbying officials in an attempt to motivate them toward action. By contrast, collective activism relates to the coordination with others to promote civic activism, for example, joining public demonstrations (Pattie & Seyd, 2003).

The concept of social capital is not only a theoretical concept, but also a descriptive term that has prevailed in the literature since the 19th century, primarily by political economists like Karl Marx, Henry Sotzg'wik, John Bates Claskey, Alfred Marshall, and Edward Bellamy (Farr, 2004). The primary meaning of the theoretical term is the collection of social capital that goes beyond personal capital, which can be transformed to promote the consumption of goods (ibid.). Although none of these theorists has directly focused on the concept of social capital, everyone treated corporations, cartels, stock companies, guilds, unions, shared companies, communes, companies of mutual aid, and cooperation as complements to one another, providing for economic needs and seeking to increase profits, control markets, enhance efficiency, raise wages, improve working conditions (such as shortening working hours), and enhance the class struggle. These scholars thus contributed greatly to the literature on social capital.

This concept developed later in other traditions, especially the pragmatist tradition, as with John Dewey (ibid.). Dewey emphasized the practical aspects of society to solve problems and deal with challenges as part of the communitarian tradition (Campbell, 1998). For Dewey, a society is an association, the coming together in a joint activity to better deal with any effort that is promoted and ratified because it is shared (Farr, 2004, p. 14). According to this perception, there is an emphasis on cooperation, sympathy, and civic education; and a priority on assisting vulnerable communities. It is this critical context and its focus on the social dimension of the economy to bring underserved communities out of poverty and to create sympathy that make the concept of social capital relevant to this discussion.

Pierre Bourdieu (1985) was among the first scholars who directly theorized the concept of social capital. He argued that social capital is manifested in the resources created by social networks or connections, which were largely formalized. Therefore, investment in social groups' membership gives people access to others' resources, thus empowering them to exist and behave in a way that would not be possible without this membership. Bourdieu perceived social capital as a resource that necessarily impacts humans' possibilities in society and explains many of the various social phenomena we see today, especially civic activism (Portes, 1998). Accordingly, unlike the financial market, where material capital is the strongest component, and unlike the state, whose power is derived by its formal authority, in civil society it is social capital that acts as its main driver and explains human behavior.

The number of social networks and their use to advance social goals become essential to understanding the extent of society's success in achieving its broad objectives. In this context, it is important to reflect Bourdieu's position on the importance of symbolic power in society:

> Symbolic power relations tend to reproduce and to reinforce the power relations which constitute the structure of the social space. More concretely, the legitimation of the social order . . . results from the fact that agent apply to the objective structures of the social world structures of perception and appreciation that have emerged from these objective structures and tend therefore to see the world as self-evident. (Bourdieu 1991, cit. Alexander, 1995, p. 141)

Putnam (2000) shifted the social capital discussion from resources into the discussion of social traits. According to Putnam, social capital refers to "relations between individuals—social networks and norms of reciprocity and the resultant trust" (p. 288). This helps people to better address communal challenges. He states that social capital "lubricates the carts that allow society to function and advance more smoothly . . . allows for the development or maintenance of personal characteristics that are good to all the society" (p. 288).

According to Putnam's conceptualization, social capital is a trait or an index for society's development and activity patterns; thus, social capital is not a developmental process, but rather an independent variable, which measures the ability of a society to overcome challenges.

Portes (1998) criticized the shift from viewing social capital as a resource into viewing it as a structural trait, and argued that both aspects are essential. He suggests looking at both resources and traits on the micro and macro levels and examining their interactions to explain social capital's influence. His criticism is important, as it tries to maintain both dimensions of social capital, while maintaining the dynamic and developmental aspect alongside the structural one.

James Farr describes social capital very efficiently. He manages to connect the three main components of social capital to the overall expression of the phenomenon, including social networks, norms, and trust. In his view, social capital is:

> complexly conceptualized as the network of associations, activities, or relations that bind people together as a community via certain norms and psychological capacities, notably trust, which are essential for civil society and productive of future collective action or goods, in the manner of other forms of capital. (Farr, 2004, p. 9)

Rojas, Shah, and Friedland (2011) accept Putnam's and Portes's characterizations of social capital, but concentrate more on its communicative quality. This includes not only social connections but also connections characterized by communicative practices that promote civic engagement. He contends that social capital is a factor in the integration of various social elements. Therefore, communicative practices are another criterion that must be examined when analyzing CSOs' behavior as well as the extent to which they use these practices to promote common goals.

These perceptions of social capital are not necessarily mutually exclusive. If we combine Portes's attitude with that of Rojas et al. and Farr, we may regard social capital as a variable comprising three major elements: a resource based on social networks; a structural social trait, which enables society to promote its common goals more effectively based on norms and trust; and communicative practices, which enable open discussions between civic associations, social movements, and civil activists.

It is important to note that the nature of social capital in one society may differ from that in another, and that these disparities ought to be addressed when examining the discourses and practices of a particular context. It would not be wise to apply general and abstract conceptualizations to concrete realities. The discussion of social capital cannot ignore the liberal slant embedded in its theorization so far. The examination of social capital must take into consideration that it may also take place in illiberal contexts and traditional societies. Voluntarism and social associationalism, social norms, the meaning of trust, and the patterns of communication could have different meanings in different contexts. Therefore, they should be employed to advance our understanding of civic activism.

The Liberal and the Postcolonial in Civil Society

It is important to note in this context that there are two other important critiques of the debates on civil society that are relevant to our discussion below. The first has to do with the sociology of civil society, and it concerns the premise that civil society is inherently egalitarian. This critique is raised by Bhiko Parekh, who points out that even in civil society there is discrimination against minorities and vulnerable groups (Parekh, 2004). In his view, civil society is controlled by the middle class, which violates the principles of equality and equal access to public resources for disadvantaged groups. This element is lost in the project- and democracy-oriented atmosphere dominant in civil society. Parekh argues that we tend to homogenize civil society and thereby undermine our ability to address its internal inequalities (ibid.). This criticism is especially true when we examine the works of Robert Putnam and his followers concerning the subject of social capital. The pluralistic tradition does not refer to inequality within civic organizations, and this lack of attention detracts from our ability to understand some of the important dynamics in civic organizations' activities. In the following pages, we demonstrate that when subaltern civil society struggles for equality and fights against discriminatory state policies, the battle is also between elitist tendencies of civil society and the normal social environment. Civic activists are often more educated than the average citizen, originate from the upper middle class, and conceive of activism as an opportunity to promote their professional careers. Moreover, civil society may entail internal inequalities, especially between those in leadership positions and support staff. These internal inequalities and professional opportunism are important to consider when studying the dynamics between CSOs and their social environments.

The second critique raised by Parekh concerns the universalization of the Western model of civil society and social capital (2004). First, not all CSOs and not all relationships within civil society are the same. Social organizations operate in different social and cultural contexts and therefore take on different roles in various contexts, depending on their respective histories and dominant social institutions (De Maggio & Anheier, 1990). Societies' common values and the ways in which these values are manifested influence the motives of CSOs and their activities (Parekh, 2004). Accordingly, the examination of civil society must take into consideration the prevailing morals and the dominant social structures of society.

Therefore, it is important to operationalize "subjugated knowledge" to critique civic activism. Such knowledge centers on the discourses and practices of those who are subjugated to the dominant power structure and find themselves underprivileged by its mere definition, let alone its policies. This means that the study of civic activism could benefit from laying alternative theoretical foundations to those common in the literature. Such an alternative requires listening to the subaltern and using methodological and theoretical tools provided in the postcolonial literature (Woods, 1992; Bratton, 1989; Bayart, 1986). This literature, according to Hall, "marks a critical interruption into that whole grand historiographical narrative which, in liberal historiography and Weberian historical sociology, as much as in the dominant traditions of Western Marxism, gave this global dimension a subordinate presence in a story which could essentially be told from within its European parameters" (1996, p. 250).

The present context departs from the universalized and homogenized perspectives that dominate the literature on civil society. Furthermore, it challenges the predominant perspective of civil society, which assumes a democratic state and a liberal society when discussing the patterns of conduct and the aspirations of civic activism.

The relevance of the postcolonial perspective is explicated by Homi Bhabha, who argues:

> Postcolonial criticism bears witness to the unequal and uneven
> forces of cultural representation involved in the contest for polit-
> ical and social authority within modern world order. Postcolonial
> perspectives emerge from the colonial testimony of Third World
> countries and the discourses of "minorities" within the geopolitical
> divisions of East and West, North and South. They intervene
> in those ideological discourses of modernity that attempt to
> give a hegemonic "normality" to the uneven development and
> the differential, often disadvantaged, histories of nations, races,
> communities, peoples. They formulate their critical revisions
> around issues of cultural difference, social authority, and political
> discrimination in order to reveal the antagonistic and ambivalent
> moments within the "rationalizations" of modernity. (Bhabha,
> pp. 245–246)

The following analysis emerges from the testimony of CSOs, which represent
a minority discourse "within the cultural and geopolitical division of East
and West, North and South." Our analysis focuses on the discourses and
practices of those who seek to reconstitute their environment and employ
their agency against a power structure that defines itself through the denial,
marginalization, and silencing of the other. It is an analysis that seeks to
reveal the rationalization of the hegemonic regime, which continuously uses
colonial tools to dominate the subaltern. Colonization is not manifested in
geography only. It is also practiced in the topography of consciousness and
memory. The mobilization of educated civic activists is better understood
when such a context is better explicated as a structural condition in which
civic activism takes place.

Thus, exploring subaltern civil society provides us with new knowledge that avoids compliance with power structures and reveals patterns of
social practices that challenge hegemonic power structures. Such an avenue
reveals how and to what extent to which civic mobilization leads to or at
least aspires to deconstruct hegemonic power structures and the normative
order that stands behind it.

Such an approach also comes to critique one of the most prominent
scholars of the postcolonial tradition, Partha Chatterjee, who is viewed to
be elitist and who operates within the confines of the modernist, colonial
state and society. The forthcoming analysis therefore may be characterized as
a form of mobilization for the subaltern in the postcolonial era (Chatterjee,
2001). Despite the importance of Chatterjee's critique of civil society the-

ory, especially his warning of falling into the traps of traditional modernist discourse when practicing anticolonial mobilization, his assertive distinction between civil society and political society may become redundant in the present context.

Chatterjee argues that the concept of civil society currently used in the literature conforms to the normative model of Western modernity, excluding from its scope the vast literature of postcolonial societies. In his view, civil society refers to "those institutions of modern associational life set up by nationalist elite in the era of colonial modernity, though often part of their anti-colonial struggle. These institutions embody the desire of this elite to replicate in its own society the forms as well as the substance of Western modernity" (2001, p. 174). He adds that this desire is "for a new ethical life in society, one that is in conformity with the virtues of the Enlightenment and of bourgeois freedom and whose known cultural forms are those of secularized Western Christianity" (ibid.). Based on this understanding, Chatterjee argues that "civil society will long remain an exclusive domain of the elite, that the actual 'public' will not match up to the standards required by civil society and that the function of civil social institutions in relation to the public at large will be one of pedagogy rather than of free association" (ibid). He argues that for us to better understand the mediating role between the public and the state, especially in the postcolonial era (after independence), one must observe the active role played by political society, which is a separate realm of action from civil society. In his view, political society is a new realm of action practiced by modern political associations such as parties and movements, which seek to strategically maneuver and resist, and are appropriated by different groups and classes in ways that are not always consistent with the principles of civic associations. Political society, according to Chatterjee, is less organized, not elitist, and not necessarily committed to the ethical values of Western bourgeois society.

This point made by Chatterjee cannot be ignored. His attempt to identify the pitfalls of Western, modern ethics of social and political organizations as part of resisting colonial power structures is worth considering. It is essential to differentiate between two aspects of Chatterjee's critique. The first is the difference between civic associationalism that falls within the ethical discourse of enlightened Western modernity and political society as strategic maneuvering and resistance of state power structures. The second aspect relates to the elitist social identity of civil society and the more grassroots-oriented political society. Both are important to consider when dealing with subaltern minority civic activism in a Western, illiberal, postcolonial context. The first critique means that civil society may indirectly spearhead colonization if it adopts the patterns of behavior and the ethics of Western societies.

Notwithstanding this important differentiation between the ethics of civil and political society, it may not be relevant in some independent, postcolonial states and is absolutely not generalizable. In the political context in which Chatterjee's theorizing operates, this differentiation may be appropriate. In a sovereign, postcolonial state such as India, there is a need to differentiate between the imagined sovereign, which is defined by nationalist elites in universal inclusive terms, and subaltern citizens, who struggle for rights that are integral to citizenship and India's constitutional framework. Furthermore, in such contexts, civil society may be professionally elitist by nature. By adopting Western patterns of collective action in a traditional society, the possibility of elitism and, as a result, inefficacy, becomes very plausible. Political mobilization based on grassroots motivations that do not submit to rigid, formal rules may be more representational. This means that the ethics of civil society in the Indian context may embody the traditional modernist discourse, and therefore Chatterjee's critique is important.

However, in a context in which the state does not identify with all its citizens, such as in ethnic postcolonial states, civic associationalism and political mobilization by those excluded from the majority's society and state cannot be separated. In such contexts, the mere definition of the civil is a realm of political struggle between the hegemonic majority and the excluded minority. In such contexts, CSOs are not only essentially political, but political parties and social movements are also civic. Such an understanding does not invalidate Chatterjee's first critique completely. The reduction of civic activism, despite being political, to patterns of associationalism that characterize Western ethics may weaken "authentic" culture and grassroots initiatives. When the civic elite becomes fully engaged in formal dimensions of associationalism, their potential social capital becomes detached from the rest of society (Harriss, 2006).

In this respect, one should also note that in the context of minority struggle against the exclusionary nature of the state, civil *and* political society may become elitist. The institutionalization of struggle could therefore be relevant to both civic as well as political society. In cases in which minority political society is not part of the legitimate power structure and as civil society is inherently political, both realms could be viewed as complementary rather than antagonistic if they do not become detached from subaltern groups within their own society. Such a view does not dismantle

Chatterjee's critique entirely. To the contrary, it draws our attention to the need to examine the relationship between CSOs, political parties, grassroots initiatives, and public attitudes toward all of them.

Chatterjee's critique encourages us to examine what forms of agency emerge from CSOs' resistance and whether they manage to avoid falling into the traps of the dominant power structures' construction group dynamics in a way that makes them malleable to power and its related disciplinary analysis (Latour, 2005, p. 29).

Furthermore, this critique encourages us to examine the extent to which subaltern CSOs formulate independent perceptions of themselves, apart from those propagated by the hegemony, and resist their own alienation as a result of the power structure's dialectics of othering. Chatterjee's critique also motivates us to examine how civil society voices its rights, needs, and freedoms, thereby defying the dominant power structure's silence toward it. This examination of postcolonial civic activism therefore focuses on the discourses and practices of resistance and struggle against repression, subjugation, silencing, and marginalization.

Such perceptions of civic activism may allow us to better examine its normative commitment and that of subaltern agency, revealing how the voices of the dominated become empowered. This examination allows us also to escape two possible analytical traps. The first is that of poststructural theory and the romanticism of subaltern voices. These serve to homogenize it, something about which Aijaz Ahmad warned us in his seminal book *On Theory* (1994). In it, Ahmad makes us aware of the complexities of the subaltern and the need to avoid falling into an "arrant idealization" of the subaltern and "ahistorical leveling" (ibid., p. 205). Chandhoke (2001) makes a similar point when arguing that civil society cannot and should not be romanticized as something that guarantees democracy. Instead, she argues that the civil sphere is better conceived as "a process whereby [citizens] constantly monitor both the state and the monopoly of power in civil society" (ibid., 2001, p. 22).

The second issue we avoid is what Gareth Griffiths calls the "myth of authenticity" in the process of the "reinstalling of indigenous cultures" (1994). In other words, we talk about the dangers of falling into the traps of the counter "hegemonic" self-perception, wherein it is presented as the only authentic form of resistance. Examples include the Islamist movements, which propagate the empty slogan of "Islam is the solution," or the discourse of nationalist movements that not only homogenize the nation, but also marginalize internal voices that seek to promote a differential regime of rights, such as feminist ones. "[M]ythologizing the authentic" is a recurring obstacle in the struggle against hegemony, which either idealizes a single self-perception or a vision. The consequence of such idealization is no less silencing than the power structure it seeks to replace.

In this context, subaltern studies and postcolonial theory facilitate our ability to study the subaltern indigenous national minorities' patterns of civic activism, in which they reside under sophisticated surveillance and a repressive regime that seeks to dismantle the indigeneity's physical and cultural presence. The following analysis enables us to do so without falling into the traps of discursivism, which focuses on a single analytical perspective that prioritizes discourse and language at the expense of the tangible world of the subaltern.

The following study takes into consideration material elements as well as the cultural conditions under which Palestinian civic activism takes place. Furthermore, the lessons learned from postcolonial studies enable us to escape the traps of idealization and provide us with a close, realistic reading of reality without losing the ability to be sensitive to the challenging circumstances in which this activism takes place. From the vantage point of postcolonial theory, we are afforded a balanced perspective that takes into consideration the literature on civil society without accepting most theoretical assumptions underpinning the topic. In this context, civic activism may suffer from the structural bias imposed by Israel's legal and political regimes, but proper study of the phenomenon must deconstruct these biases to reveal the subalterns' patterns of collective action and their meanings.

Moreover, such a theoretically conscious endeavor allows us escape the warnings of Aljandro Colas: that civil society refers only to co-opted "actors, institutions and practices [that] reproduce liberal democracy, freedom and participation on a global scale" (2005). Colas argues that CSOs, whether local or global, work to "[legitimize] and [reproduce] the system of capitalist markets," which he considers to be the "mainspring of global civil society." He also encourages us to be aware of the need to differentiate between various forms of civic activism. This critique is especially important, since it enables us to differentiate between civic activism that contributes to the reproduction of capitalist markets on the one hand and other civic practices that seek to deconstruct hegemonic economic structures and the images they produce about reality.

Chapter 3

Civic Activism, Minority Politics, and National Conflicts

It has become clear so far that most of the literature concerning civil society is located in the liberal-pluralist tradition and assumes that the society in question shares basic common values or at least common aspirations toward the state. Furthermore, most of this literature is based on the assumption of a democratic and open political system, which allows free speech as well as effective social and political mobilization (Cohen & Arato, 1992; Keane, 1998; Seligman, 1992; Berman, 1997). In cases where the literature refers to the emergence of civil society in undemocratic societies, including in the postcolonial literature, it is still an assumption that the civil society in question belongs to a majority in the state and that its internal social forces strive toward a significant political and cultural change (Chatterjee, 2001; Berman, 1997; Touraine, 1983). Even in cases of social and political revolution, the literature refers to society as a single unit and ignores internal cultural or ethno-national conflict (Skocpol, 1979).

Furthermore, the mainstream theoretical literature regarding civil society ignores the position, nature, and activities of civic activism on behalf of minorities, whether ethnic, national, cultural, or otherwise. Minorities are excluded from the theoretical discussions for many reasons. This exclusion is especially true in cases where the minorities are homeland minorities and are in conflict with the state in which they live. When the literature relates to minorities, they are usually referred to under a separate research framework (Keating & McGary, 2001; Kymlicka, 2001).

Therefore, this form of minority civic activism, particularly in complex conflict situations, such as the one we are dealing with in this context, remains relatively uncharted territory. There is a pressing need to draw attention to the importance of homeland minorities or indigenous national minorities that are in conflict with their state, for being affiliated with a different national or cultural majority. The literature on indigenous minorities covers populations in Australia, New Zealand, Canada, Ecuador, Bolivia, Mexico, and elsewhere (Haveman, 1999). This literature emphasizes indigenous people's unique features compared with other minorities and creates a firm moral ground for the variety of political and cultural identities, based on the principle of indigenousness versus the states of these people.

Indigenous peoples are defined by their existence prior to the state and their unique attachment to their homeland, which together create a distinct social culture. They are also defined by their status as a minority and the colonization of their culture by an external one. As a result of this process, the gap between attachment to the land and attachment to the state shapes indigenous peoples' self-perceptions and behavior. In this complex situation, normal civic rights are not sufficient for indigenous peoples. These rights, as defined by the state through citizenship, often impinge on the position of indigenous peoples, who conceptualize themselves as simultaneously outside of and inside the state. Formal citizenship may thus become a control mechanism through which indigenous peoples' behavior is restricted and the legitimization of their political activities challenged (Jamal, 2007a).

In light of this dimension of control, we now witness an expansion of the literature on indigeneity, which has come to describe a variety of unique rights that ought to govern indigenous peoples' situation. This literature also suggests that indigenous minorities' CSOs have special traits inherent in their political activity (Kovokin, 2001; Fox, 1996). These traits, which are unique to national homeland minorities, reveal a special relationship between state, society, and CSOs' activity, especially their level of influence on state policy toward minorities; their empowerment; and their influence in the expansion of democratization processes and the decentralization of power. Most studies in this field suggest that the emergence of CSOs strongly contributes to the indigenous society's empowerment and the expansion of its social capital, which enables homeland minorities to overcome political and social challenges (Genugten & Perez-Bustillo, 2004).

According to this literature, the connection between empowering indigenous society and the democratization of the state is obvious. Studies on Ecuador, Bolivia, and even Australia illustrate the role of indigenous minorities' CSOs in encouraging political participation and empowering their society vis-à-vis policy change, which previously ignored them, their values, and their desires (Hart, Thompson, & Stedman, 2008). CSOs and the growing number of voluntary organizations in minority societies are indications of their growing efforts to influence state policy and their increasing engagement in defining the lifestyle of the minority. According to the comparative literature, this process also indicates a rise in social capital. Hart, Thompson, and Stedman (2008) wrote in this context:

> Yet if civil society was only accessible to those who were culturally equipped, since the 1970s indigenous Australians have been remarkably effective in developing a framework of active indigenous organizations in the cities and towns of Australia. Indigenous activists have mobilized indigenous communities within the mainstream Australian legal/cultural environment so that there are indigenous organizations for research, housing, health, broadcasting, art, dance and a wide range of other areas of life. Though some of these were facilitated by government bodies they represent an indigenous civil activism within mainstream society. (56)

Kovokin makes a similar point in the case of Ecuador:

> The Otavalo experiences, however, shed light on the relationship between these struggles and the process of political democratization. Barred from official recognition as local governments, the leaders of Otavalo indigenous communities have developed into active participants in civil society, mobilizing their members against the white-mestizo authorities. This mobilization created some of the disruption so feared by liberal students of civil society. It is doubtful, however, that Otavalo communities would have been able to change local relations of power otherwise. In the context of land reform and the national drive toward democracy, indigenous struggles were perceived as legitimate by at least some segments of the national political community, including those associated with the reformist military, the Partido Socialista, and Izquierda Democratica. Conversely, the indigenous movement in Ecuador had incorporated elements of national developmentalist and leftist discourse, fusing them with centuries old indigenous values. (Kovokin, 2001, pp. 58–59)

Despite these conclusions, one cannot ignore the necessary distinction that ought to be made between the success of CSOs in mobilizing and empowering minority society and their success in promoting the state's democratization. The relationship between the two is not obvious, and they are not necessarily conditioned by each other. CSOs may empower their society, but they will not necessarily affect the state or promote its democratization. In other words, the growing strength of CSOs and the expansion of their activities may invoke a negative reaction by the state. In such cases, the state may observe the activities of certain associations—for example, human rights organizations—as offensive or oppositional to its purposes. Furthermore, the state might perceive the activities of minority CSOs as encouraging or nurturing values, customs, or behaviors that contradict the state's values or oppose its objectives.

The rise of minority civic activism, especially if it comes to promote the culture and heritage of the minority, may lead the state to respond aggressively by limiting civic activism that defies its ideology through anti-democratic legislation. Minority civic activism may be perceived or at least constructed by the state as an existential threat, using *defensive democracy* means, which compromise substantial democratic values (Pedhazur, 2004; Fischer, 2007).

Civil Society and Political Culture

The examination of the associational dimensions of civil society renders the neo-institutional emphasis on political culture relevant to our discussion and enhances our understanding of civic activism (Grendstad & Selle, 1995, Schmidt, 2008; Lowndes, 1996). Political culture is conceived as a collection of conventions and norms, which defines right and wrong and legitimate or illegitimate behavior for the various political players, including the regime and its opposition. The ideological infrastructure, even when it is not formal or openly proclaimed, grants the regime and other players the legitimacy to act in specific ways and limits their choice to behave in other ways. The identity of social and political players is inherently tied to political values, norms, and tradition (Lowndes, 1996). These values, norms, and traditions greatly influence patterns of association and spaces of action. Accordingly, we can distinguish between tolerant and intolerant, deliberative and authoritative, and peaceful and violent political values.

While a tolerant political culture is based on granting wide legitimacy to variance and disputes, which are peacefully resolved through various ideological means, intolerant political culture restricts variance and dictates uniform and fixed behavior and thinking patterns. A deliberative political culture enables debates and opinion exchanges in order to create meaningful debates regarding the good and preferred way of life. Authoritative political culture, on the other hand, is based on segregation and hierarchy and views variance as a threat that should be neutralized. A peaceful political culture focuses on handling variance through peaceful means, such as communication and deliberative understanding. A violent political culture legitimizes enforcement, aggression, and subordination of the other in the name of alternative collective ideals.

Civic activism may take place in complex cultural environments. This is especially true for homeland minorities that belong to a broader cultural nation, but live in an alien political culture. In such cases, it is important to explore the exact cultural values that influence civic associations and the way these values translate into the civic sphere. In this regard, one must pay attention to the relationship between broader cultural values and the values predominant in the discourse of CSOs. One must also consider those values manifested in civil society's organizational and procedural dimensions. There may be multiple external influences from the meeting of different cultural traditions. Such influences may be mutual and lead to complex consequences that require special attention. These cultural combinations may have external and internal influences on CSOs' modes of activism. The modern institutional structure of CSOs may entail internal traditional modes of behavior that establish a gap between what is observed (appearance) and what really happens (Sharabi, 1988). Furthermore, multiple cultural influences may lead to contradictory patterns of behavior in civil society, even within the same CSO. Such phenomena are known to us from the experience of feminist organizations, in which patriarchal power relations are sometimes institutionalized and stand in contradiction with declared norms and aspirations. This type of institutional cultural gap is even more salient in cases in which minority CSOs are caught between their own cultural tradition and an antagonistic hegemonic culture. In such cases, especially when the hegemonic cultural seeks to colonize that of the minority, parts of civil society may choose to focus on protecting the identity and traditional cultural values of the minority. Such activism can lead to direct contradictions with other civic activists within the same culture. This is most apparent when looking at the place of women in conservative religious civic associations or when examining power relations in many feminist CSOs. Further to that, the uniqueness of the present case study, which we explore later, adds to this other dimension that must be taken into consideration.

Palestinian civic activism exists within the Israeli context, which is based on Jewish-Zionist ideology and cultural history, whose ideals are foreign and even antagonistic to Arab culture. Israeli political culture is focused on the ideals of Zionism, which is dedicated to strengthening the Jewish people's stand in the State of Israel and promoting its control over its political and cultural spheres. Political Zionism views itself as part of Western culture, and its social and political values are characterized by a combination of rigid ethno-national concepts and strong liberal and republican ideals. This combination carries implications over every aspect of life in Israel, collective or individual, including CSOs.

Understanding the Israeli legal-judicial system is essential to understanding Israeli political culture and its implications over civil society. Israeli law is based on various sources, mainly British and American, which emphasize the importance of the civic sphere and social autonomy. The State of Israel has adopted the Ottoman Millet system, and in the early 1980s made adjustments to fit the social and political demands that emerged in the state's first few decades. Until 1980, CSOs were called Ottoman Societies. The enactment of the CSO Law (1980) was meant to formalize the distinction between the state and its civil society, opening the door to civic-voluntary work that would complement and balance the state. The CSO Law reveals the regime's willingness to shift some responsibilities for the public sphere into the hands of voluntary associations, which would act according to different standards than were previously accepted. It was one of many changes that occurred in Israeli political culture during the 1970s, particularly the rising trend of privatization and the decline of the welfare state and of collectivist political culture, which was replaced by a liberal-individualist and capitalist culture based on a free market economy led by the state.

These trends work hand in hand with the free market economy concept, which has become the state's main ideology along with the reappearance of national-conservative ideals in the political and social spheres (Ram, 2005; Filc & Ram, 2004; Rivlin, 2011). The combination of aggressive conservative nationalism and economic neoliberalism has had a wide-reaching influence over CSOs' activity. Following conservative politics and economic worldviews ideological differentiation processes have become prominent among CSOs. The state began to side with associations that promoted this common political-financial paradigm. It also limited the leeway of competing CSOs, which promoted a liberal civil paradigm and demanded restoration of the welfare state's values. These trends influenced the activity of Palestinian CSOs and dictated their expanse and level of influence over their environment.

The other cultural-political aspect of this complex context is the PCI's Arab-Islamic subset. The PCI, which belongs to the Arab nation and to the Islamic religion and civilization, is an integral part of the Palestinian people. This cultural-political dynamic determines society's basic ideals and dominant social structure, which is translated into social and political patterns of action and behavior, similar to those of various other Arab societies. While Arab societies have no influence on the legal and judicial aspects of the PCI, they are still a source of cultural and religious inspiration. Their social and cultural core values, as well as the social and behavioral structure of Arab society, are derived from Arab civilization—a relatively conservative one based on traditional fundamental values. Its political culture is mainly based on clans, tribes, and localities, though in large cities we may see an urban social culture with individualist tendencies. Furthermore, Arab social and political culture is deeply rooted in traditional and religious values, even in modern Arab states. Most Arab states are characterized by both a modern legal-judicial formal structure and informal, traditional sociopolitical core values. The tensions that arise from this balance often erupt and endanger the community's social and political stability, as we have witnessed since the Jasmine Revolution in Tunisia at the end of 2010 and to this day (Achcar, 2016; Jamal & Kensicki, 2016; Lynch, 2014).

Therefore, to understand the behavior patterns and development processes of the PCI, we must closely examine similar or different developments in the wider regional context, as we shall do in the next two chapters.

Contextualizing Palestinian Civic Activism in Israel

The growing presence of Palestinian CSOs in the public sphere has attracted attention to this phenomenon in the last few years. A number of scholars, including Shani Payes (2003), Oded Haklai (2004, 2008), Dan Rabinowitz (2001), Ayman Agbaria and Muhanad Mustafa (2014), and the author of this book (2008), have explored the issue. Despite the fact that each of these studies contributed to our understanding of the rise of Palestinian CSOs in Israel, all focused on specific aspects of the phenomenon, rather than the entire picture. Most provided empirical evidence and were based on fieldwork. Payes's research was the most comprehensive thus far. She focused on the expansion of the Palestinian CSO sector and illustrated the relationship between Palestinian CSOs and the Israeli State, arguing that "[a]lthough the importance of Palestinian CSOs in Israel is rarely acknowledged in scholarly literature, these organizations have in fact played a significant political role in the campaign of the Palestinian minority for civil equality in Israel" (82). She expanded on this, noting that:

> Their contribution has manifested itself in the creation of avenues for participation in public life by groups that have traditionally been under-represented. First and foremost, they have empowered the Palestinian minority vis-à-vis the state and the Jewish majority. CSOs have also contributed to the process of empowerment by enhancing the professional ability of Palestinians to oppose discriminatory state policies. (Ibid., p. 84)

Payes follows in Korten's (1990) footsteps, illustrating that Palestinian CSOs in Israel have moved from promoting welfare through development to building political awareness and mobilization (Payes, 2003, p. 83). Her conclusions from 2003 are still relevant today. The level of civic activity in the PCI cannot be ignored. Over the last two decades, we have seen CSOs flood the public agenda and organize different activities, such as conventions, workshops, educational courses, empowerment groups, and educational tours; publish in various venues, such as the media, academia, and advertisements, and make noteworthy and consequential court appearances. Many CSOs provide services in basic social fields, such as welfare, health, housing, education, sports, culture, and art.

Despite its wide scope, two of the weak points in Payes's research are that she only focuses on the conflictual relations between Palestinian CSOs and the state, and that she fails to pay sufficient attention to internal developments, such as organizational considerations, human resources, and the similarities and differences between and within CSOs. Most important, she does not address a very important avenue of Palestinian activism, namely the CSOs' affiliation with the Islamic Movement. Notwithstanding these failures, Payes's arguments remain important to any understanding of the emergence and manifestations of Palestinian CSOs. Her argument is true: The number of Palestinian CSOs has grown steadily over the last three decades, while Palestinian civil society in general has experienced ups and downs at a few historic crossroads. Payes provides a partial explanation for the rise in the number of Palestinian CSOs. However, her explanation as to the reasons behind this trend is neither comprehensive nor satisfactory.

The following analysis of Palestinian civic activism builds on Payes's efforts. However, it avoids the institutionalist bias that characterizes her treatment. Although it is important to address the organizational aspects of CSOs, only through providing a comprehensive examination of the political, sociological, cultural, and material aspect of civic activism is one able to develop a comprehensive understanding of this phenomenon and its ramifications. Furthermore, notwithstanding the importance of the institutional dimensions of CSOs, conceptualizing them as autonomous agents that precede their interaction with their environment is analytically problematic.

CSOs are structured by their environment as much as they seek to structure it. Such an understanding provides us with a dynamic view of civic activism and does not submit to a total and rigid institutionalist epistemology. It also takes into consideration developments in neo-institutional theory from the last few decades (Schmidt, 2008). Ontologically, CSOs' activism cannot be considered as given, neither normatively nor analytically. It is a constantly evolving phenomenon. Therefore, viewing it as a process guarantees a better understanding of it. This multifocal view of the process assists in comprehending the human, organizational, and normative dimensions of the phenomenon under study. One of the important aspects of Payes's observations is the rising associationalism in Arab society in Israel, manifested in the rising number of Palestinian CSOs and their intensive involvement in the public's social affairs.

Payes reflects that it has led to the emergence of new forms of social capital that did not exist before. It could be of great empirical importance to explore the extent to which social capital empowers the PCI. This social capital strengthens its political influence and has led to a serious improvement in the PCI's ability to address state policies of discrimination and repression (Jamal, 2006a). We must ask whether Palestinian civic activism contributes to the empowerment and development of the PCI.

We know that CSOs provide services in various fields including education, health, communication, welfare, religion, planning, research, gender, housing, higher education, municipalities, law, and so forth. Furthermore, they support and promote the rights of Palestinian citizens in Israel and worldwide, providing necessary information for political mobilization, identity creation, and cultural preservation. Moreover, it makes sense in this context to search for answers to questions regarding the efficacy of civic activism and the nature of the relationship between the rise of an educated middle class and the patterns of civic activism in the PCI.

Before we proceed, it is also important to point out that efficacy of civic activism is not limited to positive material achievements. It is also important to mark symbolic achievements, such as its capacity to challenge the state's image and make it react in ways that better mirror its true exclusive ethnic character. This challenge causes its institutions to react to Palestinian civil society to its own detriment. In other words, civic activism could be considered effective if it leads the state to reveal certain aspects of its character that were veiled in the past and therefore could not have been easily addressed by civic activism.

Payes suggests in her research that there are high expectations of Palestinian CSOs. According to her analysis, it seems that these organizations succeed in their mission to influence the state and change its policy. Despite this impression, partly created by the state itself, one must provide an explanation for the state's policies toward the PCI, which have been developing in an opposite direction (Democracy Index, 2011; *Sikkuy Report*, 2010). The state's policies toward the PCI have radically worsened in recent years, as new legal restrictions have been placed on their political and social activities (Jamal, 2016, 2017; Jabareen, 2014). The way this trend relates to the process of civic activism thus becomes an interesting avenue to explore.

Payes also does not address the impact of Palestinian CSOs on Arab societal culture. In particular, she does not address whether CSOs' activism has had any impact on the liberalization or religionization of the PCI, something we contend cannot be ignored. This has had a serious effect on the relationship between secular and religious civic activism, and Payes's treatment thus ignores the extent of civic associations' success in promoting liberalism and civic ideals within the PCI.

Oded Haklai (2004) provides us with a different, very well-founded study of Palestinian civic activism in Israel. He uses the terminology "ethnic civil society" to describe Palestinian civic activism in Israel (p. 165). In so doing, Haklai emphasizes the superficial commitment of Palestinian CSOs and thereby idealizes a metaphysical perception of civil society, which he applies in critically analyzing this particular case study. According to Haklai, Palestinian civic activism is limited to the services of a nationally and culturally defined society, rather than defending the principle human rights that could serve every citizen. While Haklai contributes in great measure to the understanding of Palestinian CSOs in Israel, he expresses bias when arguing that Palestinian CSOs should not be perceived as promoting civic-universal ideals, but rather as "*ethnic mobilization*, targeting the *empowerment of an ethnic community*" (ibid., p. 157, emphasis added, A. J.). Haklai's terminology of ethnic civil society is thus limited and rife with internal contradictions. For example, according to Haklai:

[E]thnic CSOs can attempt to transform the state by renegotiating the extent of state autonomy from the dominant ethnonational forces, or, they can form ethnically based institutions that are isolated from those of the state. Such associations, however, are not based on the inclusive societal ties normally associated with civil society activities. Rather, these are ethnically exclusive linkages. In constructing these bonds, as I hope to demonstrate in the ensuing discussion of the PAI, ethnically based civil society asks, explicitly or implicitly, for formal recognition of the community it seeks to represent, thus, contributing to the institutionalization of the ethnic identity of the minority group. (Haklai 2008, p. 3)

Haklai's findings are based on three significant conditions, which are briefly explained here: First, the Palestinian CSOs referred to in Haklai's research are not exclusively Palestinian. Many CSOs employ Jewish activists, who share the same values and wish to promote civic culture and democratization in Israel. Many Palestinian CSOs, including The Galilee Society, Adalah, Women Against Violence, Mossawa, I'lam, and others, are open to any social activist who shares the same civic values and wishes to join them. These CSOs' enlistment criteria have never been ethnic. Many have employed or still employ Jews as well as activists and volunteers from the international community.

Second, Haklai dismisses Palestinian CSOs' claim that they promote universal-liberal ideals by their demand for equal citizenship, just like other minorities in different countries, and insinuates that such claims are dishonest (Keane, 1998a). His concept of ethnic civil society suggests that Palestinian CSOs manipulate and use liberal ideals to serve limited ethnic causes. This may be true in some cases of Palestinian CSOs, especially antiliberal and religious ones. Yet Haklai's generalizing terminology goes even further, as he tries to reduce all Palestinian civic activism into an identity-related, collective effort, infected with cunning.

It is possible to provide many examples that demonstrate the weaknesses of such narrow conceptualizations. The civic values of the Future Vision document, published by the High Follow-Up Committee for Palestinian Citizens of Israel in 2006, reflects the efforts made to demand equal rights for all citizens in Israel. The call of this document is that the State of Israel does not subordinate the whole political, constitutional, and legal order to narrow ethnic considerations, as has been manifested in the nation-state law enacted by the Knesset in 2018 (Jamal, 2018). While a contribution of several Palestinian CSOs reinforces their national identity, the activities of other CSOs cannot be reduced to the mere politics of identity. Many Palestinian CSOs lead wide-ranging cultural and political projects, promote liberalization within Palestinian society, and sometimes pay high prices in terms of social prestige, as in the case of feminist CSOs (Yisachar, 2009). Some of the most active CSOs are feminist or LGBT organizations such as Women Against Violence, Kayan, Assiwar, Azzahra', Nissa Wa-Afaq, Aswat, and Al-Qaws; all of them promote gender equality, empowerment, and liberal education for tolerance and pluralist values. These organizations are aware of the implications of their demand for equality and its consequences on Palestinian society and Israeli society. It is not reasonable to assume that all of these organizations are ethnically manipulative or pursue ethnic values only.

Furthermore, by restricting the discussion of Palestinian CSOs to ethnic boundaries, Haklai blames this CSOs' network for the failure to democratize the state. Instead of placing the blame on the state, which ignores the demands of a significant portion of its population and promotes racial laws, such as the citizenship law, the Nakba Law, the CSO Law, and the nation-state law, Haklai's analysis renders Palestinian civic activism against such laws as ethnically oriented.

Haklai's reading of the relationship between Israel and its Palestinian population as a whole may shed some light on the origins of his definition of Palestinian civil society as ethnic. In his book *Palestinian Ethnonationalism In Israel* (2011), Haklai suggests that institutional fragmentation processes and structural changes in the state are the main sources of the Palestinian population's political mobilization. Additionally, the Jewish majority's insistence on preserving the state's ethno-national identity deprives Palestinian citizens of political influence and equal allocation of resources. This reality weakens the state's control over its Palestinian citizens and also reflects their antagonism toward the state, leading to political mobilization that creates new civic and political organizations. When explaining Palestinian political dynamics, Haklai bases his explanations on the state's actions, rendering Palestinian political and civic agents reactive if not passive. In doing so, he robs them of their agency and role as political and cultural actors, awarding the state the main role in determining and conceptualizing Palestinian mobilization. Haklai also encloses Palestinian political and civil activism in an analytical framework that singularly views them as hostile to the state; thus, he joins a series of Israeli scholars who perceive Palestinian politics from the perspective of Jewish national security and promotes an epistemology of compliance (Jamal, 2019; Matza, 2019).

Dan Rabinowitz (2001) provokes the literature on civil society, especially concerning the relationship between practices of civic activism and values promoted by it. Based on his contrasting of civil society literature in the West with that of the Arab world, Rabinowitz differentiates between civil society as a valuational project that comes to promote civic values, such as equality, and civil society as a network of institutions providing protection vis-à-vis the repressive hand of the state. Through an ethnographic examination of the Islamic Movement's practices in the Arab city of Umm Al-Fahm located in the northeastern part of Israel, Rabinowitz sheds light on the strategies adopted by the Islamic Movement and contrasts them with the main conceptualizations and features of civil society known from the Western tradition. Using the case of the Islamic Movement, he explores the uniqueness of its educational project and the way it is translated into a network of civic organizations that intervene in society, not only providing services that the state is reluctant to afford them, but also protecting society from the authoritarian policies of the state.

Rabinowitz's analysis of the Islamic Movement demonstrates the cultural bias and embedded racial underpinnings found in Western conceptualizations of civil society, based on its differentiation between progressive liberal societies and its view of the "backward" Islamic mentality (Rabinowitz, 2001, p. 352). In doing so, Rabinowitz demonstrates the fundamental gap between civic activism under the auspices of the Islamic movement and the protection of civic values, especially equality between men and women. According to his analysis, the Islamic Movement promotes constructive projects that answer basic needs of society, but does not respect basic civic liberal values, especially gender equality and personal freedoms. Rabinowitz demonstrates that CSOs affiliated with the Islamic Movement in Israel are similar to CSOs active in the Arab world that provide protection in the face of social disintegration and the fierce hand of the state. In both contexts, asserting traditional social values does not match the philosophy and ethics of human rights, known to us from the liberal tradition. He believes that it is more appropriate to speak of civil society in Umm Al-Fahm in terms of political struggle, thereby demonstrating Haklai's argument about the ethnic orientation of many Palestinian CSOs, as well as Payes's argument concerning the political impact of Palestinian civil society, taking into consideration that many of these CSOs were outlawed by the Israeli cabinet in November 2015. Being aware of the illiberal and essentialist features of the civic project provided by the Islamic Movement, Rabinowitz still asserts the importance of the civic model for resistance to state policies. Therefore, Rabinowitz seems to differentiate between the forms of activism and networking on the one hand and the values promoted by such efforts on the other. The Islamic Movement's civic activism set a model for him that ought to be adopted by other CSOs but with a clear commitment to equality and tolerance.

Rabinowitz's analysis forms a very important background for the following analysis of Palestinian civic activism in Israel. Writing almost two decades after his study enables us to revisit these same religious CSOs and see if any changes have occurred in their worldview and their practices. Furthermore, it enables us examine the relationship between CSOs belonging to the Islamic Movement and more liberal ones, especially the willingness of the former to tolerate and cooperate with the latter to promote common policies that counter the repressive state's discriminatory policies. This approach also enables us to revisit and compare their toleration for pluralism and gender equality in Palestinian society in the present.

Another important study of Palestinian civil society in Israel is that conducted by Ayman Igbariya and Muhanad Mustafa. They also provide us with a comparative study of two Palestinian CSOs involved in the field of education and identity formation (Agbaria & Mustafa, 2014). The Follow-Up Committee on Arab Education (FUCAE) is a secular organization that operates under the auspices of the National Committee for Arab Mayors and Iqraa, the Association for the Promotion of Education in the Arab society, a faith-based organization that is controlled by the Islamic Movement in Israel, which was outlawed in November 2015. According to Igbariya and Mustafa, whereas FUCAE aspires to represent Arab society as a whole, Iqraa was established by the Northern Faction of the Islamic Movement to improve its position among Arab students in institutions of higher education throughout Israel. The authors examine the ideological and functional differentiation between the two organizations, juxtaposing their goals, strategies, arenas of action, and funding sources.

The comparison of the FUCAE and Iqraa is based on the assumption that the two organizations represent two forms of civic activism, challenging state policies in the field of identity formation. The findings of the authors demonstrate that both organizations are involved in politics of recognition, based on difference. However, according to the authors, the two organizations diverge in three central areas. The first is "the arenas in which they locate their difference—the groups they wish to differ from and within" (ibid., p. 53). The second area is "the use of difference—the politics through which they wish to accentuate and/or conceal their various distinguishing boundaries within and as opposed to the groups from, or within, which they wish to distinguish themselves" (ibid., p. 53). The third is "the destination of difference—the underlying goal which motivates their politics to accentuate and/or conceal their differentiation" (ibid., p. 53). Furthermore, a comparison between the two organizations shows that "FUCAE represents the quintessence of the politics of contention: opposing the Jewish and democratic State hegemony, calling for the establishment of an encompassing, secular Palestinian Israeli identity, and demanding national recognition and differential group rights" (ibid., p. 54). Accordingly, they argue that FUCAE "seeks to achieve these goals with capacities that the hegemonic discourse allows; they seek change from within, using the tools and opportunities that democracy—e.g., protest, litigations, and lobbying provides based on the exclusive nature of the State as a Jewish State" (ibid., p. 54). By contrast, Iqraa represents the transition of the Islamic Movement's orientation from local to national activity. Thereby, "it constitutes a new breed which places Arab society, or central parts of it, at the focus of their activity. It promotes politics of difference which resist the hegemonic discourse of a Democratic-Jewish State from without, rather than from within" (ibid., p. 54).

All studies reviewed in this section are valuable. They enrich our knowledge of Palestinian civil society in Israel. Despite the fact that they represent different theoretical and methodological traditions, all of them focus on issues of identity and recognition. However, none of these studies, except for Payes's, provides empirical data from the real Palestinian civic activists. Furthermore, all of them frame Palestinian civil society within Western conceptualizations and do not devote sufficient attention to the ethical and cultural dimensions of civic activism. Rabinowitz, Agbaria, and Mustafa, who do manage to relate to Islamic CSOs, provide a thorough analysis of only some aspects of these CSOs' patterns and networking.

These theorizations of Palestinian civic activism from a purely Western perspective and the lack of sufficient empirical evidence drawn from the experiences of civic activists render the following analysis not only relevant, but also necessary. This study overcomes this gap in the literature, providing us with a better understanding of the relationship between the PCI and the state of Israel and the internal ethical and ideological differences and struggles within the PCI.

The examination of a subaltern civil society in a hegemonic context, as in the present case, expands on the literature of civic activism and reveals how activists construct an autonomous civic sphere in which the subaltern identity is developed alongside the basic values of society. The examination of Palestinian civic activism in Israel provides evidence of patterns of identity formations and modes of resistance that have not yet been presented in the literature. While it is true that the present case is unique, its particularity may be a useful, constructive tool that enriches our knowledge of certain aspects of civic activism that have not yet been deeply explored.

Chapter 4

Political Culture and Civil Society

Relevant Lessons from the Arab World

The relationship between Palestinian civic activism in Israel and civil society in the rest of Arab world may not be readily apparent. However, examining theorizations and empirical examinations from the Arab world could be valuable, as this chapter shows. The chapter argues that as the cultural values salient in Arab society are the same values that dominate the political imagination and major patterns of behavior among the PCI's civil and political elite, it is worth applying some of the same insights learned from these other contexts. This transfer of theory and empirical insight does not ignore the uniqueness of the subaltern Palestinian minority. This is also true as this study does not adopt an exclusively cultural explanation for the rise of Palestinian CSOs in Israel and their patterns of civic activism. However, because the PCI views itself as part of the Arab world and is influenced by deep cultural and political motivations and modes of collective conduct rooted in Arab social structures, it is necessary to locate Palestinian civic activism in its Arab context, as well as the Israeli one.

The historical consciousness and cultural identity of the PCI are deeply connected to the Arab world, and its common political ideologies are reflected in many other Arab countries. In this respect, there are the three major ideologies dominating the Palestinian political scene in Israel: political Islam, nationalism, and communism. These main ideological streams in Palestinian politics in Israel are reflected in the leadership dominating Arab societies, especially when talking about nationalism and political Islamism. The PCI conceives itself as part of the Palestinian people, which is affiliated with Arab and Islamic civilization, religion, language, and norms. Given that these characteristics have an impact on individual and collective patterns of behavior, understanding their place in the PCI's collective action is necessary.

Therefore, when providing an explanation as to the rise of Palestinian civic activism in Israel and exploring their patterns of behavior, especially their relationship with society, one must bring in the broader Arab social and cultural context. This context is unique from others in that its civic organizations face a social structure and set cultural values that are not neutral to its activities.

The following analysis of a subaltern indigenous civil society does not belittle the fact that Israel and surrounding Arab states are two different political contexts with different relationships between state and society. It does not ignore the fact that Palestinians in Israel are an indigenous minority in a state defined in narrow and exclusive ethnic terms and leads policies of repression and discrimination against the minority. Because the following analysis does not focus on state structures or their constitutional foundations, but rather on civic activism, and as this activism is deeply related to the dominant culture, the similarities and differences between Palestinian society and the broader Arab one may contribute to a comprehensive explanation of Palestinian civil activism, its behavior, and its goals.

Further to that and despite the fact that Israel maintains a democratic political system within the Green Line that allows for procedural, majoritarian decision making; a separation of powers; elections for parliament; and an autonomous civil society (Peled & Shafir, 2005; Azoulay & Ophir, 2008), the relationship between Israel and the PCI is antagonistic. Israel does not represent the political and civic aspirations of the PCI. The PCI's values are conceived by the hegemonic Jewish majority and the Israeli security apparatus as a threat that should be securitized and as a backward remnant of traditional society to be resocialized. These perceptions, reflected in official state documents (The Or Commission Report) and in public opinion (The Annual Democracy Index of the Israel Democracy Institute), provide sufficient evidence that when it comes to the Palestinian homeland minority, the Jewish hegemony of the Israeli state turns its regime into pseudo-authoritarian that uses majoritarian processes to maintain a democratic façade (Jamal, 2017).

When it comes to Palestinian affairs, the Israeli political system employs an automatic, majoritarian decision-making process. The state fully ascribes to a common good that solely reflects the interests of the Jewish people. This "good" is viewed by the majority of its Jewish citizenry to be antagonistic with Palestinian aspirations and rights in Israel (The Israel Democracy

Institute, 2015, 2016, 2017). Furthermore, Israel leads a project of internal colonization of Arab areas, of which the best manifestation is the "Admission Commissions Law," which enables Jewish settlements to block Palestinians' entry. Another example is the manner in which Israel confiscates land and demolishes unrecognized villages in the Negev, all of which pave the way for new Jewish settlements (Kedar, Amara, & Yiftachel, 2018). Israel's legacy of democratic decision-making processes is not based on the will of all citizens of the state. As a result, Palestinian citizens are not considered *philia* (civic friends) and therefore do not take part in determining the Israeli common good.

Moreover, notwithstanding the avenues given to Palestinian civic activists in Israel, one cannot limit the scope of collective Palestinian political behavior from the vantage point of their Israeliness only. Doing so would mean joining most studies of the PCI from the perspective of the hegemonic paradigm, namely the politics of compliance. The main characteristic of this paradigm is that it locates Palestinian society solely within the confines of Israeli citizenship and that it seeks to examine the extent to which Palestinian citizens comply with Israel's political and legal order. From this view, Palestinian citizens are usually differentiated based on their level of loyalty to the rules and values of the Israeli regime. The theory of Palestiniazation versus Israelization presented by Sammy Smooha and the theory of politicization presented by Elie Rekhess, two major Israeli scholars of the Palestinian minority, fall within the confines of the compliance paradigm (Smooha, 1992, 2012; Rekhess, 1993). The main concern of these scholars is the extent to which Palestinian citizens have accepted and internalized Israeli values and rules of the game. When such a view is historically contextualized, one can see a direct relationship between this paradigm and the views that dominated the Israeli security apparatus beginning with its first prime minister, David Ben Gurion, and ending with the current prime minister, Benjamin Netanyahu (Jamal, 2019).

In contrast to such a paradigm, one must pose two alternative propositions. The first is that, because it is only natural that Palestinian citizens resist the Israeli rules of the game, their political behavior cannot be measured via these rules, as if they are neutral. These rules were historically imposed on them and sought to force them to accept the Jewish hegemony, promoted by the state. As mentioned earlier, the PCI have never been an integral part of the Israeli "common good." This common good is exclusively determined by Jewish values and is limited to enhancing the Jewish Israelis' interests and privileges. Palestinian citizens are discriminated against and are not welcome to take part in determining the values and interests of the Israeli state. Their political representation in the Israeli Knesset is excluded from the main junctures of power (Rouhana & Huneidi, 2017). Therefore, the democratic procedures in which they take part become a questionable façade used to create a false impression of Palestinian participation.

Moreover, if Palestinian collective behavior is seen from within the sole confines of the Israeli rules of the game, then any effort to resist their surveillance or control is condemned as deviant, and any such efforts are depicted as a danger to the state security and Jewish society. Such a perspective of Palestinian citizens, well established in the Israeli media, is not only limited, but also renders the dominant paradigm in the literature on Palestinian society a tool of control. This tool justifies, or at least complements, Israel's other legal and institutional guidelines (Harlap, 2017; Lavi & Jamal, 2019). Such an understanding invites a critique that liberates the study of the Palestinian community from the grips of a hegemonic theoretical paradigm and presents us with a different starting point that overcomes Israel's confining "rules of the game." Examining the collective behavior of the PCI means that one should consider this behavior solely from within Israel's seemingly democratic Israeli regime. The PCI should also be conceptualized as something that is apart from it.

The second proposition is that the PCI's Arab nationality and culture are deeply embedded in its patterns of collective behavior, as seen in various forms of its civic activism. Many Palestinian CSOs in Israel are engaged in cultural activities, such as theater, music, art, cinema, education, literature, poetry, and media. These CSOs, such as Khashabi Theater, Al-Ma'amal, Umm Al-Fahm Art Gallery, Arab Culture Association, Fattoush Gallery, Mahmoud Darwish Cultural Center, Nazareth Fringe Theater Ensemble, and the Union of Arab-Palestinian Authors, are deeply connected to similar CSOs throughout the Arab world. Therefore, the PCI's CSOs are influenced by cultural trends in Cairo, Beirut, Damascus, Tunisia, and other Arab cities. This exchange of ideas with CSOs in the Arab world is achieved either directly through in-person meetings abroad or via new media tools and video conferences. The behavioral patterns of the Palestinian CSOs in Israel reflect their alienation from the hegemonic Israeli culture, which is gradually becoming more nationalistic and religious. This alienation is manifested in the policies of Israel's Ministry of Culture over the last few years, as well as in the PCI's inability to reconcile its national identity with its citizenship. The tension between the two has become an avenue through which civic activism is articulated.

Accordingly, the paradigm of compliance does not allow us to view the Palestinian community's collective behavior in light of its threatened identity and injured historical consciousness. To do so would enhance our understanding of the dominant culture's role and impact on the PCI and reveal how certain political formulas enable it to protect its identification with its Palestinian heritage and broader Arab culture. This perspective does not ignore the Israeli context in which this community operates. Instead, it renders this context the structure in which the diverse Palestinian community acts with collective political agency and conducts itself as Palestinian nationals and cultural Arabs. The critique expressed by Israeli officials regarding Palestinian cultural life, such as in cinema and theater, is an indication of the growing antagonism between the PCI and Israeli politics and society.

The PCI is not only deeply influenced by political and cultural developments in Arab societies in the Middle East, but also has invested significant effort in maintaining its connections with other Arab countries. Despite the fact that the legal and economic reality in the Arab countries does not directly influence the daily life of Palestinian citizens, many in the PCI closely follow their ideological and cultural developments. Witnessing these developments has inspired many Palestinians to mobilize their own political movements. This is true for the 1967 or 1973 wars, but also for smaller events, such as the nationalization of the Suez Canal in 1956, the establishment of the United Arab Republic in 1958, Black September in 1970, the assassination of Sadat in 1981, and the Arab Spring in 2010–2011 in many Arab states (Jamal, 2017).

It is true that most Arab states are authoritarian and, until the Arab Spring, had no legacy of an autonomous civil society that acts freely and promotes social values or interests vis-à-vis the state (Achcar, 2016). The authoritative regimes—republican or monarchic—existed and still exist in all Arab states except for Tunisia. The Arab Spring raised the possibility for democratization in the Arab world, even if it enjoyed only limited success (Jamal & Kensicki, 2016; Brownlee, Masoud & Reynolds, 2015; Lynch, 2014). The political culture and regimes in these revolutionized states have not developed favorably toward democratization and the emergence of an autonomous civil society. Therefore, the issue of civil society is still young and fragile in Arab states, especially where CSOs failed to lead the revolutions' mobilization and where protests were mostly disorganized. Though CSOs were among the leading forces that called for the public to demonstrate, they were also the first to be attacked and investigated in Egypt and Tunisia (ibid.).

Notwithstanding the above, the PCI has always sought to maintain its cultural and social affiliation and identification with Arab societies. On the state level, Palestinian leaders, especially members of Knesset and heads of major political parties and movements, have always met with Arab officials. This is only true for the post-1967 period, as before that such contact was not possible. One could register many meetings between Palestinian leaders from Israel with officials of Egypt and Jordan, two countries that signed peace agreements with Israel, as well as other Arab states, such as Syria, Libya, and Lebanon.

Furthermore, the Palestinian cultural elite in Israel have been deeply impacted by Arab cultural elites from other parts of world. Palestinian novelists, poets, musicians, and painters have been influenced by events and developments in the cultural scene throughout the Arab world. They also sought to establish personal contacts with Arab institutions and personalities, bridging the legal and political separation between themselves and the Arab world. These efforts took a serious turn after 1993, when the peace process between Israel and the Palestinian Liberation Organization (PLO) was still shedding an optimistic light on the Middle East.

The relationship between the Palestinian community and the Arab world, especially with the broader Palestinian diaspora, is an important factor in the social, cultural, and political conduct of the PCI. The majority of the PCI are Muslim and share religious values and norms with the rest of Arab society. In particular, the Islamic Movement in Israel maintains deep ties with ideological streams of thought and Islamic Movements in other parts of the Arab world.[1]

Therefore, the uniqueness of the Israeli context should not deter us from exploring the relevance of Arab society and culture for explaining the collective behavior of the PCI. This relevance is based on its social-cultural, rather than its legal-political, context. This is true in the field of civil society as well, despite the fact that we are speaking of the civic as an avenue of collective action of the PCI. The civic in this context is not a given, but is an open field in which various CSOs compete to construct its meaning and features. As we demonstrate later, the tension between secular and religious CSOs mirrors the tensions taking place in other parts of the Arab world, especially between communists, nationalists, and Islamists. As well, these tensions highlight the presumption that the civic is an open avenue of collective conduct rather than a closed field, which is predetermined by the hegemonic political order in Israel.

Therefore, it is important to understand the developments or obstacles in the development of civil society in the Arab world as a background for the development of the PCI's civil sphere. The following discussion focuses only on the relevant aspects to our case and therefore deals mainly with the social-cultural dimension. However, we do not ignore the fact that this dimension challenges the legal-political context in which this behavior takes place: Israel.

Conceptualizations of Civil Society in Arab Culture

The meaning, characteristics, and future of civil society in the Arab context have been widely debated over the years, especially during the rule of the authoritarian regimes prior to the Arab Spring (Lutterbeck, 2012). The main elements of this debate are 1) the definition of civil society and the distinction between what is commonly called in Arab literature *mujtama' madani* (civil society) and *mujtama' ahli* (communal society); 2) the relationship between civil society and traditional society, particularly the tribal structures, and the average citizens' loyalty to their primordial affiliation groups vs. the individual's autonomy; 3) the relationship between civil society and the dominance of Islamic values and religious practices associated with communal-religious based associations; 4) the development of civil society vis-à-vis authoritarian political regimes, and the state's affiliation with a narrow, dominant elite; and 5) the relationship between Arab states' financial dependency as developing states in an era of economic, technological, and cultural globalization and the development of a young, global, and educated class whose members are active in the international arena and in the virtual world. The latter has created a demonstrable conflict between authoritarian political structures, built on a narrow political and financial elite, and a growing class of globally aware youth who use civic activism and information and communication technology (ICT) as a means to challenge political regimes.

As mentioned previously, only some of these aspects of Arab civil society outside the Israel/Palestine context are relevant here. In particular, two major issues lend themselves to a deeper analysis of the current discussion: The first is the relationship between Arab social structure, its dominant communal rather than individualistic social character, and the development of civic associations that are detached from this structure and present an organizational basis for new social and political values. The second has to do with the relationship between Arab society's resilient religious beliefs, especially since the return of political Islamism to the center stage, and their civic ideals, as manifested in the Arabic concept of "Madani" (Al-Jabari, 2005). We now present each of them separately.

Arab society is overwhelmingly traditional in its social structure, norms, and values (Reynolds, 2015; Al-Azm, 1997; Sharabi, 1988). Two aspects of this tradition are relevant here, and they are dialectically connected to each other. The first is the tribal-clan structure, and the second is individual autonomy, or the lack thereof. Both are vital for understanding Arab behavior and political activism as well as the status of CSOs in the overall social sphere.

Many have researched the challenges of Arab society in the modern age, including Anouar Abdel-Malek, Halim Barakat, Hisham Sharabi, Burhan Ghalioun, Abdalla Belakliz, Mohammed Abed al-Jabri, Sadiq Al-Azm, George Tarabishi, Mohammed Arkoun, Saad Eddin Ibrahim, and Aziz al-Azmeh. Almost all of them referred to Arab society's typical tribal-clan structure and to the development of a despotic regime, which used this structure to promote its interests, favoring it over social associations based on profession, politics, or ideology. Many of these scholars were inspired by Ibn Khaldun (1967) when they attempted to clarify the scale of the challenge facing Arab society in dealing with the clash of clan and tribal loyalties versus associations' alternative motivations, either ideological or civic (Harb, 2014; Al-Maskini, 2011).

Ibn Khaldun (1967) made an important distinction between rural and urban societies when he described the transformation processes in society and their organizational and behavioral patterns. His distinction is relevant to this day. Most recently, Mohamed Abed al-Jabri (2005) used it to describe a dichotomy between a tribal-rural society, with its traditional characteristics, and urban society, with its modern characteristics. This distinction may be too simplistic in the context of a diverse and complex Arab world, which is constantly changing and whose differences among many Arab societies are quite large. Of note in this regard is the PCI, which has experienced increasing urbanization of its villages, both demographically and culturally. Yet al-Jabri's analysis remains salient to this analysis, as it illustrates the distinction between social organization and activism based on tribal, communal, and religious worldviews, in which activists are more loyal to the social structure or to the existing set of values than to the basic logic of the association and activism. In these instances, social mobilization is led by national left-wing activists, who frustratingly note their inability to impact formal politics because of the regime's authoritarian nature (Cavatorta & Durac, 2010; Lnagohr, 2004).

Associations of this kind are based on modern ideas and mainly promote civil and human rights as defined by Arab liberal scholars at the turn of the 20th century through the last few decades (Al-Maskini, 2011). Al-Jabri used an etymological analysis of the term *al-mujtama' al-madani* (civil society) to reconnect it with its urban roots—*al-madina* (the city)—where one can develop discrete relationships on an individual, rather than a traditional, basis, thus creating a public sphere that goes beyond any tribal or clan commitments. His analysis is significant not only in geographic terms (the city versus the village) but also culturally, because the main traits of the city are the relative anonymity and the ideological and political loyalties that trample rural, tribal affiliations.

Hence, the concept of civil society in Arab language and culture is more intuitively linked to the concept of the city rather than to citizenship. The city is the place where society is likely to disengage from clan and tribal loyalties and commitments, as well as traditional social values attached to those social institutions, and develop organizational patterns based on an alternative set of values, characterized by loyalty to goals, values, and worldviews that are common to individual citizens and not necessarily relatives. Such a characterization illustrates clearly the similarities between the concept of *al-mujtama' al-madini* (urban society) and *al-mujtama' al-madani* (civil society).

That said, civil society as related to the city emphasizes the cultural-symbolic dimensions of society, established by people who are not necessarily relatives, instead of those determined by primordial ties. This distinction embedded in the historical sociology of Ibn Khaldun reflects one of the most central tensions in Arab societies, especially considering the traditional conceptualization of religion as a community of believers with almost no say as to how their social organization should be. This closed, identitarian view struggles against a more open and dynamic interpretation of Arab culture and thought, which emphasizes the autonomous spaces for individuals. Such a struggle is necessary for progress and civilizational life (Harb, 2014; Al-Maskini, 2011).

The debate over the origins and meanings of civil society in the Arab world is relevant to Palestinian civic activism in Israel, especially when relating to the urban roots of the concept. Palestinian society that remained within the borders of the Israeli state after the Nakba in 1948 was mostly rural. The Palestinian Nakba represented the devastation of Palestinians' social fabric and the destruction of their cities. Among these cities were Jaffa, Haifa, and Akka, which served as centers for social mobilization and transformation before 1948 (Hassan, 2005). The destruction of these Palestinian cities led not only to physical disarray, but also to the destruction of urban lifestyles that had been emerging since the 1920s. The re-ruralization of Palestinian life after 1948 has had major ramifications for the community. The resulting expulsion and flight of hundreds of thousands of Palestinians, many of whom were living in cities, caused these communities to turn to family ties as their only safety net, a process that has a strong impact on the nature of social capital in society and on the process of individualization in it. This process of re-ruralization slowed down the reemergence of city life in the PCI. Notwithstanding, when examining Palestinian CSOs in Israel, one notices that most emerged from cities such as Nazareth, Haifa, and Shefa'amr, where urban life has been thriving in the last few decades.

In researching Arab society, many scholars use historical evidence to prove the legacy of pluralist civic spheres, which reflect the presence of a developed Arab civil society (Al-Sabihi, 2000). Some evidence can be traced back to the earliest and most salient periods of Arab history—the times of Muhammad, the Umayyads, the Abbasids, the Arabic Renaissance (*al-nahdah*), and the independence era—proving that CSOs had existed, provided various social services, and promoted ideological views in favor of collective interests (Khadouri, 1970; Abd Al-Malik, 1978; Al-Naqeeb, 1991).

Many researchers described civil society's decline as a result of the despotic state, which had penetrated society and at once suffocated all civil, autonomous, and independent associations (Al-Naqeeb, 1991). Sabihi (2000) writes in this context:

> In the name of the State's building and development, two spheres were conquered: the financial and the political, both deeply connected to the establishment of civil society. Thus, every aspect of civil life was nationalized. One expression of this phenomenon, of conquering the political sphere, is the transformation of the party or the union from a representative body into an organizing one. Both parties and unions started claiming that they are means of expression, but only in theory, therefore reduced to speech only, away from society and controlled by the regime. These institutions have become means for organizing and monitoring civil society and its members; they were tied to State's institutions, became

their underlings and lost their independence. Their connections to civil society were severed, and they stopped representing their members and their members' ambitions. (p. 73)

Sabihi's statements are relevant to understanding the development of the PCI. Although there are differences between regimes and legal circumstances, the behavior of Israel vis-à-vis its Arab society could be easily characterized as a policy of internal colonization, surveillance, and control (Zureik, Lyon, & Abu-Laban, 2011; Zureik, 1979). Such was the case as a result of the high degree of direct despotism until 1966. Although it abolished the military government in 1966, Israel has developed a sophisticated and complex control system to monitor and control Arab society and the developments taking place inside it (Lustick, 1980).

This control system continues to exist today through various economic, political, legal, and technological mechanisms (Zureik, Lyon, & Abu-Laban, 2011). Moreover, government policy further encourages the strengthening of Arab society's clan structure and tribal politics by blocking the rise of new, young, and challenging leadership (Jamal, 2006b). Clan leaders have received both formal and informal support by the Israeli government to challenge these new social forces, which would pose ethical and behavioral alternatives to the traditional patterns of thinking and behavior in Palestinian society (Bäumel, 2007; Lustick, 1980).

New civic organizations were attacked and in some cases were outlawed, as was the case with the Al-Ard movement, which did not receive recognition as a civic organization or a business (Nassar, 2017; Frisch, 2011; Jiryis, 1976; Zureik, 1978). At the same time, Israel expropriated Islamic Waqf (trust) institutions and property and used it for its own needs, thus weakening Islamic philanthropic organizations and civic activities based on the support of the Waqf (Reiter, 2013). In addition, the Committee for the Protection of Arab Land, which was established in the early 1970s, was the subject of deep suspicion and became a target of direct surveillance by state security services (Cohen, 2006).

Although the legal situation changed following the dismantling of the military government, especially following the passage of the CSO Law in 1980, the state did not and still does not financially support Arab civic organizations, as it does in Jewish society. According to our analysis of the CSO's Registrar of the Justice Ministry in early 2018, only 25% of Arab CSOs receive funding from the state, compared to more than 80% of Jewish

CSOs. Furthermore, CSO legislation in recent years (as we discuss in next chapter) illustrates that Palestinian CSOs in Israel face circumstances that place them in an antagonistic relationship with the state, despite the fact that Israel is much more sophisticated than most Arab states in regulating its relationship with CSOs that oppose its policies and criticize its regime.

Religion, Civility, and Civil Society in Arab Culture

Many Arab scholars and thinkers have discussed the dominance of religious values in Arab society, and these discussions are relevant to the present context (Harb, 2014; Jamal Amaney, 2006; Abu Zayd, 1994; Galion, 1992; Daher, 1990). In this regard, we identify three analytical camps affiliated with different political paradigms and find a strong conflict between them. The first camp views Islamic culture as the opposite of modernity, or as an element that delays democratization and therefore calls to strengthen secularization of the Arab world (Al-Azmeh, 2008). Members of this camp side with undermining religious associations and removing the Mosque from the center of politics (ibid.). Its members are secular, liberal, and connected to global politics, where they derive inspiration and financial assistance. Many of this camp's members see an inherent link between religion, underdevelopment, and a lack of democracy in the Arab world (Al-Madani, 1997; Ibrahim, 2004).

The second camp acknowledges the possibility of combining religiosity with modernity and even bases modernity on existing ideals in religion and in the scriptures. This camp points to the appearances of democratic and civic values in various verses of the Quraan, such as the *shura* (the principle of consultation), pluralism, equality, well-being, and so on. Verses like "Mankind was but one nation, but differed. Had it not been for a word that went forth before from thy Lord, their differences would have been settled between them" (*Surat Yunus*, p. 19); "Let him who will believe, and let him who will, reject (it)" (*Surat al-kahf*, p. 29); "To you be your Way, and to me mine" (*Surat al-Kafirun*, p. 6); and "Let there be no compulsion in religion: Truth stands out clear from Error" (*Surat al-Bakara*, p. 256)[2] represent, according to many scholars, the foundation of pluralism, tolerance, variance, mutual respect, and equality as fundamental Islamic values. These values were the core of the doctrine of liberal scholars such as Rifa'a al-Tahtawi (1801–1873), 'Abd al-Rahman al-Kawakibi (1854–1902), Khayr al-Din al-Tunisi (1810–1887), Jamal ad-Din al-Afghani (1838–1897), and Muhammad Abduh (1849–1902).

This camp's contemporary representatives are many, including Muhammad Amarah, Abd al Wahab Al-Massiri, Muhammad Shahrour, and Rashid al-Ghannushi; all of them see no contradiction between religious ideals and modern social associations, including CSOs (Tamimi, 2001; Ghannūshī, 1994). They argue that communal organizations were always part of Arab society and operated within the Islamic tradition to serve charity and individuals' well-being. Islam's high regard for variance and equality is represented by the principle of the *shura*, a fundamental, constitutional Islamic principle that leaves the nature and structure of the regime open for discussion and adaptation to different periods in history. This camp also includes moderate secular thinkers like Burhan Ghalioun, Mohammed Arkun, Mohammed Abed al-Jabri, and Fathi Al-Maskini, who do not call to abolish Islam from the public sphere, but also warn against religious organizations taking control over public life and the regime. This camp supports the view that Islamic social and political culture has been always tolerant toward civic patterns of organization that provide autonomous, safe spaces away from state intervention. Many supporters of this camp argue that there is sufficient historical evidence of the rise of a vibrant network of civic organizations under Muslim rule. Where such organizations are suppressed in Arab states, they posit that it is for the benefit of authoritarian secular regimes, rather than a result of Islamic religious beliefs.

The third camp is radical and dogmatic, and legitimizes social associations based on religious tradition and delegitimizes any alternative value system. As this camp has no control over any independent state, despite its influence in many, it is not worth relating to broadly. The only relevant aspect we must relate to is that, theologically, this camp does not see any place for separation between religion and state and that all the social order must be organized around a strict interpretation of religious scripts.

We do not intend to decide which camp is right and which is wrong so much as claim that, based on common religious ideology and our present and historic reality, the second camp is the most central in the Arab world. Mutual tolerance between religious and nonreligious values is fundamental in this camp, as reflected in participants' willingness to compromise on the nature of the public sphere and the regime, as long as all players respect each other's freedoms and rights. One such example is the current Tunisian regime.

Recent developments in the Arab world have shed new light on the debates regarding civil society (Achcar, 2016; Brownlee, Masoud, & Reynolds, 2015; Lynch, 2014). After a long period of pessimism and disbelief in CSOs' ability to effect political and social change, the Arab revolutions in

Tunisia, Egypt, Yemen, Libya, and Syria have proven that civic activism, especially when accompanied by the appropriate tools to enable activists to overcome the authoritarian regime's security apparatus, could have a very strong impact on people's lives. Through these recent Arab upheavals—despite having ultimately failed to transform the authoritarian regimes and lead to democratization in most cases—civic networks comprising CSOs, social movements, advocacy groups, clubs, and workers' unions were able to mobilize large parts of society to resist the authoritarian political reality (Cavatorta, 2012). The popular upheavals in several Arab countries eventually proved that civic activism, motivated by a firm faith, can bring change and overcome even the most untouchable and violent regimes, as in the case of Tunisia, Egypt, Libya, and Yemen.

So far, attempts to explain these Arab revolutions have entailed revisiting the literature dealing with the Arab societies in general and with CSOs, new media tools, and social movements in particular (Lynch, 2014). Arguments calling into question Arab civil society's ineffectiveness against authoritarian regimes and the lack of civic values have been replaced by new arguments, which differentiate between civic activism and the ability of authoritarian regimes to curb civil protest, impose their will, and silence oppositional voices.

This point of departure, namely avoiding limiting the judgment of civic activism to its instrumental efficacy, namely the immediate success to realize the aspired for goals, is what makes the process taking place in Arab countries relevant to analyzing the civic activism in the PCI. Palestinian CSOs are active in criticizing the Israeli regime and the discrimination against Palestinians while materially and symbolically privileging Jewish citizens. Despite the difficulties in providing tangible evidence of broad successes of Palestinian CSOs, they have become part of the social and institutional fabric of society, whose long-term and not unidirectional impact on their environment is worth examining.

When it comes to the presence of religious values in society, the PCI is very similar to the patterns found in the revolutions described above. Accordingly, the PCI's civic activism can be divided according to worldviews between modern-liberal and religious. While the first camp is based on liberal fundamental values of human rights that highlight the autonomy of the individual, including women and secular people, the other camp is based on a religious worldview—Islamic or Christian in this case—and promotes religious values through preaching and the provision of basic social services like education, health, charity, and welfare. The distribution between these two camps is not evident in every aspect of their work, but it is highlighted by the different funding sources of their associations. Most, if not all, secular CSOs raise funds from Western sources with a liberal-modern agenda. By contrast, religious associations are strongly tied to religious sources, whether Muslim or Christian, and fund raise based on religious affiliation. The resources of religious CSOs are allocated according to internal considerations, mainly for the promotion of a communal and religious agenda, despite the fact that they use modern organizational tools and show much institutional efficiency, often much higher than those of secular associations.

One of the important aspects of the relationship between social structure and civic activism has to do with the necessary differentiation between institutionalized and professional organizations, which operate according to defined legal and administrative rules governing their human and financial resources and un-institutionalized associations, such as "popular committees" and "youth movements." These last two types of associations seek to meet specific goals and mobilize popular movements by convening committees of a more fluid and informal nature. These associations operate according to traditional values of mutual aid and mediation, using most of their resources for solving internal disputes and conflicts. Many such "popular committees" have thrived over the last couple of decades in a response to the inability of formal institutions, such as municipalities, to handle the growing challenges of the PCI, especially social strife and its rising levels of violence. Popular and un-institutionalized committees operate in many cities and villages and successfully engage in social matters and in many cases manage to reach solutions to social conflicts that could not have been addressed via state institutions. The involvement of traditional public figures in such initiatives, the use of traditional norms to appease antagonists, and the lack of any need to secure financial resources to finance these efforts render these initiatives a successful model of civil society.

One of the best examples to demonstrate the fusion of traditional norms with modern patterns of behavior is the *Sulha* (reconciliation) committee that handles conflicts on the basis of traditional values separate from and simultaneously alongside the state legal track. This national committee composed of local leaders reflects the preservation of tribal values considered essential to social survival, while engaging in a central civic mission, namely civility and civic peace. The existence of such a committee suggests that the state's handling of conflicts does not meet all social expectations or satisfy all needs. Traditional values, cultural norms, and social clan structure are still important in Arab society, something that has profound implications for the nature of its civic activism. Any study of the latter must address the existence of life-worlds separate from the state's official plane. Such life-worlds have led to the rise of civic activism, which cannot be captured by a formalistic, modernist conceptualization of civil society. The existence of traditional and religious civic organizations, which are actually closer to the daily lives of Arab citizens in terms of values and culture, necessitates looking beyond a simple dichotomy between modern and traditional types of civic organizations and activism.

The emergence of many communal organizations, based on conservative or religious worldviews that simultaneously run counter to modern principles, highlights the importance of Arab and Islamic values in our understanding of the PCI's civic activism. Not all such activism results in a direct and interactive relationship with the state. On the contrary, the distance between the state and the PCI, especially regarding the allocation of resources, causes many religious and traditional leaders to establish organizational and institutional alternatives based on religious ideas. One such example is the *zakat,* a taxing system controlled by Arab society, to address its own unique challenges and goals.

Chapter 5

Neoliberal Nationalism and
Civil Society in Israel

This chapter addresses state-civil society relations in Israel, which form the contextual structure in which Palestinian civic activism takes place. The Israeli context—legal, political, economic, and cultural—is crucial to understanding the PCI's collective behavior. Therefore, to understand its civic activism, we must thoroughly address the most important factors that circumvent it. The chapter begins with a review of the civil society literature in the Israeli context and then moves on to address the legal regulations that set the framework in which Palestinian civic activism takes place. In this regard, we address the recent legal developments in the CSO Law, which is representative of the political trends taking place in Israel over the last decade. Next, we highlight the economic conditions that circumvent civil society in general and carry major implications for the development of a growing number of welfare CSOs, including those in the PCI. Finally, we address the rise of Israeli nationalist trends and their ramifications for the rise of nationalist and conservative CSOs that cooperate with political parties to curb liberal and human rights organizations, delegitimizing their activities and seeking to silence their critique of government policies.

There has not been very much research on civil society and civic organizations in Israel. Despite the increasing number of studies addressing the topic in the last few decades, this body of literature remains small relative to the media attention and critiques of human rights organizations on state policies toward the occupied Palestinian territories (OPTs) (Ben Eliezer, 2015, 2003; Herman, 1995; Yishai, 2003, 1998; Kaufman and Gidron, 2006). It seems that the few studies in this area are based on a hidden presumption that civil society in Israel is a residual phenomenon, especially when taking into consideration the centrality of Israel's military industrial complex and its neoliberal economic policy. Israeli society is also often depicted as very advanced high-tech compared with other states. Israeli civil society has not managed to define itself as autonomous from the state, nor does it identify itself with civic values known from the Western tradition, such as equality, tolerance, freedom, and pluralism. Civil society, although an old phenomenon, remains a new development. According to the Ministry of Justice, 70% of the registered CSOs in Israel were established after 1998. This means that civic associations have not yet stabilized as a field of political and social activity. Furthermore, one notices a clear commitment of political research to the formal plane of politics and society in Israel (Bel Eliezer, 2017; Gidron, Bar, and Katz, 2003).

The emerging debate in Israel regarding civil society's nature and goals indicates the growing presence of civil society in Israel. This statement comes without committing to or assuming that it maintains the ability to influence state policies, especially in the field of social justice and civic equality (Chazan, 2012; Peled, 2005b). The political and media coverage of CSOs' activities has increased exponentially over the last decade, particularly with regard to its activities during and following the Second Lebanon War and two years later during and following the Gaza War ("Operation Cast Lead").

During these periods, CSOs' provision of services became vital for handling the adversities caused by the war. When the north was shut down and roughly one million civilians had to take cover in shelters, the state's inability to satisfy the immediate needs of the populations resulted in the shelling of residential areas by Hezbollah in 2006 and by Hamas in 2008 and later. CSOs' members worked tirelessly to deliver the services that state agencies had failed to provide. These activities, which drew much attention, invite a deep examination of the place and impact of civil society in Israel. In particular, with the state's battle against liberal CSOs, two critiques have emerged: the continuous and severe violation of Palestinian human rights in the OPTs and the ramifications the Israeli economy's neoliberalization has had on the living standards of a growing number of Israelis.

Therefore, it would be accurate to say that civil society's activities, goals, and regulations are widely disputed. These disputes illustrate Katz's argument that civil society reflects the political and social disputes within Israeli society (Gidron, Bar, & Katz, 2003). Yishai (2008), on the other hand, warns against the disintegration of Israeli society, which is reflected in the erosion of civil society's civic nature, and the flattening of citizens' political engagement, as well as their willingness to perform civic duties, which are vital for the survival of democracy. This contention is further supported by the increasing commercialism of civil society, which causes CSOs to adopt business-like thinking patterns. Thus, civil society becomes less civic and social and does not necessarily encourage citizens' mobilization in favor of the civil-political process (ibid.). Yishai's arguments focus on the roles of civil society and its contribution to the resilience of state and society, something that has become a widespread topic of theoretical and empirical discussion in Israel; it is based on the idea of a connection between civil society and civic engagement, taking responsibility and assisting and preserving democracy (Yishai, 1998).

This notion is also part of an interesting and productive debate between advocates of the liberal point of view, focusing on the existence of thousands of CSOs active in various fields and promoting liberal core values, and advocates of the critical point of view, who disapprove of the mere existence of CSOs, focusing their discourse on their level of success in promoting their core values (Ben Eliezer, 1999; Limor, 2010).

A debate of a different nature revolves around CSOs' level of autonomy. Some argue that these associations should be almost completely independent from governmental interference, while others point to market failures, which could potentially compromise these associations' functioning and their internal relationships, therefore requiring legal regulations to mitigate the balance between government supervision and the preservation of CSOs' autonomy (Limor, 2010).

According to some researchers of civil society in Israel, most CSOs operate within the common ideological concept of a Jewish and democratic state; therefore, they accept the state's existing structure, and if they demand any change, it is only for the purpose of adjusting this formula to align with the social and political reality (Ben-Eliezer, 1999; Menuhin, 2011). Yet a significant number of CSOs operate outside this consensus, mainly human rights organizations like B'Tselem, The Association for Civil Rights in Israel, Gisha, Yesh Din, Physicians for Human Rights, and Breaking the Silence, along with organizations that are active in other fields, like New Family, Itach-Women Lawyers for Social Justice, Israel Religious Action Center, Zochrot, and others.

Based on this introduction, it goes without saying that the major developments taking place in Israeli society in general and in civil society in particular demand special attention. The structural economic, functional, and legal conditions in which CSOs act in Israel have undergone dramatic changes. These changes are important for the understanding of the role of CSOs and the special circumstances in which Palestinian CSOs operate. The following chapter cannot address all changes taking place. Therefore, we start with a brief historical overview of civil society in Israel since its inception and then concentrate on the three most relevant processes taking place over the last few decades.

The first process is the Israeli economy's intensive neoliberalization and the state's withdrawal, which has led to growing gaps in average incomes between different segments of society and the dependence of growing number of citizens on CSOs' aid provided (Palatnik & Shechter, 2012; Rivlin, 2011; Shalev, 2004; Swirski, Connor-Attias, & Lieberman, 2019; Gidron, Bar, & Katz, 2003). This process empowers many CSOs, but also renders them dependent on the state for funding. This process has been behind the major social protests that took place in summer 2011, in which hundreds of thousands of Israelis marched the streets to protest the high living costs in Israel and the withdrawal of the state from the provision of social services, such as education, health, and welfare (Yona & Spivak, 2012). The place of CSOs in supporting weak social segments, on the one hand, and their role in providing back winds to the privatization of a growing number of social services, on the other, is also crucial.

The second process is the legal and juridical efforts made by rising nationalistic and religious powers in Israeli society and the curbing of liberal civic CSOs, especially human rights organizations, and in the narrowing of democratic spaces available to activists through legal means (Jamal, 2017; Asseburg, 2017).

The third process is the rise of nationalist and religious civic activism manifested in seeking more influence on state policies while silencing, shaming, and delegitimizing liberal CSOs. The former uses public diplomacy as a means to cut the funding sources of the latter.

Historical Development of Israeli Civil Society

The State of Israel has played and continues to play a powerful role in shaping the characteristics and values of civil society. In the past it harnessed civic activities to serve national needs and the priorities consistent with the worldview of the labor movement; this was a hegemonic movement for many decades (Yishai, 2008, 1998). Scholars of Israeli politics and society argue that, historically, many CSOs operating in Mandatory Palestine predated the state (Horowitz & Lisak, 1977). The various CSOs that operated within Jewish society at the time in education, health, welfare, and so forth contributed to the welfare of Jewish immigrant society and their national objective to establish an autonomous Jewish entity that can later lead to independence. Since that period, a strong link has been forged between the state and its CSOs, especially those operating as a part of, or alongside, the Histadrut (the Jewish labor union). As Yishai (2003) argues: "The most prominent quality of the pre-State civil society is its devotion to national missions. Groups and organizations worked for the flag and responded to a call up that wasn't issued by any authority, but rather by a strong faith and solidarity" (p. 71). CSOs became integral to the formation of the state; they provided services and attended to society's needs as part of the Zionist ideology, even when they criticized the state over the best policy for implementing national objectives. Civic organizations provided many services as part of the state's socialist economic views and welfare policy (Yishai, 1998; Chazan, 2012; Peled, 2005b).

The labor movement, which dominated the state until the late 1970s, succeeded in mobilizing and tying most civic organizations to its national project. Uri Ram described this situation as follows: "Until recently, there has been in Israel one version of national Zionist identity. This identity played a key role in committing the Jewish population to the goals of the labor movement first and then to state's goals" (Ram 1996: 19). Peled and Shafir claim that the universal rhetoric of the labor movement and many of its practices of nation-building veiled its exclusive policies against Palestinians, Mizrahi Jews, and all women (Peled & Shafir, 2005, p. 49).

The relationship between the state and CSOs continued to be of special nature in the first few decades following the Israel's founding (Yishai, 1998). A collectivist political culture survived the first few decades among all ideological sectors; they all saw the individual as the nation's agent, one who should sacrifice his destiny for the sake of the state (Peled & Shafir, 2005). Furthermore, most CSOs were ideologically or politically attached to one of the large parties of the time, mainly Mapai, Mapam, and Herut (Horowitz & Lisak, 1977). The Labor parties had their own CSOs, as well as the Herut party, the religious Zionists, and the orthodox. Some of these CSOs were registered as Ottoman associations and provided various services and activities (Yishai, 2003). Because of their attachment to political parties, these associations were not perceived as independent. This was particularly true for associations attached to the ruling political parties. Because the Israeli market and economy were largely corporate during the first three decades of the state, the political and financial autonomy of associations attached to political movements were naturally limited (Peled & Shafir, 2005). CSOs were loyal to their political parties or to the state and therefore focused on the individual and provided community services.

Only since the mid-1970s, and especially at the end of this decade, did we see a rising number of CSOs operating outside the dominant political consensus and presenting ideological alternatives. The Likud party's victory in the 1977 elections and the wider acceptance of the liberal economic paradigm, striving to minimize the state's involvement in the market and in society, was a watershed moment. The first signs of CSOs' institutionalization were seen in the early 1970s, when the Association for Civil Rights was established. The Association called for empowering citizens as social-political actors, independent of ideological and political structures that enslave citizens to the state or the party. Another prominent indication for this growing trend, which included hundreds of CSOs, was the establishment of the New Israel Fund, which intended to fund the activities of CSOs that empower civil society and create a balancing force vis-à-vis the state. The Fund was established following the Likud's victory in the 1977 elections. This period was marked by a deep fear created by the rise of what has been conceived as "fascist" forces (Mautner, 2002; Peled & Shafir, 2005). The intellectual and political elite that dominated the state since its foundation and until the late 1970s expressed its fear of losing democracy in favor of the conservative right wing, which sought to use the state's power to promote a nationalist political agenda (Pedhazur, 2004).

The Socialist-Republican ideology that dominated political discourse under the leadership of the labor movement lost its rigorous power to a liberal discourse, which boosted the free market economy (Galnoor & Blender, 2013). This process also went hand in hand with the decline of the Labor movement and its impetus, the concept of a welfare state as part of the national mission to empower state and society (Doron, 2003). Notwithstanding the loss of the hegemonic labor movement, it had a positive effect on the growth of civil society.

The civic organizations that emerged in the eighties conceived of the liberalization process—economic, political, and legal—as a guarantee of the maintenance of civic values and a protection against possible nationalistic tendencies, apparent in many conservative segments of society, especially Jews of oriental origin and ultra-orthodox communities, which led to the rise of the Likud to power and to the emergence of the Shas movement in the 1980s. The decline of the hegemon and the veteran Ashkenazi elite (Kimmerling, 2001) and its anxiety for the future of democracy and liberal values (Mautner, 2002) led to the search for alternative ways to maintain its influence in face of the new political coalition between the nationalist Likud movement and the ultra-orthodox Shas movement.

The privatization and economic liberalization policies of the Likud aimed not only to materialize the liberal ideology of the party, but also to weaken the infrastructural power of the labor movement that controlled many of the industrial facilities via the Histadrut (Mandelkern & Shalev,

2010; Mundlak, 2007; Nitzan & Bichler, 2002; Shalev, 1992). This policy of the Likud gave emerging social elites disappointed by the corruption of the labor movement but unable to join the conservative nationalist camp the chance to institutionalize its power in the liberal economy and the emerging field of civil society.

For that purpose, several attempts were made to enact a liberal CSOs Law, which would institutionalize CSOs' activity, minimize the state's involvement in this activity, and at the same time establish a large fund that would financially support CSOs. This led to the establishment of the Israel New Fund in 1978, a process that had begun six years earlier with the establishment of the Association for Civil Rights. This was also the foundation that helped enact the CSO Law in 1980, a liberal law that was meant to institutionalize CSOs' activity as part of an organized effort to preserve political liberal culture. This culture was perceived by human rights organizations and left-wing parties as the only guarantee to prevent Israel from becoming a radical nationalist state, especially in light of its colonialist tendencies in its occupation of the Palestinian territories in 1967 and the rise of Gush Emunim and other nationalist right-wing organizations in the early 1970s (Zertal & Eldar, 2007).

The rising power of the Supreme Court, the Bank of Israel, the business community, and civil society are presented in the Israeli sociological literature as clear expressions of Israeli architectural changes that occurred in the 1980s and 1990s (Shafir & Peled, 2002). The liberal elite and its institutional manifestations became more vibrant and expressive, combining its values with a patriotic-militaristic flavor to counter the conservative nationalistic trends in the right-wing camp (Ben Eliezer, 2012). Given that the privatization of state services under the guise of liberal ideology and the free-market economy continued, many civic activists used this opportunity to establish CSOs that either provide services to the poor or advocate for the protection of basic liberal values, state transparency, and human rights.

As a result of the major social changes in Israeli society (Galnoor & Blander, 2013), the conservative right has also become stronger in recent decades and has established itself in many junctions of power in the bureaucracy, economy, security services, and civil society. As a result of the increase in privatization (Harris et al., 1997), the government's retreat from the welfare state, and the enforcement of the notion that the market economy is integral to the nation's resilience, a growing number of CSOs with a right-wing, chauvinist worldview have emerged over the last few decades. These CSOs combine nationalism with liberalism and support the retreat of the state from the market and economy and the reduction of services provided by the state, while at the same time calling for more governability. This means, among other things, empowering the executive branch vis-à-vis the judicial system, the weakening of the media through its fragmentation and surveillance, and strengthening the regulatory power of the state. While one should note that these processes are not one-dimensional and the big picture of civil society suggests great variance and pluralism among civic organizations, we can definitely identify a growing conflict between liberal CSOs (of which some are active in service provision, advocacy, and lobbying) and CSOs that support a combination of a communal-national political and neoliberal economic worldview.

The widespread network of CSOs working in various areas, from educational organizations to healthcare, welfare, advocacy, and research, occupies a growing space in the public sphere as they increasingly attempt to influence state policy and determine its character. As of mid-2018, 43,714 nonprofit organizations are registered in Israel. The number of active CSOs that have submitted reports to the Registrar in the last five years is 14,810. The distribution of these CSO according to year of establishment and specializations reflects an interesting map of the development of Israeli civil society.

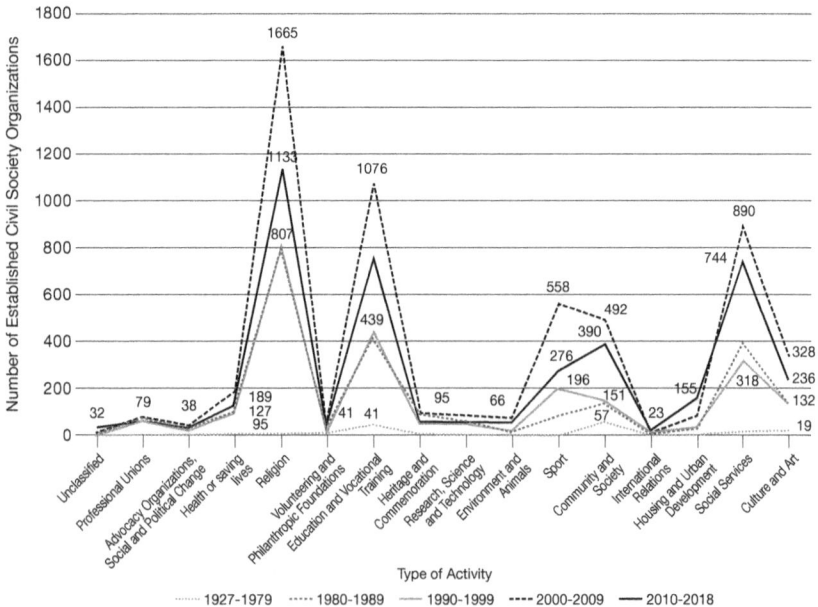

Graph 1.

As one can see from the data above, the number of CSOs in the following five fields are the most apparent: religion, education and professional training, sports, community services, and social service. This mapping shows clearly the major trends taking place in Israeli society and economy, and the need for services provided by CSOs is on the rise. The CSOs in the fields indicated above seem to fill a void in basic social services that were abandoned by the state. This picture also reflects the neoliberalization of the Israeli economy and the mobilization of CSO to provide services in central fields, such as education, professional training, and sports. Only 1.7% of these CSOs are engaged in common projects with governmental offices, with large funds from the state, but 25.2% of them receive small funds from the state based on article 3a of the Funding Eligibility Law.

According to the Central Bureau of Statistics in 2011, the GDP of all nonprofits was approximately 48.4 billion Israeli shekels, 5.6% of which belonged to nonprofit organizations (Limor, 2012). Nonprofit organizations' total revenues in 2011 amounted to approximately 119 billion NIS, with 48% of revenue representing transfers from the government, 31% from the sale of services, 10% from domestic donations, 9% from foreign donations, and 2% from interest and property (ibid.). It is important to note that, in 2011, Israeli nonprofit organizations' workforce included more than 400,000 jobs, or about 13% of all jobs in the Israeli economy. These data indicate the importance of the third sector in Israel's economy and the labor market.

Civil Society and the "Nationalizing Neo-Liberal State"

Since the early 1980s, Israel has adhered to a liberal economic philosophy that includes increasing the privatization of services and the shrinking of the welfare state (Shalev, 1992; Gal, 2010). The neoliberalization policies of the state taking place in recent decades highlights the state's growing withdrawal from service provision in an increasing number of areas, including education, health, welfare, and more. One of the most prominent trends from the last two decades is the retreat of the welfare state and the strengthening of economic liberalism (Swirski, Connor-Attias, & Lieberman, 2019; Filc & Ram, 2004). Under the auspices of this process, the state seeks to shape the character of civil society through political, legal, and economic means. This trend has led to the growth of many civic organizations that sought to fill the void and took on some of the responsibility that the state has abandoned. This structural transformation is reflected in a number of CSOs identified as social service providers. The number of such CSOs that were active in the 1980s was 318. The number of such CSOs active in the first decade of the 21st century went up to 890, and in the years 2010–2018 fell to 724.

Although this trend has imposed increasing responsibilities on civil society, the state did not withdraw financial and legal regulations over the activities of civic organizations. The hegemony of the national right-wing parties has led to the state's selective involvement among various civic organizations, according to their ideological and political affiliation with political parties and member of the ruling coalition. The patterns of aid to certain CSOs and the exclusion of others, combined with new legislation seeking to impose procedural restrictions on foreign aid granted to associations characterized as "problematic," began mirroring the bias of the state vis-à-vis civil society. CSOs' closeness to the ruling parties became an important factor in determining the amount of financial support CSOs are allowed to receive. On the other hand, liberal CSOs began searching for the support of external funds that extend financial resources to serve their liberal agenda, especially human rights.

The openness of the state to external influences led to increasing efforts of the business community and civil society to lobby its institutions. Each sought to receive financial benefits in its own way, to promote its interests and worldviews. Therefore, it is difficult to identify even one area relating to public policy in which civic organizations are not working to exert their influence in a variety of ways. As the involvement of CSOs in state policy making grows, their strength is also increasing. This does not, however, firmly establish that CSOs are able to effectively influence policy, but that the struggle between different organizations, especially those who define themselves as human rights organizations and those with national-conservative orientation, grows ever stronger. This process is strongly influenced by structural changes in the role of the state in education and welfare, mainly because of the contraction of the welfare state, but also as a result of changes in state policy in various fields, including planning, settlement, development, construction, and maintenance of heritage sites. In education, for example, there are very powerful struggles between various CSOs, which seek to influence the curriculum or to be subcontracted by the ministry to gain financial support; in this way, these CSOs can enter schools on a broad scale and shape the educational content and pedagogies of the schools. The involvement of liberal CSOs in the 1980s and early 1990s in influencing educational policies, promoting democratic liberal values, has been replaced by a wave of conservative nationalist CSOs that seek to promote national and religious beliefs. The promotion of these values has been supported by the ruling parties and enabled these CSOs to draw on a rising amount of private funds from the United States, United Kingdom, and Australia (Shizaf, 2015; Hasson, 2011). A growing number of CSOs are requesting permission from the Registrar to keep their funds discreet. In 2016, there was a 130% increase in the number of CSOs asking for this permission, a vast majority of which are right-wing CSOs (Ilan, 2017). Similarly, there is a major struggle between CSOs in the field of heritage site conservation, a field that is predominantly controlled by religious national CSOs, which have managed to capture the scene and claim full control over this domain.[1]

When considering civil society in Israel, we must consider the summer 2011 social protest, which enables us to shed light on the civility of Israeli civil society from the vantage point of welfare and social justice. This occurrence, which developed out of internal changes in the relationship between state and society, is very telling in two ways. The first is the nature of the role played by CSOs in mobilizing the broader public to march the streets, and the second is the ability of CSOs to influence the neoliberalization of state policies.

The 2011 summer protest impacted hundreds of thousands of people, requiring society to raise new questions regarding the role, engagement, and contribution of CSOs. Here too we find disputes regarding CSOs' level of engagement. Equally important is civil society's relationship with the market forces on the one hand and the state on the other. The reasons that mobilized so many citizens to go into the streets also create an interesting context for studying CSOs' self-perceptions in Israel vis-à-vis a new cause. In this way, the 2011 protest revealed a distinction between advocates of the socialist perception—who criticize the collapse of the welfare state, the state's retreat from service provision, and the increasing privatization of more public services—and advocates of the market economy and the "thin state."

Despite the rise of civic engagement related to the structural economic changes taking place in Israel, the social protest in summer 2011 was surprising for most CSOs in Israel (Yona & Spiveck, 2012). The leaders of CSOs testified that these associations neither initiated the protest nor were involved in its organization (Tauben-Oberman, 2014). These CSOs joined the protest in its early stages, but they had no clear policy on how to handle the crowds that were flooding the streets. The protest's length and especially the CSOs' provision of tents to cover many of the protesters enabled them to contribute to the protest and promote their civil agenda. However, this was a response to the protest and an attempt to extend it, rather than a planned operation that initiated it.

The fact that hundreds of thousands of citizens came to protest the cost of living and express their lack of faith in the state's political and economic leaders indicates the level of dissatisfaction and discontent among citizens. While the political and financial elites were the main source of this dissatisfaction, the protest may also be seen as a testament to either CSOs' inability to change government policy or their marginality in the economic field, in which CSOs could be divided into two major camps. One camp is composed of those service providers that aid needy families, especially before big holidays. As a result of their engagement, CSOs benefited from the economic policies of the state. The second camp is composed of CSOs that campaign against the neoliberal policies of the state and provide information concerning the problematic consequences of these policies. For example, the Adva Center provides information and advocacy, addressing a great need for the public in a time when such CSOs and the media reports on this information are heavily criticized and often attacked by governmental officials. Despite its importance, the impact of such CSOs on the public agenda remains very marginal.

One cannot ignore the fact that the protest was focused on socioeconomic issues, while political and human rights issues were left aside. In fact, the protest brought together civic activists from within the entire spectrum of Israeli politics, from human rights activists to settlers from the OPTs. This fact alone illustrates the marginality of political issues in the protest. Thus, we can say that the social protest was based largely on the common interests uniting the majority of the Jewish population while preserving balance and preventing internal conflicts. The distinction between the social and the political was meant to concentrate power in an effort to achieve the protestors' socioeconomic objectives and focus their influence on the government's economic policy.

This strategy suggests that human rights organizations hold a very different perspective from that of the general Israeli population. The gaps between the positions held by human rights organizations and the wide network of CSOs that do not express support for the former demonstrate that most CSOs in Israel support the view that the Jewish hegemony is an expression of a democratic majority. Accordingly, it seems that only a small minority of CSOs perceive silencing human rights organizations as contradictory to civic and democratic values. The gap between these perspectives distinguishes the majority of conformist CSOs from the critical minority. According to this distinction, Palestinian CSOs in Israel belong to the second group and therefore exist in the margins of Israeli society.

Compared to the large numbers of CSOs in Israel, the number of Arab-Jewish organizations is very limited. The trend of common civic activity expanded throughout the 1970s and 1980s, especially in the field of education. Organizations like Givat Haviva, Beit Hagefen in Haifa, Neve Shalom, and the Adam Institute have been active in promoting an educational agenda based on a civic worldview. But the number of Jewish-Arab organizations, which is very limited according to the data obtained from the Registrar, currently hovers at 84 CSOs and has been dwindling since the mid-1990s. One unique organization that operates in the rather sensitive area of Jewish-Arab relations is Sikkuy, an association that promotes civic equality by presenting data on discrimination and inequality as well as advocacy and lobbying. Most CSOs active in the field of civic equality are divided according to national affiliation, though many Palestinian civil activists are members of Jewish associations, like the Civil Rights Association. One of the major developments in the aftermath of the October 2000 protests is the emergence of joint Jewish-Arab organizations and associations, which presented a different way of thinking and behavior compared to the traditional organizations like Givat Haviva or Neve Shalom. These new organizations did not present themselves as coexistence organizations per se, but rather focused on terms like partnership or coexistence. The most important among them include Shchenim-Neighbors for Joint Development in the Galilee, A Different Voice in the Galilee, Ta'ayush, and Tarabut. Their importance does not stem from the scale of their activities or from their influence; it stems from their discourse, which presents an alternative worldview, calling for common civic life based on mutual recognition and respect, compared with traditional CSOs that propagate separation and mutual suspicion. By contrast, shared society organizations enter into coalitions and partnerships with each other to enhance their influence and multiply their effect on the public sphere. Some of the activities of these CSOs are focused on issues that interest both communities, such as housing, regulation of land ownership, or construction of roads in urban areas.

Setting Legal Limitations on Critical Civic Activism

The first attempts to institutionalize CSOs' activity in Israeli law occurred in the mid-1950s. This attempt was repeated unsuccessfully in 1964, and a new law was introduced in the late 1970s and legislated in 1980 (Yishai,

2003). This law, including all its amendments since 1996, regulates the institutionalization of CSOs and defines their spheres of function and activity. The law and its amendments give the state a wide influence over the registration and operating procedures of these organizations (ibid.). Though the state never used its power to actively undermine CSOs' ability to register or operate, it definitely interferes, directs, supervises, and even brings about the disintegration of CSOs that exceed the limits of what is considered appropriate. The unwillingness of the state to allow the institutionalization of the Al-Ard movement in the 1950s and 1960s (Haider, 2017), and the use of emergency regulations to declare the Northern Branch of the Islamic Movement and its CSOs as illegal by the cabinet in November 2015, are clear examples of the long political hand of the state. It was not possible to achieve reliable information concerning the number of times the Registrar refused to register new CSOs or intervened by setting administrative limitations on active CSOs. Nevertheless, it is well-known that such interventions, despite being limited, are a common tool used in either curbing certain developments in the field or establishing conditions that make it difficult for certain CSOs to operate. Such state interventions would not have been noted if not for two main points that are of political importance.

The first point has to do with the legislation in the early 1980s, which came to regulate one of the most important aspects of the Israeli economy and enable its privatization, liberalization, and globalization. As noted earlier, the liberal forces in the Likud and its coalition partners were interested in opening the Israeli economy to global markets and through the large-scale privatization of the Israeli industrial complex. This process included the transfer of ownership from the state to private businesses. An important dimension of this process is the subcontracting of public companies or CSOs to conduct some of the functions previously addressed in the public sector. This trend encouraged the rise of new public companies and CSOs to take a growing role in the provision of services for the public. One of the major ramifications of this process is not only the privatization of essential services, but also the reduction of the quality of these services. This last point, which is deeply related to the lack of sufficient funding, is evidenced by the gap between the number of CSOs registered in each of the social fields in which some of the services were subcontracted and those that have remained active after a few years. From the data made available by the Registrar in the Ministry of Justice, it is clear that only one quarter of registered CSOs survive. As indicated earlier, of the 8,042 registered CSOs in the field of social services and of 8,014 in the field of education, only

2,359 and 2,730, respectively, remained active in 2018. This reality reflects the fragility of the field and the chaos that characterize it.

The second important point has to do with the state's attempts to interfere in CSOs' activities, which could be mirrored through the frequent and subsequent amendments of the CSO Law since 1980. Various amendments to the law were made in 1996, 2007, 2008, and 2009. The aim of most of these amendments was to enforce the state's supervision and surveillance over CSOs' activity, financing, and organization, especially by the CSOs' Registrar in the Ministry of Justice.

One of the most prominent amendments to the law that reflects the state's attempts at surveillance and interference is Amendment 36a in 2008, which requires CSOs to reveal their sources of financing and reinforces previous state supervisory provisions. This amendment was part of the state's effort to prevent political pressure on Israel by CSOs, especially human rights organizations financed by foreign sources, including states or associations of states like the European Union.

Other attempts to impact CSOs' reach were led by right-wing political parties in Netanyahu's second coalition established in 2009, especially Yisrael Beytenu and Shas, and assisted by key members in the ruling Likud party and significant segments of the Kadima party. These parties attempted to tighten state supervision over critical CSOs, especially human rights organizations, arguing that they endanger national security and serve foreign interests.[2] These efforts were particularly intensive following the publication of the Goldstone Report, which provided a comprehensive report on the Israeli army's conduct during Operation Cast Lead in Gaza and suggested that Israel had committed war crimes against Palestinian citizens.[3] Right-wing leadership claimed that Israeli human rights organizations provided the committee with most of the information that led to its critical report against Israel and its army.[4] Although this argument was not true, this accusation came to undermine major human rights associations. The right-wing parties' aspirations to restrict human rights organizations based on claims that they were financed by foreign governments and hostile organizations led to many attempts, including legislative ones, to undermine the status of human rights organizations and to restrict the impact of all CSOs.

Knesset member Ofir Akunis presented a proposal for the amendment of the CSO Law (Amendment-Prohibition of Foreign Political Entity's Support of Political Associations in Israel) in March 2010.[5] The purpose of the bill, according to the Knesset's website, is "to prevent associations in Israel from receiving donations from foreign governments and Institutions (the UN, the

European Union). Since many so called 'human rights organizations' act provocatively in their attempts to influence Israel's political discourse, its nature and policy." Furthermore, it is suggested in the bill that "each non-profit association . . . receive small scale donations of up to 20,000 NIS a year, which will be supervised and transparent as specified in the Law of Disclosure for Anyone Supported by a Foreign Political Entity 2001."[6] This proposal is based on the amendments made to the bill between 2008 and 2009. Section 36a in the CSO Law clearly explains the state's intentions when referring to donations from a "foreign political entity," which is broadly defined. According to the Law:

36(a). (a) In this section:

"A foreign political entity" is any of the following:
(1) A foreign state, including—
    (a) A union, organization or a collective of foreign states (in this section—a foreign states union);
    (b) An organ, authority or representing body of a foreign state or a collective of foreign states;
    (c) A local or regional authority, a governmental authority of a foreign state or of a state belonging to an alliance of states in a foreign state (in this section—a foreign body);
    (d) A union, organization or a collective of foreign bodies;

(2) The Palestinian authority, as defined by the Law for Extending the Validity of the Emergency Regulations (Judea and Samaria—Judgment of offenses and Legal Aid) 1967;

(3) A corporation formed by a legislation of one of the entities described in sections (1) or (2), or that one of the aforementioned entities holds more that a half of the corporation's control means or appointed the corporation to act on its behalf; in this regard "control means," "holding"—as described in the Securities Law 1968.

"donation"—except for a tax relief, full or partial, granted outside of Israel.
    (b) (1) A CSO whose financial turnover exceeds 300,000 NIS will mention in its financial report, according to section

36, whether or not they received, during the relevant year, donations from foreign political entities in a cumulative value of 20,000 NIS; in this section, "turnover"—as defined by the second addition.

(2) If such donations as described in section (1) were received by the organization, the following details must appear in the financial report concerning each donation from a foreign political entity:
   (a) The donor's identity;
   (b) The amount donated;
   (c) The donation's purpose or mission;
   (d) The donation's pre-requirements, if exist;

(3) The CSO must do all within its power to find out whether the donation is originated by a foreign political entity, and the aforementioned the duty to report will apply if it was known or should have been known that the donation had originated form a foreign entity as specified.
   (c) The CSO will post on its website information as specified in subsection (b); if the CSO informs the Registrar it has no website, the Registrar will post the aforementioned information on the Justice Department's website.

Knesset member Ofir Akunis subsequently presented another bill in November 2011, stating that CSOs would not be allowed to receive donations of more than 20,000 NIS per year by "foreign political entities." The law's explanation, documented by Knesset members' discourse and the impacted organizations themselves, clearly shows that its purpose is the political persecution of CSOs that protect human rights. In his explanation, Akunis writes: "Many so-called 'human rights organizations' act provocatively in their attempts to influence Israel's political discourse, its nature and policy." When the bill proposal was discussed by the Ministerial Committee on Legislation and approved with minor changes, The Civil Rights Association published a newsletter stating that:

The bill proposal in its new version, as it has been in its previous versions, is nothing but an attempt to impinge a legal civil activity, which displeases the current political majority. Most of the Israeli CSOs targeted here are active in the field of defending human rights in the occupied territories, fight against the occupation, defending the rights of Israel's Arab minority and so on—positions, which contradict the political agenda of the Knesset members and Ministers, who are trying to damage these organizations.[7]

The attorney general, Weinstein, referred to the proposal regarding the CSO Law in early December 2011 and said it is "un-constitutional."[8] Weinstein continued to argue that the proposed law "restricts the freedom of speech, the freedom of association as is disproportionate." The state, which tries to undermine these rights through direct legislation or indirect policy, evidently perceives these associations as a threat. The government's intention to approve this bill elicited worldwide critique, including responses by the foreign ministers of the United Kingdom, the Netherlands, and the United States. U.S. Secretary of State Hillary Clinton said in the Saban Forum that she is concerned by the erosion of democratic values in Israel.[9]

The trend of nationalist right-wing Knesset members issuing bills to restrict CSOs continued through the beginning of 2012. On February 27, 2012, five right-wing Knesset members—Michael Ben-Ari, Aryeh Eldad, Nissim Ze'ev, Ronit Tirosh, and Uri Ariel—proposed an amendment regarding maximum wages in CSOs (2012), intending to "[block] attempts for unsuitable and unbalanced exploitation of public funds in public CSOs."[10] This general description seems honest, but it is obvious from these five Knesset members' discourse on liberal CSOs that this bill was an attempt to restrict the activities and recruitment for Israel's large and successful CSOs, which happen to be affiliated with civil and democratic values.

The hostile atmosphere and the state's aggression toward an autonomous civil society is also reflected in the approval of the ministerial legislative committee on December 15, 2013, for the bill proposed by Ayelet Shaked, a member of Knesset (MK) of the "Habayet Ha-Yehudi" (Jewish Home) party, who became Israel's minister of justice after the 2015 elections. This bill sought to impose a tax of 45% on all organizations receiving a donation from a foreign entity and included punitive measures for activities involving calls to boycott Israel or attempts to put soldiers on trial in international courts.

While Shaked's party welcomed this decision, left-wing Knesset members argued that the law was primarily designed to silence critics of government policies. Opposition leader MK Isaac Herzog of the Labor Party clearly reflected this argument by saying:

> [T]he Committee's decision on behalf of the Government of Israel is a dark, anti-democratic, and shut the mouth of those who dare to think differently from it. The next phase of the implementation of the law is the establishment of thoughts police that will determine who will pay a fine because of his views and who does not, who will enter the black political list and who is not. Israel is becoming less and less democratic. The prime minister and the Knesset plenum needs to annul the decision and cancel the committee of Ministers' decision immediately.[11]

Legislative efforts to curb civic activism and put pressure on human rights organizations continued in 2015–2017. These efforts were deeply influenced by the massive involvement of right-wing nationalist CSOs in policy making, something we turn to deal with in the following section.

The Rise of Nationalist "Bad" Civic Organizations

The legislative activism in the field of civil society is deeply related to the disconcerting development within Israeli civil society in recent years, namely the emergence of a number of CSOs promoting a public and political agenda that opposes or even contradicts civic core values. These organizations reflect the hegemony of nationalist forces in the Israeli public sphere and their attempt to mute or even eliminate alternative voices.[12] The main grounds for dispute is these CSOs' loyalty to the right-wing conservative political formula represented by the rising number of nationalist elites in Israel and the shifts in public opinion toward a more conservative nationalist ideology (IDI, 2016, 2017). Naomi Chazan, a former member of Knesset and former head of the New Israel Fund (NIF), argued in an article on the rise of active nationalist CSOs that "[t]hese forces have carried out a systematic, well-planned and extremely sophisticated campaign against those who dare to diverge from the dominant discourse. Instead of dealing with the content of the criticism raised by progressive civil society organizations, purveyors of the new nationalism consistently question their loyalty" (Chazan, 2012).

In other words, recent developments in Israel reflect an ideological struggle between different types of civic organizations seeking to influence state policy and use of civilian tools and resources to promote goals that are not necessarily consistent with the characteristics of a political, civil, and democratic culture.

A central argument in this regard is that even if the "civil society argument" is correct to some extent, mainly from the late 1970s to the late 1990s, as several Israeli scholars argue (Ben Eliezer, 2015; Chazan, 2012; Peled, 2005b), one notices in the last few decades that there has been a steady growth of "bad civil society" or "incivility" in Israel (Ben Eliezer, 2015). Such civic organizations aim to promote values and norms that are incompatible with a democratic liberal worldview and do not respect civic equality or the equal value of human beings and their autonomy (Adalbert, 2010). These emerging nationalist CSOs intervene in state policies and seek to influence legislation in an effort to promote antidemocratic and racist laws. These organizations attempt to exert their influence over all civic organizations that base their activities on equality and human rights (Chazan, 2012). The latter are attacked by national civic organizations as antipatriotic and said to be treacherous, and therefore there is a need to scrutinize their activities and impose legal restrictions on their resources and funding. The massive publications made by NGO Monitor and its critique of the "misuse" of funds by human rights organizations provide us with sufficient examples to amplify this trend (Steinberg, 2012). Steinberg, the head of NGO Monitor, targets human rights organizations, seeking to chastise them for their use of European funding in order to expose the misconduct of the Israeli army in the occupied Palestinian territories (2013).

The examination of several examples help illustrate not only the practical dimensions of the discourse, activities, and campaigns promoted by nationalist CSOs, but also enables us to reveal the strategies used in order to achieve their goals. Before moving ahead, it is important to make two preliminary notes. The first is that bad civil society is not determined by the fact that CSOs struggle to promote their ideology and political agenda. This goal is fully legitimate, even when these CSOs' agendas are sectarian and conservative, nationalist or religious (Boyd, 2004; Oakeshott, 1990). The "badness" of civil society, as used in this context, is related to the efforts and tools used by CSOs to dismantle opponents, silence their voices, and delegitimize them through the use of various types of disinformation, "fake news," and manipulative measures, leading to the mobilization of state agencies to limit CSOs' freedom to organize and express themselves. Bad civil society crosses the line between legitimate deliberation and ideological campaigning against an opposing camp. The difference is not always easy to conceive, but when CSOs invest their human and financial resources in lobbying the state against liberal and human rights organizations, it is possible to see that instead of aiming to enlarge the public space and enable better deliberation, bad CSOs aim to contract civil society and limit it to those who either accept their worldview or act without daring to critique the government and the CSOs affiliated with it.

The second note has to do with the fact that we are referring to nationalistic CSOs that emerged in the last few years and that act in concert with the state and its various organs to silence, dismantle, and stigmatize liberal CSOs and human rights organizations. This note is important, first, because it comes to differentiate between these new CSOs and religious ones that were always part and parcel of Israeli reality. Despite the latter's sustained engagement with the state, they have not tried to influence the mainstream public. These CSOs, which are identified with religious parties, sought mainly to lobby for their communities without having to intervene in mainstream public affairs and influence general public opinion in Israeli society.

By contrast, the new generation of nationalist CSOs differ from old ones in that they are deeply involved with and exhibit unlimited enthusiasm to influence public policy and engage with state agencies to transform the entire Israeli reality. These CSOs seek to push the state to clearly differentiate between patriotic and antipatriotic political activism and delegitimize any critique of state policies that do not align with the nationalistic ideology they seek to promote. The new generation of nationalistic CSOs are deeply involved in the Israeli public sphere and seek to shape public consciousness through the mainstream media.

The second difference between the new generation of CSOs and the older generation is the fact that the former are nationalistic. This means that their main discourse revolves around defining the identity of the nation and debate about the main characteristics of Israeli Jewish nationalism. These organizations do not necessarily have the same worldview when it comes to defining the identity of society and the state, for some of them are secular and come from a revisionist background, and others come from national religious background. These two camps compete against each other when it comes to defining the role of religion in the public and private spheres. Nevertheless, both agree that national values should have an elevated status in the Israeli constitutional tradition and its public sphere. An illustration of such a position is the Kohelet Policy Forum and the Center for Zionist Strategies' introduction of the recently passed Basic Law–Israel the Nation State of the Jewish People in 2018 (Jamal, 2018).

Before delving into these strategies of these CSOs, it is important to note that it is impossible to provide a comprehensive illustration of these

CSOs' activities. What is addressed here is the broadly defined processes and activities of these CSOs as a piece of the puzzle in Israeli society's overall transformation. This transformation could be summarized by referring to the rise of a historical block composed of orthodox communities, conservative Jews of oriental origin, new immigrants from the former Soviet Union, and the settler community in the OPTs (Yadgar, 2017; Kimmerling, 2004). Each of these communities has its agenda, and their interests do not always match. Nevertheless, they agree on a nationalist-religious value system that enables them to cooperate in establishing their hegemony over the state and in sharing power to guarantee their success.

To illustrate the practical meaning of the theoretical arguments made in this section, we concentrate on three forms of activities that mirror the three strategies used by nationalists CSOs to achieve their goals. The first strategy is silencing, and it is illustrated through the campaign made against academic institutions, especially liberal professors who critique the policies of the state, especially in the OPTs. The second strategy is that of delegitimization through stigmatization, and it is illustrated through the campaigns against human rights organizations and activists. The third strategy is targeting the financial sources of human rights organizations, aiming to blocking their financial support by differentiating between financial support received from political entities and states, which are depicted as supporting intervening in Israel's internal affairs and those characterized as private funds, considered fully legitimate and confidential. This third strategy is illustrated through the activities of NGO Monitor and the legislation processes taking place in the Knesset.

Silencing: To illustrate this strategy, it is worth looking at the efforts made by nationalist CSOs to silence liberal and critical voices in the academia. Im Tirtzu[13] and the Institute for Zionist Strategies[14] opened in 2009–2010 as a media campaign seeking to limit academic freedom in Israel. They sought to intimidate academic institutions based on the political worldviews of some of their professors. These CSOs demanded that academic institutions distinguish between their staff according to their loyalty to Zionist values of the state. The well-orchestrated campaign of these two nationalistic CSOs started with presenting selective data concerning teaching the syllabi of professors, measuring their pro- or post-Zionist commitment. The two organizations argued in their "studies" that most of literature covered by professors in the departments of sociology and political science are critical of Israel and represent an ideological bias of post-Zionist or anti-Zionists tendencies, thereby questioning the moral justifications of the state of Israel.[15] The well-orchestrated campaign sought to shame publicly funded academic institutions, mobilizing public opinion against them. The two organizations lobbied the education committee in the Knesset, which is dominated by nationalist parties. In doing so, members discussed their reports and demanded that universities act against critical professors.[16]

This campaign against academic freedom manifested itself again with the efforts made in the years 2017–2018 to draft an "ethical code" for all academic institutions in Israel. The involvement of Im Tirtzu in lobbying for this ethical code—which was condemned by most academic institutions in Israel except for Bar Ilan University, which is identified with the conservative Habayit Ha-Yehudi party—was made clear by the public support it gave to the code and to its involvement in its promotion.[17] The conservative nationalist CSOs, which act as a very strong lobby in the Knesset and in government offices to promote nationalistic policies, especially to block and silence liberal voices in the public sphere, expressed their satisfaction with the ethical code and stated that it is a result of their efforts to prevent liberal academics from using their positions to promote a political agenda.[18] Although it is not possible to delve deeply into the contents of the code, it is sufficient to say that the code sought to limit academics from expressing any views on publicly disputed topics in their teaching, something that was understood by most academic institutions and liberal intellectuals and student unions to challenge the principle of academic freedom and silence critical voices. Given that the governmental coalition is composed primarily of nationalistic and religious parties and that this composition is not likely to change in the near future, the promotion of this ethical code by a nationalist education minister with the support of nationalistic CSOs such as Im Tirtzu is viewed as a clear sign of how bad CSOs are successfully imposing a conservative nationalist worldview and shrinking the spaces given for freedom of expression.

Delegitimizing through stigmatization: The second strategy used by the new generation of nationalist CSOs is illustrated through its attack on human rights organizations, especially those promoting equal civic rights for all citizens in Israel and those involved in campaigning against the Israeli occupation of the OPTs. The best example to illustrate this strategy is the harsh critique on 20 human rights organizations compiled in Im Tirtzu's selective—and largely inaccurate—report published in 2015. The report, "The Planted Agents 2015," depicts the activities of 20 human rights organizations supporting equal rights and a discourse of liberal citizenship in their quest to protect Israeli democracy. This report depicts projects seeking to protect human rights in the OPTs as "political propaganda organizations that act from within with broad financial support of foreign countries against Israeli society, against soldiers of the IDF and against the ability of the state to protect itself in its war against terror."[19] This language, which depicts human rights organizations as cooperating with the enemies of the people in a situation of war, not only delegitimizes them, but also challenges the public and the state to take action against them. This challenge has come to fruition and is reflected in right-wing parties' attempts in 2017–2018 to establish a parliamentary investigation committee to examine the behavior of the accused, as well as the passage of recent legislation previously addressed in this chapter.

In its response to the report, the Association for Citizens Rights in Israel (ACRI) states that

> human rights organizations find themselves under harsh attack for several years already. This attack is led by extreme right wing organizations that seek to undermine the promotion of human rights in Israel . . . What those who incite against ACRI seek to achieve is silence the substantial critique that ACRI voices against certain actions of the Israeli authorities.[20]

ACRI's comments adds that "reports like this one and activities like those of Im Tirtzu disenfranchise democracy."

Blocking Funding from Foreign Political Entities: The example employed to illustrate this strategy is the work of NGO Monitor, led by a Bar Ilan University professor, to block foreign aid to human rights organizations in Israel. NGO Monitor was established with the intention of providing information about the activities and practices of human rights organizations in Israel.

In its mission statement, the organization states clearly that "NGO Monitor provides information and analysis, promotes accountability, and supports discussion on the reports and activities of NGOs (non-governmental organizations) claiming to advance human rights and humanitarian agendas."[21] To distance itself from the government, especially because of its deep connections with Bar Ilan University and the Ha-Bayit Ha-Yehudi party, which was the leading party of the coalition and whose members support nationalist legislation against human rights organizations, NGO Monitor states on its website that "NGO Monitor was founded jointly with the Wechsler Family Foundation. All our funding is provided by private donors and foundations, and NGO Monitor receives no governmental support."[22]

Many of the human rights organizations in Israel receive some funds from the NIF. Therefore, the first target of the attack made by right-wing affiliated CSOs is the NIF. The circumstances surrounding the Goldstone Report were fully exploited to attack human rights organizations and accuse the NIF of supporting CSOs that provided most of the information resulting in accusations of Israeli war crimes in Gaza. The NIF issued a press release reporting on the attack, stating, "Recently, the New Israel Fund became the latest target of what appears to be a coordinated effort to stifle dissent and shut down the human rights community in Israel. Although the crisis began with a smear campaign devised by a new right-wing group, the most significant threat to NIF and its work was a proposed 'commission of inquiry' in the Israeli Knesset, a proposal that was at least temporarily shelved when the Kadima party refused to endorse it in early February [2010]."[23]

This attack on the NIF, which did not stop at the media, shows clearly the relationship between right-wing nationalist CSOs and policy making on the legislative level. The efforts to establish an inquiry committee to examine the sources of CSOs' funds and, later on, to monitor the activities of human rights organizations continues to this day. Although this committee has not been established, legislation requiring CSOs funded by foreign sources to wear a tag when in the Knesset has been passed. This specific requirement was taken out of the proposed CSOs bill, but the government remained committed to it, as stated by Prime Minister Benjamin Netanyahu in early 2016.[24] Netanyahu argued that "[t]ransparency is the heart of democracy. When you hear about the use and abuse of CSOs here—transparency is the least we want and is much warranted and it is common sense. Israel is being held to a different standard here."[25] This argument made by Netanyahu reflects a sophisticated attempt to instrumentalize democratic transparency to apply pressure on human rights organizations, which are mostly funded by foreign governments. The bill does not relate to CSOs funded by private sources, which is the case in most major CSOs identified with the conservative nationalist right. The wording of the proposed bill has not been naive and aims to target certain types of left-wing CSOs. Ambassadors of Germany, Great Britain, France, Holland, the European Union, and the United States expressed concern about the proposed legislation. In particular, the European Union criticized the bill, saying that its demands on NGOs go "beyond the legitimate need for transparency" and that it is seemingly "aimed at constraining the activities of these CSOs working in Israel."[26]

The American Embassy in Tel Aviv issued an unusual press statement after a meeting of the American ambassador and the Israeli justice minister, Ayelet Shaked, in which he said, "Among the topics discussed was the government's draft NGO bill, which would require Israeli NGOs who receive a majority of their funding from foreign governments to be labeled as such . . . Ambassador Shapiro sought more information about the draft legislation from the Minister, and noted the U.S. government's concerns on the matter."[27] Furthermore, German Canceller Angela Merkel expressed her concern about the proposed CSOs transparency bill in a meeting with Prime Minister Netanyahu on February, 17, 2016, in Berlin.[28]

The bill passed in the Knesset on July 16, 2016.[29] Yariv Oppenheimer, former head of Peace Now Movement, claimed "We are portrayed as 'foreign agents' . . . Promoting the idea we are working for foreign money is a way of branding us as 'traitors' that aren't part of society. NGOs are almost 'the enemy from the inside.' This is the language we are seeing."[30] Debbie Gild-Hayo, policy advocacy director at Association for Civil Rights in Israel (ACRI), argued, "In the last few years it has become more severe. What is really worrying is that it is coming from high up in the government, as well as from the mainstream press."[31]

The role of right-wing nationalist CSOs in promoting restrictive legislation and in propagating policies that accuse human rights organizations of being enemies of the state and society in Israel is best reflected in the intensive and vibrant international activities of NGO Monitor. In the last few years, NGO Monitor managed to establish a broad network of connections with various international organizations and governments, seeking to pressure them to cut funding for what it considers to be anti-Israel activities. The reasons given were the purported defense of human rights. Gerald Steinberg, president of NGO Monitor, argued, "Large-scale foreign (mostly European) government funding to Israeli political groups, under facades such as civil society, human rights, peace or democracy building, and which does not take place in any other democracy, is seen as an attack on Israeli sovereignty and democratic self-determination."[32]

This statement by Steinberg reflects the cynical use of democratic discourse to promote antidemocratic policies. The efforts made by NGO Monitor do not aim to increase transparency, for this is also supported by all human rights organizations, which submit audited reports that include clear statements about their sources of funding on a yearly basis, according to Israeli law. The statements made by NGO Monitor concerning the classification of pro- and anti-Israel civic engagement and the targeting of funding sources that support human rights organizations reflect its clear efforts to cut or reduce funding for what it views as political CSOs.

In NGO Monitor's annual 2013 report titled "A Year of Impact," it clearly states, "A primary NGO Monitor objective in Europe is to significantly reduce the massive government funding for radical NGOs, directly from the European Union, its 28 member states, Norway and Switzerland, as well as indirect channels through European Christian aid frameworks. In 2013, we made significant progress in a number of key areas, following a strategy based on 'naming and shaming.' Our systematic research reports and follow-up activities have produced important results, including the discontinuation of European funding for a number of politicized NGOs active in the Arab-Israeli conflict."[33]

The naming and shaming strategy of NGO Monitor and its right-wing political partners active in the Israeli public sphere demonstrates their political and ideological goals, which is to reduce the spaces of freedom available to human rights organizations. The shaming of human rights organizations and activists as foreign agents and thereby traitors of state and society in Israel renders their delegitimization possible. This strategy of differentiation between friend and foe comes not only to ignore violations of human rights conducted by the Israeli government, the Israel Defense Forces (IDF), and radical settlers, but also to silence witnesses who can provide any evidence as to these violations.

When adding these efforts of shaming and silencing to efforts made by other CSOs to promote nationalistic legislation, such as the promotion of the nation-state law by the Kohelet Policy Forum and the Center for Zionist Strategies, one can see the broader picture of a clear effort to transform the entire Israeli regime and power structure. These efforts are about restructuring the Israeli power relations, promoting the influence of the nationalist-religious agenda and transforming Israeli political culture into one that is more Jewish than democratic (Jamal, 2019). The religionization taking place in Israeli society, as reflected in many public opinion surveys and research reports, supports the efforts made by nationalistic CSOs, making these efforts into not only legitimate but actually natural and even taken for granted (Peled & Peled, 2018; Yadgar, 2017).

Summary

Arguably, the strengthening of civil society in Israel has increased exponentially in recent years because of two key processes: the retreat of the welfare state and the rise of nationalist trends in the Israeli public up to the point that nationalist parties are now central to any government coalition. Also prominent among CSOs are those related to economic, neoliberal policies. The state has been a central player in strengthening such organizations, as it entrusts these CSOs with many of its welfare responsibilities, such as daycare, shelters for battered women, and educational institutions. However, the state's reliance on them also simultaneously promotes political and legal restrictions on human rights organizations, which are inclusive of some of these activities.

The processes described in this chapter confirm once more the critical arguments raised in the limited literature concerning civil society in Israel. Israeli society did not develop a civic political culture that lends legitimacy to activities of CSOs as protecting civil rights in the face of the state's penetrating power, and market culture, and intensive commercialization of private and public life. There are many dangers that civic organizations, especially those that define themselves as social change and human rights organizations, must face.

These dangers stem from three main sources, raised in the discussion above. The primary source of danger is the state, which not only fails to provide resources to human rights organizations, but also promotes laws and regulations that negatively affect the activities of these organizations and portrays them as treasonous. The second source of danger is the market forces, due to changes in the economic structure of Israel and the withdrawal of the welfare state. CSOs are forced to fill the void left by the state, making them collaborators with the privatization of basic public services. The social protests in Israel during the summer of 2011 inspired a resurgence in civil society and made a strong impact on the public agenda. But the protest fizzled out, and its lack of direct results, as well as the inability of many CSOs to create a direct link between their activities over the years, left many disillusioned. Furthermore, these widespread protests obscured the extensive activities of the network of civic organizations in various areas, something that did not help to improve the public's perceptions of their effectiveness. Additionally, the struggles between human rights organizations and conservative civic organizations with nationalist tendencies further obstructed genuine discussions of civil society's effectiveness in influencing the public agenda.

A third source is the growth of "bad" civil society, which not only seeks to influence public policy, but also attacks liberal human rights organizations' democratic and civic values and activities. These attacks are defended by a narrow nationalist agenda and are based on accusations of disloyalty and treason. These conservative organizations also stand behind waves of new legislation designed to limit human rights activities and cut foreign funding.

When it comes to Palestinian civic activism, these trends pose a serious challenge to its work. The state's interventions through legal and economic means place a heavy burden on the PCI in general and its civic activism in particular. The hegemonic ethno-nationalist ideology promoted by the state forms a repressive system that clashes with the PCI's aspirations for equal civil rights. The religionization of state and society leaves a narrow space for civic activism to lobby for the transformation of the Israeli political structure. Despite the fact that the Islamic Movement and its CSOs are not liberal, their activities, which were outlawed in November 2015, operated within the same civic spaces made available by the state. However, the outlawing of the movement and its CSOs is a clear sign of Israel's dwindling tolerance of and shrinking spaces for civic and political activism (Asseburg, 2017). Furthermore, the prime minister's assault on the Freedom Protection Council established by I'lam and the efforts he and his government invested in pushing the EU to stop funding the project are a prime example of the atmosphere in which Palestinian CSOs have to act.[34] One of the radio stations affiliated with the ruling conservative coalition described the announcement made by the prime minster as a strategic victory.[35]

Chapter 6

Transformations in the PCI, the Emerging New Elite, and Civic Activism

Since the state's founding in 1948, which resulted in the demolishing of the Palestinian political, financial, and cultural elite in what is now the State of Israel, a rising number of educated Palestinians, intellectuals, and professionals is emerging (Jamal & Bsoul, 2014). Since then, Palestinian leadership in Israel underwent several extreme transformations, some of which are discussed here. During the first few decades following the establishment of Israel, the remaining Palestinian leadership was a direct result of the *Nakba* (Manna, 2016). The vast majority of the political, financial, and cultural Palestinian elite vanished in 1948 from the territories that had become the State of Israel (Sa'di & Abu-Lughod, 2007). Any leader who was involved in some way in opposing the Zionist movement was deported, and those who remained in their houses were living in areas outside Israel's borders (Manna, 2016; Pappe, 2006). The Israeli security forces gathered information about any influential figure, marking them as targets (Cohen, 2006; Pappe, 2006). Low-level Palestinian leadership who remained within the state had to submit to its new rules (Lustick, 1980). The military regime imposed on the Palestinian population after the war posed heavy limitations on freedom of speech, freedom of movement, and freedom of assembly, practically preventing any real potential for political mobility (Bäuml, 2007; Ozacky-Lazar, 2002). In the meantime, as part of their efforts to enhance control over Palestinian society, Israeli authorities began to nurture young and ambitious members of large clans (in many cases, these were clans that previously had been marginalized in Palestinian society), who were willing to cooperate with the state in exchange for positions of power, including a seat in the Israeli Knesset (Lustick, 1980). Many of these people were members of the political lists affiliated with the dominant Jewish Mapai party (which later would become the Labor Party) in the Knesset elections until the late 1970s.

Hence, most of the members of the post-1948 Palestinian leadership were traditional leaders who based their power on religious and family ties, held a utilitarian worldview, and submitted to the state's dictate without posing any challenge. Most of the leaders of these Arab parties did not even have a basic level of formal education (Jamal, 2006b). Many of them had only graduated from elementary school. Some were members of prominent clans in their villages, and others managed to raise the support of these large clans, which offered them the social support needed to compete against their opponents. Still others blindly obeyed the state's dictates and provided services that other leaders could not or would not provide, such as paving roads, connecting houses to the grid or the water supply network, and so forth.

The only two movements that were not supported by the Israeli government during these early years were Al-Ard, which carried the Palestinian national banner and demanded the establishment of a Palestinian state based on the UN 1947 Partition Plan (Nassar, 2017; Frisch, 2011, Bäuml, 2007), and the Israeli Communist Party (Kaufman, 1997).[1] Similar to their counterparts in the Mapai-affiliated political lists, the leaders of these two movements were also relatively young and at the beginning of their careers. However, their level of education was higher, and they paved their own path (Jamal, 2006b). The leaders of Al-Ard were mainly the descendants of Palestinian families that had been displaced and robbed of their main sources of income and social power because of Israeli's land expropriation policy (Manna, 2016). Some of them were members of lower-middle-class families that had a strong national consciousness and viewed Israel as a purely colonial project, clashing with their ambitions and the basic interests of the Palestinian people. The leaders of Al-Ard, including Anis Kardosh, Habib Kahwaji, Jabur Jabur, Zaki al-Karmi, Naim Makhul, Sabri Jiryis, Mohamad Miari, Nadim Al-Kassem, Abdel Aziz Abu Isba'a, Tawfik Odeh, Mohamad Sruji, and Sami Nasser, were more educated than the average leaders in the Palestinian community. We might say they were directly connected to pre-1948 national leadership, but possessed a more realistic worldview and a greater understanding of the Zionist movement's power and its inherent clash with the basic aspirations of the Palestinian people and the Arab nation (Haider, 2018).

The Palestinian leaders of the Israeli Communist Party were also younger and more educated than the leaders of Mapai's Arab political lists. Mostly in their 20s, they had been part of the Palestinian Communist Party prior to 1948 (Jacobson, 2018). Because of their support of the UN Partition Plan, they were granted permission to stay, despite their critical views of the government (Manna, 2016; Kaufman, 1997). The senior party leaders, including Emile Habibi, Tawfik Toubi, Emile Touma, Saliba Khamis, Nimer Murkus, and others, were mostly members of the Greek Orthodox Christian community (ibid.). Loyal to their Marxist-Leninist ideology, the party leaders viewed Jewish-Palestinian relations mostly in terms of a class struggle, and their criticism of the state's discriminating policy against Palestinians focused on class exploitation. Communist Palestinian leaders supported the establishment of a Palestinian state, demanded the return of Palestinian refugees to their original homes, and objected to the state's land expropriation policies (Jamal, 2010). At the same time, they also recognized the right of the State of Israel to exist and the legitimacy of Jewish immigration to Israel. They spoke of Jewish-Arab camaraderie in a struggle against the discriminating state's policies. Despite their very compromising positions, these leaders were persecuted by the state for their mere support of equal rights for all Israeli citizens, irrespective of their national affiliations and for raising particularly sensitive issues, such as the status of refugees, the military regime, and land expropriation (Bäuml, 2007).

These three groups of political elites underwent major changes in the last few decades. It is not my intention to review their evolution, but to argue that new social, economic, and educational conditions have led to the growing socioeconomic differentiation within the PCI, including its elites. Leading figures from broader socioeconomic backgrounds, including from poor families and internal refugees, have begun to emerge. As a result of the growing differentiation among these emerging elites, their ideological fabric has undergone major changes. These Palestinian leaders became less united on the ideological level and as different elites adopted different ideological beliefs that could be defined broadly as communism, nationalism, and Islamism. These ideological orientations were institutionalized and became central to the Palestinian public sphere. The debates among them show that whereas they differ on their social philosophies, when it comes to their relationship with the state, they agree on most issues, except for those elites who were not willing to participate in the Israeli elections (Second Strategic Report, 2018).

Education and the Changing Characteristics
of PCI Leadership

Today's Palestinian elites are decisively more representative, as their members are far more diverse. Recent decades have witnessed a constant rise in the level of education in the PCI. As a result, a large group of Palestinian academics specializing in various fields and disciplines has emerged. Today, the PCI's leadership includes experts in various fields, such as medicine, pharmaceuticals, engineering, law, social work, science, behavioral science, and so forth. One of the key features of this group is that this diversity in expertise is not the exclusive product of the Israeli education system, but also of other educational institutions in Eastern and Western Europe, Jordan, the Palestinian Authority, as well as the United States. This trend began with student missions to Soviet states arranged by the Communist Party and continued with individual ventures of medical and legal studies in European countries (such as Italy and Germany) and in graduate studies across the United States. In the last decades, thousands of students from the PCI are studying in Jordan and in areas of the Palestinian Authority. The rising level of education among the PCI resulted in a process of cultural and political awakening and, as a result, a rise in the political expectations of the PCI. This change was reflected in the growing mobility of Palestinian academics as well as their increasing involvement in civic activism, including infiltrating the Israeli labor market and fighting against the government's exclusionary policies in the provision of services and social integration. Furthermore, this newly educated Palestinian political leadership began to enact internal changes in the PCI's self-perception and behavioral patterns. Among the Palestinian political leadership acting on the national level, one could notice the growing number of academics in Arab parties and political movements, which explains their global worldview and their attempt to transcend state boundaries and make contact with the rest of the Arab world (Jamal, 2017).

In the past, the rates of academically educated Palestinians in Israel were extremely low (Al-Haj, 2003). In the academic year 1956–1957, there were 46 Palestinian students in Israel, an overall 0.6% of the entire student population. In 1979–1980, there were 1,634 Palestinian students—about 3% of the student population. Between 1988 and 1998, the rate of Palestinian students had risen from 6.7% to 8.7%. In 1998–1999, there were already 7,903 Palestinian students—7.1% of the entire student population in Israel (Manna, 2008). According to the Central Bureau of Statistics, in 2000–2001, there were 7,200 Palestinian students, compared to 9,967 in 2004–2005. The number of Palestinian college students was 2,000 in 1999–2000 and 4,553 in 2004–2005. In 2004, the number of Palestinians with 16 or more years of education was 94,486—a testimony to the fast-paced growth of the Palestinian academic and professional elite (ibid.). According to the CBS data, in 2007–2008, the proportion of Palestinian students in the entire population of undergraduate students in Israel was 11.6%. In 2008–2009, they were 11.5%, in 2009–2010 they were 11.9%, in 2010–2011 they were 12.1%, in 2011–2012 they were 12.5%, and in 2012–2013 they were 12.9%. These numbers jumped to 18% in 2019. These data clearly show a rise in the rate of Palestinian students studying in Israeli higher education institutions, yet the rate of growth remains low when compared to the overall Palestinian population in Israel, which amounts to 28% in the ages 18 to 21, the years for higher education.

The numbers of students studying for graduate degrees are even lower, though also constantly on the rise. In 2007–2008, 6.4% of the master's degree students and 3.5% of doctoral degree students in Israel were Palestinians. In 2008–2009, the rates were 6.5 and 3.7, respectively; in 2009–2010, 6.9% and 4%; in 2010–2011, 8.2% and 4.4%; in 2011–2012, 9% and 4.4%; and in 2012–2013, 9.2% and 4.9%. These changes reflect a slow but significant growth in the number of Palestinian citizens who are pursuing higher education, developing a career, and becoming interested in improving their chances of translating their education into higher incomes. These graduates are an important human resource contributing to the creation of an educated Palestinian middle class, which is developing expectations for a better socioeconomic reality. This group spearheads the overall political project aimed at improving life conditions for the Palestinian population in the shadow of the state's discriminatory and exclusionary policies.

Only a small group of Palestinian citizens have managed to be accepted as staff members in academic institutions in Israel, but these individuals have made significant contributions to the development of the academic discourse in issues related to the status of Palestinians in Israel, particularly vis-à-vis their political and human rights. Palestinian academic staff, although few in number, helped to introduce the debate over the PCI's rights into the academic and political agenda in Israel, as well as in various international forums. They are joined in their effort by a large group of Palestinian professionals, particularly lawyers and human rights activists, who are active in CSOs across Israel and abroad (Jamal, 2008). The latter are connected to international human rights organizations and are well aware of the changes in global politics concerning individual and collective human rights. These Palestinian academics and professionals are at the forefront of the Palestinian public, aiming to promote its civil, political, financial, and cultural rights. Gradually, they are creating the moral, legal, and political foundations for the full integration of the PCI in policy-making processes in Israel, particularly the realization of their right to effective representation in the private and public spheres (Jamal, 2011). New-generation Palestinian leaders demand to institutionalize the Palestinian public in national-level forms of representation as an integral part of their attempt to create external protection for the PCI.

A look at the Palestinian elected officials, particularly in the Knesset, reveals vast changes within this group as well. The number of academics among this small group of elites is constantly growing, and these academics are slowly but tenaciously shaping the political orientation of the leadership, affecting its modes of operation versus the state, as well as their own patterns of political mobility. Until 1981, most Arab Knesset members, particularly the ones in the Labor party, were not educated. Of the 70 Arab Knesset members between 1949 and 1984, only seven had an undergraduate degree, and 19 of them never gained official education. By comparison, since 1984 and until the 20th Knesset (elected in 2015), 93 of the 102 Knesset members had at least an undergraduate degree, and the rate of graduate-degree recipients has been growing in recent years. Five of the Arab representatives in the 19th Knesset had a PhD or an MD, one had an MA, and four had a BA degree. Of the thirteen members of the Joint List in the 20th Knesset, four have either a PhD or an MD, one has an MA, and the rest have a BA degree. These data reflect an actual change in the intellectual qualities of the Palestinian elites' political leadership in Israel. It is important to note that this trend does not accurately represent local leadership in Arab municipalities; however, here there are major changes taking place. An increasing number of Arab mayors have pursued higher education. Many are either medical doctors, engineers, lawyers, and so forth. This trend has major implications on society, despite the fact that many of them use the patriarchal familial social structure to be elected. The very small number of women active in this field reflects its patriarchal and gender bias, as evidenced as late as the October 2018 municipal elections.

Unlike the previous generation of leaders, who were nurtured and sometimes even invented by the Israeli establishment, this younger generation has had to fight to establish its status in the state's formal democratic institutions. This was the case for many of today's prominent leaders who have affected the social and political reality of the PCI. Leaders such as Mohammad Barakeh, Raed Salah, Haneen Zoabi, Ayman Odeh, Ahmad Tibi,

Aida Touma-Suleiman, Yusef Jabareen, Masud Ghnaim, Kamal Khatib, Azmi Bishara, Jamal Zahalka, Abdel Hakim Haj-Yihya, Awad Abdel Fattah, Abbas Mansur, Osama Sa'di, Ibrahim Hijazi, Abdallah Abu Maaruf, Juma Azbarga, Mazen Ghanayeem, Heba Yazbak, and Mudar Yunis, alongside many local leaders, such as Shawki Khatib and Mohammad Zidan, former chairs of the Follow-Up Committee, the most important representative body of the Palestinian public in Israel, and Ramiz Jaraisy and Ali Sallam, former and current heads of the Nazareth Municipality, reflect the broad socioeconomic differentiation of the PCI's leadership. Many of these leaders come from low socioeconomic backgrounds and represent different segments of society; this may explain their legitimacy, despite the very modest achievements they manage to realize in face of the state's discriminatory policies.

It should be mentioned here that the prominent presence of second-generation Palestinians does not contradict the continuous development of younger generations' elites in Palestinian society and additional changes in Palestinian leadership. The technological development in the fields of communication and information in recent decades has allowed for greater social mobility, enabling young leaders to develop a reputation and influence public consciousness using the new information technologies (Jamal, 2017). Young leaders active in social movements are very powerful, even though their power is not backed by any formal authority or an official position. They offer a significant contribution to the shaping of public consciousness. One of the areas representing young leadership activity is student unions at institutions of higher education. In this field, one witnesses the mobility of a new generation of young women and men and their commitment to the aspirations and interests of the PCI. This generation of leaders speaks the language of social media, especially those who enable new forms of networking beyond the local level. This mobilization is manifested in various initiatives, which could be illustrated by the commemoration of the Palestinian Nakba in various universities (Sorek, 2015). Internet activity and the use of new media for political mobility and social protest were often found to be extremely important tools for this generation (Ben Beri, 2018). The best example is the protest against the Prawer Plan (a proposed governmental plan to resettle Arab Bedouins living in unrecognized villages in the southern part of the country and concentrate them in exiting towns), which eventually resulted in delaying its implementation. The ambivalence of influential hierarchies among young activists makes it more difficult to present clear arguments regarding changes in today's Palestinian leadership, but these young leaders will definitely have a critical impact on shaping the PCI's social and political fabric in the future.

Active Citizenship and Political Mobilization

Through the first three decades of the state, Arab demands for equality were based mainly on distributive justice and the concept of individual rights, derived from its aspiration to insure the survival of what was left of Palestinian society within Israel following the *Nakba*. Accordingly, the state should include its Palestinian citizens as equal participants in its society and economy. Dominant political movements within the Palestinian minority, particularly the Communist Party, believed for a long time that a joint Arab-Jewish identity could be established, dismissing the role of Zionism as the state's dominant ideology (Kaufman, 1997). Based on this kind of political vision, the majority of Palestinian society tried to advance their interests within the formal political system through the state's official representative body, the Knesset. Adjusting to this new system and searching for ways to influence it from within was perceived as the best strategy under the circumstances. This strategy was also enforced, as it served the interests of the Communist party, the dominant political force that acknowledged the state's Jewish identity, but still presumed to authentically represent the Palestinian minority's interests. The Communist Party challenged any opposing voice and tried to eliminate any separate political force, such as the Abnaa al-Balad Movement, which was established in 1972. It was also one of the reasons for the establishment of the Socialist Front in 1958, which later supported the emergence of Hadash (The Democratic Front for Peace and Equality) in the 1977 Knesset elections. Here, the Communist party aspired to integrate nationalist Palestinian intellectuals in all-inclusive political groups to avoid the growth of competition. Its members thus tried to expand the party's representative base and include politicians who could empower the party despite the fact that they were not communists (Rekhess, 1993).

This adaptive pattern of political behavior has remained in every political party that represented Palestinian society since 1984. The Progressive List for Peace, established as a Jewish-Arab party, exhibited similar behavior in its attempts to influence official politics through the Knesset, despite the extreme rhetoric of its members. For example, the Progressive List presented a new political-national discourse, which emphasized the identity of the PCI and demanded a solution for the Israeli-Palestinian conflict that would include them. Similarly, the Arab Democratic Party had the same objectives. Ex-Labor party members before the 1988 elections established the Arab Democratic Party as a pure Arab party, with a platform based on equality and integration in the state's institutions and in Israel's society and economy. This party expanded the integration discourse and demanded to be a part of the coalition so they could exert greater influence on policy and decision-making processes. While the communists and nationalists based their political moves on firm ideological ground, the Democratic Party was a pragmatist party, which sought any effective way to promote its leaders and integrate them into the state's institutions.

This strategy was adopted by Arab political parties for a variety of reasons. The experience of the 1948 war and the disintegration of Palestinian society that lived in what is now Israel played a major role in determining the PCI's mind-set. Until the 1967 war, this group suspected that their presence in the Jewish State was merely temporary and that any "wrong" behavior on their behalf would lead to their expulsion (Manna, 2016). Furthermore, the installation of a military regime over the areas settled by Palestinians helped to control and eliminate any alternative pattern of collective behavior (Cohen, 2006). The state also tried to monitor and manipulate the PCI's consciousness through less overt means. One of the main objectives of these ideological and disciplinary means was to create a local consciousness that would accept Israel as a Jewish state (Jamal, 2010). The education system and the media, alongside the General Security Service (Shabak) and Police Intelligence, attempted to dictate a Palestinian collective consciousness that would be subordinated to the state's ethnic ideology.

Hundreds of textbooks printed since 1948 were written with the intention of educating the PCI to accept the vision of Israel created by Jewish teachers and academics (Mari, 1978; Al-Haj, 1995; Bar-Tal, 2005). The state even presented new media outlets in Arabic in an attempt to dictate the Arab public's agenda (Jamal, 2010). The Hebrew media also contributed to the delegitimization of any Palestinian opposition to the state's policy (Wolfsfeld, 2000). According to a study published by I'lam, 68% of news items about Palestinian society published in the Hebrew media frame the former as either a security threat or criminals (Massalha & Jamal, 2012). The police and the Shabak were highly active in Arab cities, spreading fear among separatists and encouraging traditional clan and other leadership to cooperate in stopping any opposition to the sophisticated system of control employed since 1948 (Lustick, 1980). While its methods underwent many transformations, the state's aspirations for its acceptance and the taming of Arab civil or political opposition toward its policies remained constant.

Despite the state's material and ideological hegemony and the fact that the Palestinian public never abandoned official politics, Palestinian civil society managed to open new ideological horizons, leading to the development of an oppositional consciousness (Jamal, 2007b). This process is not only about participation in the political game, but also how it determines its rules and who takes part in it. The PCI's attempts are evident in the moral and political justifications used by Palestinian citizens to challenge the Israeli discrimination policy (Jamal, 2006a). The Palestinian refusal to be subordinated to the Israeli control mechanism started in the 1950s, but it was relatively latent until the mid-1970s. The main reason for the latency of oppositional political engagement is the fear of being outlawed by the political system on security grounds, as happened with Al-Ard movement in the 1960s (Nassar, 2017; Frisch, 2011). This experience demonstrated to many Palestinian citizens that the margins of tolerance in Israel's political systems are limited and determined by a security mentality that represses any political debates challenging the way the system was established, who participates in it, and by which means.

Since the 1970s, we have witnessed the emergence of new political leadership, which successfully initiated new patterns of political ideas and political and civic engagement. Palestinian politicians continue to operate within the Israeli political establishment, complying with the dominant rules of the political game, but at the same time challenges Israeli policy and presents new demands for equal, active, and meaningful citizenship, including representation in the state's institutions. This political leadership, which is fragmented on ideological and sectarian grounds, still managed to translate its political engagement into active organizations and institutions in areas that were neglected by the state, like education, welfare, and others.

Over the last two decades, we have seen Palestinian intellectuals and politicians rephrase their struggle for equality in Israel by highlighting the state's obligation to recognize them as a national indigenous minority (Jamal, 2011). Many demand official recognition as an indigenous people and are entitled to collective rights, which by their account should be interpreted in terms of self-governance (Jabareen, 2001; Bishara, 1993). The demand for collective rights does not replace the demand for full and equal citizenship, but rather completes it. This demand creates a challenge for Israeli authorities, who are bound by their own laws to address it. One of the PCI's main arguments in this regard is that collective rights are a prerequisite for individual rights (Bishara, 1993). The demand for self-governance is relevant in several public realms of the PCI, including education, media, planning, management of resources, social welfare, and development (Haifa Declaration, 2007; The Future Vision, 2007). More and more Palestinian citizens have also begun to demand proper representation and full participation in defining the state's policy and priorities. This demand includes participation in deciding the future of the country's resources that belong to the state, particularly its land, which was taken from Palestinian citizens through Israel's planning and resettlement policy, based the notion that these lands are meant for exclusively Jewish use (Yiftachel, 2006).

Furthermore, the political, cultural, and intellectual elite have created widespread connections with Palestinian society in the Palestinian territories and elsewhere in the Arab world (Nassar, 2017). One can point to a range of communication channels at the political and cultural level, such as meetings between Palestinian members of Knesset and leaders of the Palestinian Authority, active engagement of local poets and authors in cultural events taking place in the Arab world, and the building of communicative networks between Arab youth from the PCI and Arabs from Arab states though social media. In other words, Arab cultural activities in Israel have become part of the cultural landscape in the Arab world, something that strengthens the ability of the PCI to resist the state's policies toward them.

Beyond the elite's attempts to influence policy from inside Israeli law, a growing number of Palestinians have become disillusioned with their ability to influence state policy through formal means (Jamal, 2006b). Different political initiatives, some of which became institutionalized, called for resisting the entire epistemological underpinnings of the Israeli system. They pointed out that participating in the political game according to the hegemonic rules means legitimizing them, no matter what one says and does. The question they argued is not the patterns of conduct within the system, but rather the exclusion embedded in the system and manifested by who takes part and who doesn't and by what means.

The main manifestation of such politics remains the boycotting of formal elections to the Knesset. This has been one of the major ideological elements in the worldview of Abnaa al-Balad (Sons of the Land), dating back to the 1970s. Members of the Islamic Movement, led by the Sheikh Raed Salah, also adopted this ideology in the mid-1990s. Salah encouraged citizens to boycott the Knesset elections and called for the establishment of a self-sufficient society, where Palestinian citizens are totally independent of the parliamentary system that is fully and exclusively dominated by the Jewish majority (Ghanem and Mustafa, 2019; Rubin-Peled, 2001). A few Palestinian academics adopted this idea after examining the imbalance between the Palestinian community's (minor) ability to influence the state's resource distribution through Knesset representation and the price paid by the community for legitimizing the dominance of Zionism in the political establishment. According to these academics, Arab parties cannot run on a platform that rejects Israel's definition as a Jewish state or calls for a change in the state's identity. This limitation prevents Arab parties from using legitimate democratic means to challenge the Jewish hegemony in the state's institutions. The civil sphere is thus perceived by many as a more viable avenue for promoting socially, culturally, and politically unique objectives. To fulfill this need, dozens of Palestinian CSOs were established.

Yet the development of an opposing consciousness was not limited to a particular political or ideological stream of thought. Palestinian activists tried to realize their desire to influence their reality through civic activism and sought to establish associations that provide support and services to the Palestinian community. As a result, the number of local, regional, and national civil society institutions, which presented a new model of political activity, grew steadily. Many CSOs were active purely for social motivations and became active areas in which the state's services did not provide what was expected from them. These areas include sports, healthcare, education, and agriculture. Additionally, formal networks were established in many Arab villages to meet local challenges. Such networks have routinely emerged since the development of the digital revolution. Many social initiatives used digital spaces to make new contacts and promote general social interests (Jamal, 2014). The mobilization of widespread social resistance to the Prawer Plan in the Negev is just one example. Many Palestinians, especially Palestinian youth, have harnessed the power of new media to bypass formal party institutions and independently coordinate, monitor, and mobilize local and international support. It remains to be seen if the informal political engagement of youth via social media will translate into formal political processes in which parties and elected leaders will take online youth engagement into account and respond accordingly.

Formal Political Activism and
Strategic Dilemmas of the PCI

The PCI have been participating in the Israeli political system and taking part in the elections since 1949. This participation has been based on the strategic interest of protecting the interests of the community in remaining in the homeland and the hope that they might influence government policies to deliver effective, positive changes in its future. This pattern of conduct, especially the notion that the differences between the Palestinian minority and the Jewish majority must be dealt with through legal means and from within Israeli's state agencies, was accepted by the vast majority of the PCI's leadership. Since then, most Palestinian citizens act in concert with this position and use the spaces of political mobilization afforded to them by the Israeli political system, despite their mistrust toward government offices as a result of their policies of discrimination and neglect. That said, it is possible to generalize by stating that there is a feeling of growing disappointment among many Palestinian citizens and a rise in an oppositional, ideological consciousness among nationalist and religious Palestinian citizens. This trend has led to a continuous decrease in the percentage of Palestinians participating in the formal political process, especially the elections to the Knesset. Whereas more than 80% of Palestinian citizens participated in the elections before the 1980s, resulting in a rising number of Palestinian members of parliament in the Knesset, the decades since have witnessed a growing number of Palestinian citizens boycotting the elections and seeking alternatives to the formal political system. Election participation by Palestinian citizens declined from 79.3% in 1996 to 49% and 60% in April and September 2019, respectively, while more than 80% of Palestinian citizens boycotted the special election in 2001.

This steady decline in participation is an expression of Palestinians' growing disillusionment in the capacity of the Israeli political system to represent their needs and the search for alternative means of practicing power and pressure vis-à-vis the Israeli state. This long-term decline was slightly affected by the establishment of the Joint Arab List, which united all the Arab parties ahead of the 2015 election (shown in Table 1). The reversal

Table 1. Participation in Elections by Palestinian Citizens of Israel, 1996–2020

Year	Participation (%)
1996	79.3
1999	75.0
2003	62.0
2006	56.3
2009	53.6
2013	57.3
2015	63.5

Source: Central Elections Committee—Knesset.

of the decline in participation between 2009 and 2015 marks an important trend but one that is likely to continue only if the Joint List manages to demonstrate political efficacy or if future elections take place in the wake of a major clash between the State of Israel and Palestinians in Gaza, as occurred in the 2013 and 2015 elections. The Gaza conflicts of 2012 and 2014 led to rising national sentiments among Israel's Palestinian citizens, which translated into higher turnout for Arab parties as an act of protest.

Many Palestinian leaders in Israel call on members of the PCI to use every structural opportunity to advance their interests. Notwithstanding its limitations, the Knesset does provide some resources to Arab parties that may in turn provide the PCI with venues to articulate its needs and desires in a sanctioned Israeli forum. Others reject such participation on the grounds that it legitimizes the Israeli system and enables Israel to assert its "democratic" character without yielding any real influence for the PCI on Israel's discriminatory policies. If the Joint List does not manage to significantly change Israeli policy—and this is the most likely scenario, given its dwindling legitimacy in the eyes of most Jewish parties and the unwillingness of the latter to integrate it into their decision-making processes—the influence of the latter camp will grow, and the percentage of Palestinian citizens participating in Israeli elections will decrease further. If this happens, an increasing number of Palestinian citizens will seek alternative means to express their dissent and protest against their secondary status in the Jewish state.

One might generalize that the PCI has so far preferred to avoid adopting "either/or" diagnoses of the present Palestinian reality and the proper strategies for improving it. The PCI has demonstrated much political maturity, managing to avoid falling into the traps set by the far right, which views them as enemies and seeks to push them into a direct clash with the state. Instead, the PCI tends to pursue a "selective" strategy, remaining committed to its Palestinian nationality while simultaneously struggling for full, individual, and collective citizenship rights. This approach represents the most effective use of the structures of opportunities available to them. Through this selective engagement, the PCI seeks to overcome its "double marginality," imposed by both Israelis and occupied Palestinians, and to use its double consciousness to promote the best reality possible for all parties, including itself. In other words, the Palestinian community in Israel does not aspire to be a bridge for peace, as if it were the United Nations. Instead, it seeks to use what influence it has to end the suffering of millions of fellow Palestinians living under brutal occupation. This community also demonstrates that it is deeply concerned with the struggle of its Palestinian brethren under occupation and that it seeks to play its own distinct role in equalizing the asymmetric power relations, which enable Israelis to solidify their hegemony over the entire Palestinian homeland.

The double consciousness of the PCI is deeply related to the rise of the Palestinian middle class, which is both nationally conscious and has accrued great economic wealth in recent years. Growing prosperity—despite the fact that around half of the PCI still lives under poverty line—has raised this group's expectations and demands, but also its fears that existing gains might be lost. This class resents Israeli discrimination, but elects nevertheless to participate in the economy to raise Palestinians' standard of living. It seeks to integrate with the Jewish-Israeli population and expects to be given a chance, not only on the economic but also on the political level. This same class anticipates that the state and the Jewish majority will permit it to translate its growing economic power into political influence without having to entirely submit to perpetual Jewish hegemony. It also believes it can achieve this delicate balance without disengaging from the national Palestinian question, especially in the form of opposition to Israeli policies in the occupied territories (Ghanim, 2009).

Having said that, and notwithstanding the many commonalities among Palestinians in Israel, this group is nonetheless split over its future visions and strategies. Broadly speaking, three different approaches have gained support in the community. All three strategies are driven and articulated primarily by the rising Palestinian middle class.

The first is based on seeking the best measures possible to enable the community to reconcile its Palestinian-ness and Israeli-ness. This camp sees itself as realistic, arguing that international, regional, and local constraints require a pragmatic strategy that accounts for political realities without sacrificing principles. It maintains that the coercive power of the state, the determination of the Jewish majority to expand and violently defend its hegemony, and the international realities of a Trump presidency and an Arab world in disarray all set sharp limits on what can be achieved in the present situation. The Palestinian minority must deploy its resources strategically, pursuing quiet popular and civic resistance while promoting better communication with state agencies to increase access to its resources as part of their rights as citizens. This camp enjoys the support of at least one-third of the PCI, manifested politically in the Hadash party as well as a small number of voters in Zionist parties. It also maintains some presence among supporters of Balad and even the Islamic Movement.

As regards the broader Israeli-Palestinian conflict, supporters of this camp argue that there is widespread international support for the two-state solution; that Palestinians in the West Bank and Gaza live under a brutal occupation that must be abolished, and that Palestinians in Israel have acquired rights and gains that should not be jeopardized. The disintegration of many Arab states and the upheavals that took place in several have weakened partners that were once viewed as strategic assets of the Palestinian people. Palestinians must therefore choose realistic, rational policies that recognize their weakness and lack of leverage vis-à-vis Israel. The pragmatic camp also understands that Palestinian elites in the West Bank and Gaza are not united and that the Israel will employ any means to suppress them, especially when the PCI demonstrates sympathy for Palestinian resistance against the occupation. This group argues that Palestinians have recognized the legitimate right of Jews for self-determination. Therefore, they conclude, Palestinians should seek compromises with Israel, while insisting on partition and the establishment of an independent Palestinian state in the West Bank and Gaza Strip. In this regard, they advocate for a realistic and just solution of the Palestinian refugee problem, whose implementation is compatible with the right of Jews to self-determination but recognize the Israeli government's role in blocking any serious and genuine solution of the conflict. Therefore, this camp argues against the formal definition of Israel as a Jewish state and sharply criticizes the discriminatory policies that have been grounded in this definition.

The second camp more firmly situates the PCI within the broader Palestinian reality, focusing on its national identity and the search for just solutions of the Palestinian problem in all its aspects. It argues that all Palestinians have paid the price of Zionism and the establishment of the State of Israel. Furthermore, it maintains that the state does not fundamentally differentiate between Palestinians when it comes to its colonization and settlement policies and in its brutal coercion and discrimination against Palestinians. The expansion of settlements in areas occupied in 1967 have rendered partition unrealistic; continued talk of a two-state solution serves merely as a diplomatic tool for Jewish nationalist leaders to reduce the reputational costs of their continued occupation. The rise of the settler movement and demographic changes within Israel point toward a one-state condition that will persist for the foreseeable future. This camp, which attracts the support of more than 20% of the community and finds institutional homes in the Balad party and the Abnaa Al-Balad Movement (Sons of the Village), criticizes the "pragmatic" approach of the Palestinian Authority, which, it maintains, facilitates the occupation and contributes to the fragmentation of the Palestinian people. Politically, this group believes Palestinians should reject the Jewish character of the Israeli state and assist Palestinians under occupation to struggle not just for national independence but also for comprehensive liberation, using all means legitimated by international law, including boycott. Many members of this group envisage a democratic one-state solution for Israel/Palestine.

Finally, there is the Islamic camp. While ambiguous about its ultimate political aspirations, it is subdivided into two groups. The first argues that, as a minority in a non-Muslim state, Muslims in Israel should exploit all opportunities available to promote the well-being of Muslim citizens, including representation in official Israeli institutions. The second is more dogmatic and less open to engagement with Israeli social and political institutions. It views the conflict as religious and asserts that only religious beliefs, values, and practices offer any hope for resolving it. This group is affiliated with the more conservative and dogmatic elements of the Muslim Brotherhood movement and seeks first and foremost to transform the values and behavior of the Muslim community in Israel. It supports the movement for boycotts, divestment, and sanctions (BDS) against Israel, without announcing its position bluntly. These two groups together win the support of more than half of the PCI.

All political forces in the PCI share the belief that the Jewish majority is radicalizing. They agree that it should not be given any excuses to use force against the Palestinian community. This results in a broad strategic consensus, notwithstanding their underlying political and ideological differences. Most opt to use tactics least vulnerable to persecution, such as establishing CSOs to resist governmental policies and protect the safety of their members by legal and international advocacy. As a result, as long as the state's policies do not precipitate a major crisis, whether in the occupied territories or inside Israel, the Palestinian minority will maintain its current approach: combining daily civic resistance to state policies of discrimination with an eye toward improving community relations with state agencies to achieve better understanding and empathy and greater material resources to improve communal well-being. This strategy makes use of the tools available—with growing reluctance—by the Israeli political system. It is complemented by efforts to strengthen social, economic, and cultural ties with Palestinians in the West Bank and the diaspora, as well as with the wider Arab world. This strategy is pursued in a variety of ways, including shopping in Palestinian cities, intermarriages, and interacting with political activists in the Palestinian world.

This "bonding and bridging" strategy seeks to maximize the resources available to the PCI to endure and challenge the state's policies of Israelization, subjugation, and economic and cultural neglect. This balance between Israeli and Palestinian societies reflects the double consciousness of the Palestinian community in Israel and its ability to transform this duality from a weakness into a source of strength.

Chapter 7

Palestinian CSOization, Active Citizenship, and the Politics of Contention

The struggle against the policies of the newly established state toward the Palestinians who remained within its borders began immediately after it became clear that the new status quo meant that Palestine had been divided and that they were to live for the time being under Israeli rule. This recognition was apparent among communist Palestinians, who initially supported the partition plan and accepted the establishment of two states in Palestine—one Jewish and one Arab (Ghanim, 2017). The miserable reality and the poverty caused by the war plagued the Palestinian community, especially the internally displaced who lost their homes and properties and sought refuge in neighboring villages. Such a reality has motivated more established members of the PCI to extend help and assist in others in overcoming these hardships (Manna, 2016; Arraf, 2007; Bäuml, 2007; Ozacky-Lazar, 2002).

New networks began operating in various areas, seeking to invigorate the community and collect the resources needed to support neighboring families who as a result of Israel's rigid legal system were rendered refugees (Kanaaneh & Nusair, 2010; Al-Haj, 1988; Sa'di & Abu Loghud, 2007). These networks operated in the shadow of the newly imposed military government and martial law on Palestinian areas (Lustick, 1980; Ozacky-Lazar, 2002). Therefore, they had to be defined in humanitarian terms and remain local. This pattern of volunteering is a well-known social behavior in most Palestinian villages, which, unlike the uprooted communities, remained in their place and hosted thousands of refugees (Yazback, 2019; Kanaaneh & Nusair, 2010; Al-Haj, 1988). Women were very active in this pattern of social volunteering for two main reasons. The first had to do with the fact that, in a patriarchal society, the responsibility for the household, especially cooking, is fully organized based on gender, and women took care of these affairs (Abu-Baker, 2009). Providing food and the basic needs of the refugee families had been left for women, notwithstanding the men's decision to host these refugees in the first place. The second reason for the deep involvement of women in volunteering with refugees was that they were less surveilled by the Israeli authorities and not suspected as politically active in a traditional rural society. This oriental view left women a narrow space to operate a local welfare system, without which it is hard to imagine how the internally displaced could have survived the miserable circumstances in which they lived prior to finding permanent refuge (Yazback, 2019).

On a more formal level, one could speak of several attempts to institutionalize a limited set of civic activities in fields that were not suspected by the authorities of being political. The first is the establishing of Al-Nahda Al-Nisaiyah (Women Renaissance), a women's organization headed by female activists in Nazareth in December 1948. While not much is known about the particular developments of this organization, we know that it was part of the local networks established to provide help to refugees and was initiated by educated women, mainly Christian families, affiliated with the Communist Party (Kaadan, 2019). This local organization remained active until 1951, when it was united with the Jewish women's organization, Progressive Women's Organization, which together established The Movement of Democratic Women in Israel (Fleischmann, 2003). This organization was officially registered as a civic association in 1982 and is still active to this day (Kaadan, 2019).

Another type of civic activity that was partially institutionalized had to do with workers' unions, especially in Nazareth (Dallasheh, 2012). The Communist Party, which framed the Israeli-Palestinian conflict in terms of class, pushed to establish workers' unions to protect the rights of Arab workers while integrating into the emerging Israeli job market. The Union of Nazareth Workers, established after 1948, and other workers' unions that were established before 1948 continued to operate after the war. Their work reflected the efforts made by communist activists to organize workers in civic organizations that operated in their name and sought to protect their interests.

The Communist Party's efforts to organize civic activity among the PCI were not the only ones. National activists, especially after the 1956 war, began organizing civic activities to serve the PCI's needs and promote certain worldviews. The Al-Ard movement's work was the most well-known in mobilizing people based on ideological lines that centered around the Palestinian identity of the PCI and the rejection of Israel's efforts to integrate the community based on civic values only. The Al-Ard movement propagated the Palestinian identity of the PCI and sought to reflect the paradox between being Palestinian and being an Israeli citizen (Manna, 2016; Lustick, 1980; Sorek, 2015). To mobilize the PCI, Al-Ard avoided operating as an independent political party. Rather, activists in the movement tried to remain a civic association, based on the Ottoman law legally valid in Israel (Kahwaji, 1972). They established many clubs in Arab villages and towns and issued several publications that made their ideology apparent, marking the difference between themselves and the Communist Party and their affiliation with the Nasserite Pan-Arab ideology, voiced by Gamal Abdel Nasser from Egypt (Jiryis, 1976). Al-Ard was not satisfied with local civic activism and its efforts to mobilize and transform the Israel reality. This dissatisfaction was reflected in a letter sent by the movement to the United Nations in July 1964 (Nassar, 2017; Frisch, 2011; Bäuml, 2007). The letter pointed out the discrimination against the PCI, demanding the implementation of the partition plan and Resolution 194 of the Security Council, which addresses to the return of Palestinian refugees to their homes (ibid.). This letter facilitated Israel's decision to outlaw the movement, clearly marking the acceptable limits of the PCI's political protest and civic engagement in the public sphere.

The civic activities promoted by Palestinian activists demonstrate their efforts to find the right path to address the challenges the PCI faced following the Nakba. The services provided by these activists, whether social, educational, trade-unionist, or welfare, reflected their efforts to overcome the hardships caused by state policies, especially the military government. Although one cannot speak of a vast and active civic sphere in the PCI at that time, given the circumstances following the Nakba, the networks established at the time and the volunteering activities aiming to provide the necessary services mark the seeds of Palestinian civil society in Israel.

The 1970s mark a shift in the PCI's efforts to establish civic initiatives in order to meet social and economic needs. These efforts were mostly politically motivated and orchestrated by the Communist Party, which sought to overcome the cliental political patterns promoted by the Israeli government in the PCI (Jamal, 2006b). Whereas the Arab Lists affiliated with the dominant Mapai Party in Israel since 1948 were based on tribal coalitions, the Communist Party, seeking to win the loyalty of the PCI, had to overcome the familial connections and generate new types of civic activities based on ideological grounds. Civic associations, clubs, unions, and other types of civic movements were thus adopted by the Communist Party in order to promote their goals.

Among the prominent CSOs established in the mid-1970s were the Nationwide Committee for the Protection of the Arab Lands. Its goal was to lobby against the state's policy of confiscation and dispossession of Palestinian lands.[1] The Arab Student Organization and the Arab High-school Student Union were also established at about the same time. These CSOs were hyperpolitical, and their aim was to represent the fundamental rights of the PCI. This wave of civic institutions was welcomed by the Communist Party, which used it to promote its own political interests vis-à-vis the Israeli authorities as, despite being a legal political party, it was still perceived by Israel to be illegitimate (Bashir, 2006). These CSOs were characterized as political and representative, despite the fact that their leaders were not elected by the public. Their leadership was instead a group of volunteers tightly linked to the Communist Party and acted discretionally, according to the party's goals. This unique relationship enabled the party to anchor itself in the PCI and express its true needs and desires. This dynamic also enabled it to operate with little or no internal resources, unlike most CSOs today.

Thereafter, the number of Palestinian CSOs grew consistently, continuing throughout the early 1980s and into the last few decades, which saw exponential growth. In 2006 there were 2,609 registered Palestinian organizations, 1,517 of them active. These included 1,358 service providers, while 132 organizations provided other types of nonmaterial support, such as advocacy and consulting.[2] However the CSO scene in 2018 was different and reflected the major challenges CSOs have faced as a result of the state's neoliberal economic policies, the nationalizing processes taking place in the Israeli politics and society, and the growing competition over resources in the international arena. In 2018, there were 3,895 registered CSOs (Graph 2). Of this number, only 947 were active ones. The main indicator used to define active CSOs is the submission of a financial report to the Registrar in the last five years, namely 2013–2018. Only those CSOs having submitted a financial report are able to legally act as an employer.

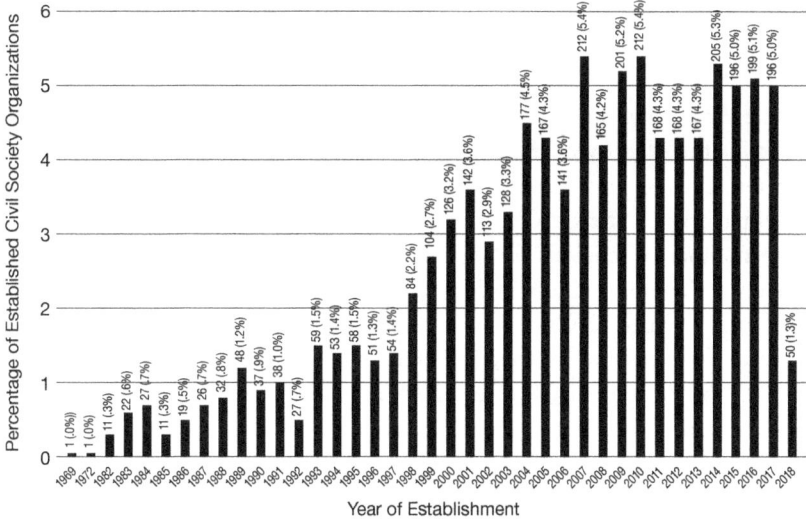

Graph 2.

As the graph above (No. 2) demonstrates, there has been a steady rise in the number of CSOs registered every year. Despite the slight fluctuations, one could confidently say that the last two decades mark the emergence of most registered Palestinian CSOs in Israel. This pattern reflects a broader process that the entire PCI has faced, namely the merging of two broader developments—the first is the Oslo Accords, which assumed the PCI would remain in Israel in every peace agreement between the Palestinian national movement and Israel, and the continuous shrinking of the Israeli welfare state. The PCI's recognition that it must take care of its own affairs has led to major changes in the PCI's politics, namely the rise of the Balad Party, the split in the Islamic Movement, and both parties' decision to enter the Israeli Knesset elections in 1996. These major developments are connected with the rise of new CSOs that sought to defend the PCI's political and civil rights.

Furthermore, when it comes to the centrality of the second indicated development impacting the rising number of Palestinian CSOs since the early 1990s, namely the shrinking welfare state, one could indicate that a large number of the established CSOs provide services such as education, religion, sports, social welfare, and so forth. The graph below (No. 3) demonstrates this trend and reflects the soaring number of CSOs that came to fill the void that the state created as a result of its privatization in all fields and the

PCI's sense that it must take care of the many challenges it faces because the state has adopted, in its view, a politics of neglect.

When looking at the numbers in the graph below, one cannot but notice that many established CSOs provide services that have clear implications for the identity of the recipients, especially in the fields of education, religion, culture, and even social services. Although it is not always possible to differentiate between CSOs based on their ideological commitments, a large number of religious CSOs demonstrate the split between secular and religious orientations in the PCI. By comparison, the low number of advocacy and social change CSOs are mostly nonreligious and reflect the culture of society. Notwithstanding these differences, all CSOs share the demand for the PCI to be recognized on equal footing with the Jewish citizens of the state, regardless of their ideology.

In this regard, one could generalize that the wide network of Palestinian CSOs could be seen as a kind of a counter-public; that is to say, Palestinian civil society, particularly its active associations established since the 1990s, forms a unique network of associations based on its special social, political, and cultural agenda, which is vastly different from that which is promoted by the state. While the state strives to fully subordinate the PCI to the interests and considerations of Jewish-Israeli society, many Palestinian CSOs promote a different self-perception and a collective vision of a whole new Arab and Jewish reality. While Islamic associations call for an Islamic future, secular associations promote a civic future of liberalism and equality.

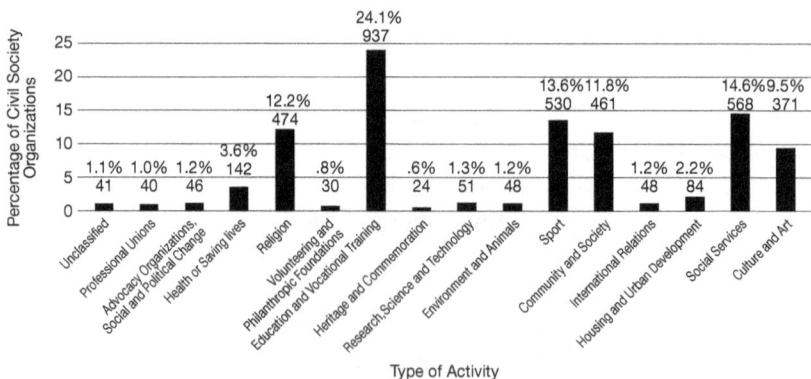

Graph 3.

The massive rise in the number of Palestinian CSOs since the 1990s can be divided into two major waves. The first wave occurred after 1994 and the second after 2000. Before presenting the direct and indirect causes for these two waves, we should explore the general background for their emergence. The first wave can be attributed to two circumstantial factors that created a powerful structural constraint on the PCI and thus brought these waves to fruition by necessity. First, the Oslo Accords and the establishment of the Palestinian Authority enforced the understanding that the PCI should take responsibility for its own fate. During this time, a growing number of leaders and academics began to reflect on new ways to promote the rights and attend to the needs of the PCI.

Following the Likud party's victory in the 1996 elections, the structure of the Israeli economy began to change; the welfare state underwent a serious process of contraction, and the subsidies policy (employed by Rabin's second government and allocated more resources to the PCI) was dissolved (Reiter, 2009). When much of the funds allocated toward improving the status of the PCI were blocked, the crisis of the PCI deepened, and new action had to be taken to alleviate its growing social and economic distress. Many Islamic and secular leaders supported the idea that associations should be established to provide services or challenge the state in areas that had been neglected.

Another factor to consider during this time was the Israeli municipalities' crisis, particularly in Palestinian villages and towns. Many municipalities stopped or reduced the provision of services, leaving the PCI even more

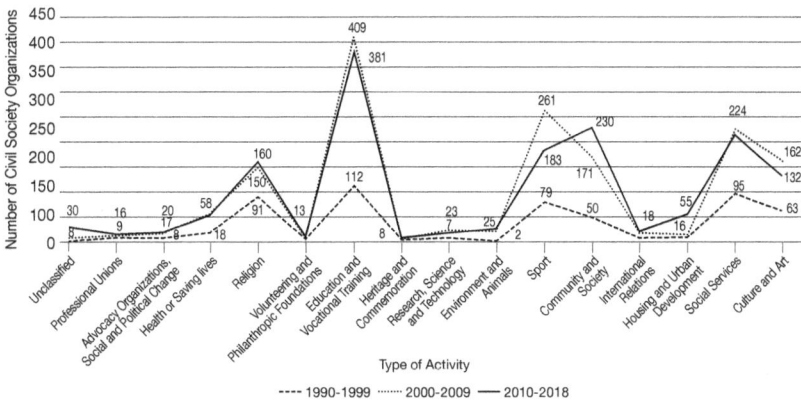

Graph 4.

vulnerable than it had been previously (Ben-Bassat & Dahan, 2009; Haider, 2012; Ghanem & Azaiza, 2008; Abu-Habla, 2012).

The second wave of Palestinian CSOs can be attributed to the October 2000 protests, which caused great disappointment among the PCI as to the state's conduct during the protests and its failure to provide new services to the Palestinian community (Haider, 2010). After almost a decade of hope following the Oslo Accords and the establishment of the Palestinian National Authority (PNA), as well as the policy changes toward the PCI initiated by Rabin's government, the October 2000 protests shattered all hopes and effectively rolled back the state's relationship with the PCI (Reiter, 2009). Palestinian civilians were killed, hundreds were wounded, and the Jewish population boycotted Palestinian cities and commercial centers. Its aftermath was the practical deterioration of the relationship between the state and the Palestinian minority to an extent unseen in recent decades (Jamal, 2007a). This reality encouraged many Palestinian leaders to establish CSOs that would provide new services, defend Palestinian citizens' rights, and promote change in the government's policy.

Today, this network of CSOs continues to grow, and, in particular, national associations have begun to develop and empower the PCI, simultaneously defending its basic rights vis-à-vis the state. The activities of these Palestinian CSOs challenge state policy in an attempt to bring change in significant fields like law, planning, housing, education, media, and others. Adalah's contribution, for instance, is evident in the legal discourse in Israel; it has managed to influence the dominant policy in several areas, such as housing, land allocation, and educational policy. Mossawa exposed the state's biased allocation of resources; Women Against Violence raised awareness as to the importance of gender equality, although women's status in Palestinian society has been slow to change; al-Aqsa Association has made a direct impact on the preservation of Palestinian religious and historical sites; The Arab Center for Alternative Planning exposed the biased planning policy; Mada Al-Carmel published many studies on the political behavior of the PCI and influenced Israeli academic discourse; I'lam Center has exposed the important role played of the media in founding antagonistic discourse against the PCI; Iqraa and Al-Qalam assist college and university students with getting ready for academic education in a new cultural environment; Al-Zahraa provides employment and professional education and training to women; Arab Human Rights Association (HRA) provides educational programs in the field of human rights at schools; Al-Manarah provides services to people with disabilities; and Al-Sadaqah al-Jaririya helps families in distress and assists in several social development projects.

These examples illustrate the PCI's efforts to contribute to its own welfare. CSOs undoubtedly address the basic social, economic, and cultural needs of the PCI and therefore are authentic in their representation of major trends taking place in it.

The reasons for the emergence of Palestinian CSOs and their fields of activity cannot be explained solely by the distresses of the population. These distresses may have been significant factors that motivated many civil forces, especially service providers, but they are not enough to explain the massive growth in the number of Palestinian CSOs since the 1990s. This growth calls for a comprehensive explanation as to Palestinian civic engagement. This engagement can take the form of individual voluntarism, organizational engagement, or participation in the elections. In this case, increased engagement in CSOs is characterized by its collective needs and the way it intervenes to alleviate them. When discussing engagement, we refer to activity beyond family or friends and those actions intended to influence the lives of others without requiring personal acquaintance. This activity entails a strong motivation for rationalization, choice, and autonomy based on one's worldview and desire for personal gain, both direct and indirect. It is possible to argue that civic engagement for public benefit is influenced by many structural and behavioral circumstances.

It is our belief that in recent years we are witnessing a new wave of civic associationalism, which complements the PCI's attempts to provide for the population's needs and draws attention to areas that thus far have been neglected. Associations like Baladna, Injaz, and Al-Qaws demonstrate the PCI's attempt to tighten the CSOs' network and introduce the key challenges faced by the PCI to the Palestinian-local and Israeli public agendas.[3]

Moreover, it is important to also draw attention to new trends in the digital activity of Palestinian society. There is much greater mobility today among younger generations than in the past, who are now able to use digital tools to promote and address public issues. Good examples of such mobilizations are the digital resistance to the Prawer-Begin plan run by a group of youth in 2013; I'lam center's "Ma-Esimhash hek" campaign ("It is not called this way") to raise awareness of the Arabic names of junctions and sites that have been renamed by the state to match the Zionist narrative; the campaign called "Love in the Time of Apartheid," opposing the citizenship law and its impact on family reunification; and the campaign "Urfud"

("Refuse")—Your People Protect You, which was launched in March 2014 against compulsory military or civilian service among Palestinian youth of Druze origin. These campaigns and many others use social media to promote their goals, especially when it comes to shaping public consciousness and generating debates and deliberations regarding challenges facing the PCI.

This pattern of online activism has become central in the PCI's civic activism today. Most, if not all, CSOs have active websites and Facebook pages that attract audiences and seek interaction with the community. Many of the CSOs' activities are either broadcasted live on Facebook or uploaded to the internet and made available to the wider public. When it comes to online activism, our survey reveals that Palestinian citizens have been active in various fields between 2016 and 2017. Interviewees were asked to mark whether they have taken part in online protests and deliberation on several topics. The topics were chosen from their life environment and related to daily issues as well as broader interests, such as having been active in the online communications during the Arab Spring.

The data show that 62.3% said that they were active when it came to protecting holy sites, 42.7% were active in protesting against the Israeli wars on Gaza, 37.8% protested against policing of the PCI, 36.6% protested against the policies of house demolition in the PCI, and 36.6% participated online during the political upheavals of the Arab Spring. These data are not surprising when compared to political participation in participants' offline activities.

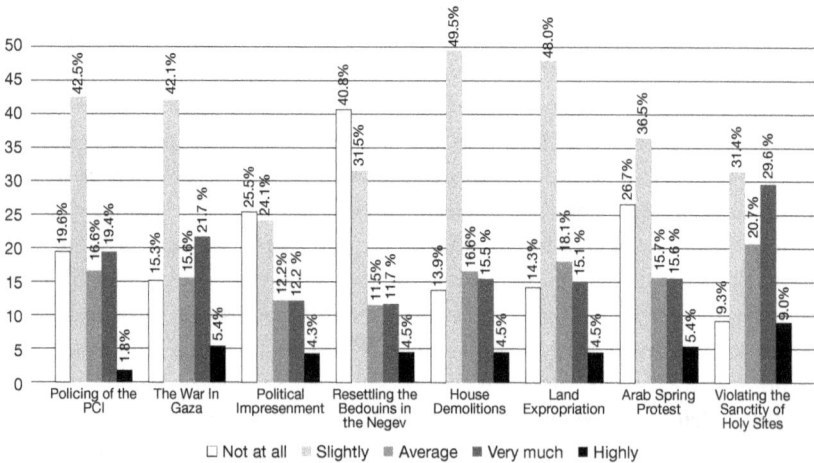

Graph 5.

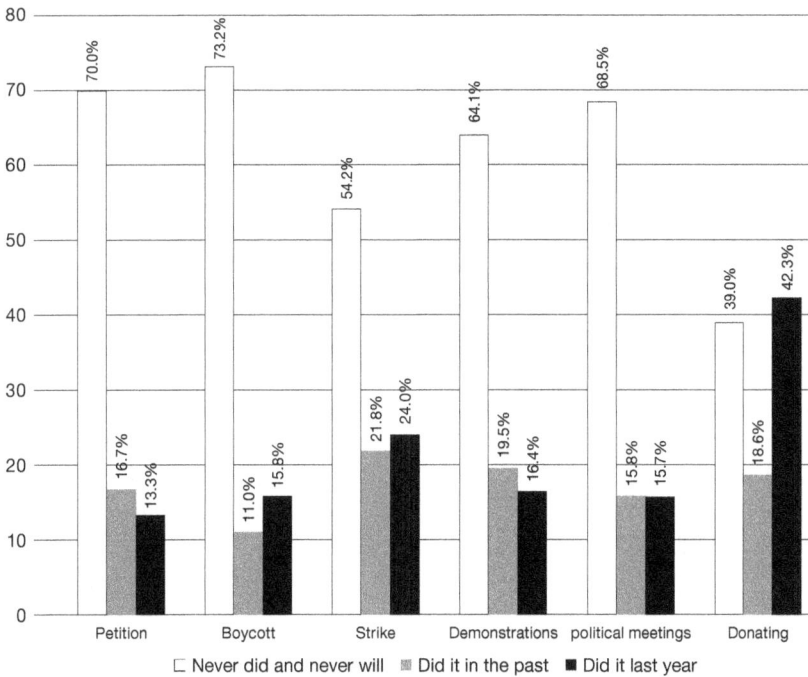

Graph 6.

As we can see from the above graph, the average participation in offline protests amounts to only 15%. Most people answered that they have never took part in petitions, boycotts, strikes, demonstrations, or political meetings. Only around one-third reported ever having taken part in such activities. Donation is an exception, as it reflects the political culture dominating Palestinian society. The PCI is mostly Muslim and therefore participants would have been required to participate in the *zakat* (religious donation). These data reflect a serious gap between online and offline civic engagement. They go along with the data in the broader field of digital activism, which posit that the effort needed to participate in protests on the ground is far beyond that which is needed to "like" something on Facebook, something that has become a central factor in the transformation of modern civic engagement and political participation (Vraga-Kjerstin, Thorson, Kligler-Vilenchik, & Ge, 2015; Zuniga, Jung, & Valenzuela, 2012). It is important to note that in online civic engagement, the average level of participation when it comes to religious issues is much higher than in other fields, mirroring the higher commitment of believers to take part in political activity when it is related to their belief system.

These trends present a striking illustration of the changes taking place in Palestinian civic engagement. Civic organizations are increasingly using digital instruments to empower Palestinian society and to influence Jewish society in Israel. This engagement illustrates the will of young Palestinians to influence public awareness and preferences outside their political parties. The leaders of these digital campaigns emphasize the importance of promoting civic activity that is not subject to the hierarchical authority of existing political parties, seeking to achieve two main goals. The first goal is to overcome the deep disagreements among Palestinian political leadership, which caused fragmentation of their civic initiatives and crippled much of their activity. The second goal is to make it difficult for the authorities to monitor events, which would allow the authorities to neutralize a large portion of this activity.[4]

The Roots of Palestinian CSOization in Israel

When discussing the intensive rise in the number of Palestinian CSOs over the last two decades, we must recognize the fact that this is a complex phenomenon, which cannot be explained by a single factor. There are many reasons for and causes of this process, both structural and behavioral. The reasons and causes behind Palestinian CSOization can be divided according to the following: While some of these factors are immediate and direct, others are related to long-term processes and indirect influence; some are internal and others are external; some factors are negative and others positive. To provide a comprehensive and satisfying explanation for the rapid increase in the number of Palestinian CSOs, it is worth combining all of the above into a single model. The following pages briefly detail these reasons and present a model, which provides the most comprehensive explanation for the emergence of Palestinian CSOs. Because it is difficult to delineate a clear hierarchy or priority between the different elements of the model, we present them according to the following classification.

Table 2. External and Internal Factors of CSOization

External Factors	
Positive	*Negative*
1. Globalization of human rights and liberal values.	1. Ineffective participation in the Knesset.
2. The rise of social movements around the world.	2. Lack of satisfactory social and financial services provided by the state.
3. Access to external financial resources.	3. A segregated market and a lack of financial opportunities relevant for educated Palestinian citizens.
4. The internet revolutions and the rising accessibility to a growing number of people.	
5. The expansion of Israel's CSO sector and its active presence in the public domain.	

Internal Factors	
Positive	*Negative*
1. The development of individual autonomy in the PCI.	1. Deterioration of the traditional forms of social solidarity and mutual support.
2. The growing numbers of academy-educated Palestinians and the improvement in their professional skills.	2. The weakening of Arab political parties and municipalities.
3. The development of sociopolitical awareness among the PCI and its demand for equal citizenship.	3. Ineffectiveness of social services provided by Arab municipalities.
4. Development of social ingenuity among young Arab leaders and the success of Arab CSOs.	4. Dissatisfaction with the social and cultural reality in the Arab villages, especially the increased violence and alcoholism, vis-à-vis the weakness of local and national leadership.

We now expand on the discussion of each factor:

Internal Negative Factors

1. Deterioration of the traditional forms of social solidarity and mutual support

Arab social structure has changed dramatically all over the Arab world in recent years, particularly in Israel (Barakat, 2005; Hopkins & Ibrahim, 2006;

Joseph, 1999). In particular, familial solidarity, which characterized Arab society and provided one of the main sources of support for the individual, has eroded. While the Arab family is still present in the life of average Palestinian citizens, the extended family cannot be seen today as a coherent sociological entity as it was before (Abu-Baker, 2007; Karkabi-Sabah, 2009), and especially not as a financially autonomous unit. The traditional extended Arab family has shrunk, and the nuclear family's power is constantly on the rise (Sharabi, 1988). The change in the familial structure is neither homogeneous nor universal, and it differs widely across Arab communities; while in the mixed cities and in the big towns this change has occurred speedily and is nearly universally, these change have been slower and more complex in the village communities. While familial social solidarity has been declining, individual and family mutual commitments have radically changed and become a kind of informal contract (Moghadam, 2004). This decline has resulted in an alternative social model that aims to accommodate this lack of solidarity and support. Local, regional, and national philanthropic CSOs play a major role in providing these kinds of social needs, particularly religious civic associations, such as the long-standing Islamic ones based on the Islamic pillar of zakat or Christian associations that have been part of the social scenery for a long time and provide basic social services, such as education and welfare, based on the Christian values of *grace* and *service*. These new service-providing CSOs have expanded to include alternative educational institutions, like the kindergarten network established in Arab villages and towns. Educational associations like Masar in Nazareth and Hiwar in Haifa were founded by parents who felt frustrated by the formal education system. They developed independent educational programs based on national and cultural priorities, unlike the programs delivered by the state. Many Islamic associations have also established schools as part of their attempt to create an alternative educational system to the one controlled by the state.[5] These schools promote Islamic values and customs and challenge secular tendencies that have become widespread in some parts of the PCI, especially in mixed towns and cities. The family model promoted by these two different types of schools have alternative values systems that reflect deep transformations taking place in society. Whereas the Islamic social model promotes communitarian values and conservative family structure, secular schools, although they do not give up on basic social values, instead promote individual autonomy, equality, dignity, mutual respect, and liberty. CSOs established in the PCI are deeply related to this ongoing debate, which demonstrates that social activists from both camps use CSOs' resources to promote their goals and impact broader society.

2. The decline of Arab political parties

The decline of political parties is a universal and complex process. This decline has been witnessed across most democratic political systems (Dahl, 2005). This process can be attributed largely to changes in political mediation that are required in a democracy, and the crisis of their legitimacy (Habermas, 1975). Political parties in Israel, both for Arabs and others groups, have gone through the same process (Jamal, 2011). Of note, Arab political parties were never considered legitimate partners in the coalition in Israel. They are thus excluded from the political process and from contributing to crucial decisions. With the exception of one stance in 1993, when Yitzhak Rabin formed a minority government, after the Shas party quit his coalition in preparation for the approval of the Oslo Accords by the Knesset, did Arab parties play a role in the decision-making process, which was condemned by nationalist parties and was framed as illegitimate (Neuberger, 2010). The first explanation for this special deal with the Arab parties is the state's exclusive and ethnic nature. We must remember that Arab parties were first established only in the late 1980s. Except for the Arab-Jewish Communist Party, which has been controlled by Arabs since the 1960s, the first Arab political party, the Arab Democratic Party (Mad'a), was established in Israel only in 1988. The United Arab List (Ra'am) and the National Democratic Assembly (Balad) first participated in the elections only in 1996. This late entry into the political arena contributed to Arab parties being marginal in the political system's power center and, as a result, only had minor influence over this system (Rouhana & Ghanem, 1998). Therefore, even for decisions that carry direct consequences for the PCI, Arab parties and politicians are not given the opportunity to impact decision-making processes.

Arab politicians are not part of the social networking that is controlled by the Jewish hegemonic elite. Because military service creates one of the major mechanisms of social and business networking in Israel's militaristic culture and regime, and because most Arabs are not recruited to the Israeli army, Palestinian citizens remain outside significant power centers, especially when these networks are transferred into other social or business fields or translated into a financial or political elite (Shefer, Barak, & Oren, 2008; Ben Eliezer, 1998). The number of officers in the political elite demonstrates the influence of connections made during military service when seeking to enter the political circle of decision makers, which creates most of Israeli policy (Shefer, Barak, & Oren, 2008; Levy, 2007). This accumulation of symbolic capital, created by the shift from one field to the other, effectively skips the PCI. Despite their power over their immediate surroundings, which is derived from their respective positions within them, Palestinians are still marginal within Israeli society's power distribution, especially regarding policies that affect their society.

Thus, while most Arab citizens still vote for Arab political parties, especially for the Joint List since it was established in the 2015 elections, Arab parties are not effective when it comes to influencing state policies. Therefore, many of the Palestinian educated elite have sought alternative avenues to either strengthen the impact of political parties or provide other avenues to the available formal participation in the political sphere. That is why many educated politicized activists have started in recent decades to seek alternative methods and mechanisms that would influence the state. While some leaders remain oblivious to traditional forms of politics, many have become disillusioned with the formal political system and with traditional forms of participation, such as voting. The disillusioned have thus begun to establish professional CSOs that deal with key issues concerning the PCI's welfare, society, culture, art, and sports. Many of these associations' activists or leaders are still connected to a specific political party or movement, as is the case with al-Aqsa Association, Women Against Violence, The Follow-up Committee on Arab Education, Mossawa, The Arab Culture Association, Injaz, Hirak, Al-Tufula, Mada Al-Carmel, Iqraa, Al-Qalam, and many others. The link between the CSOs and political parties has gone through a major transformation in recent years, yet no one can say that all of them are disconnected, as we shall see later in the focus groups' sessions.

3. Inefficient social services of the Arab municipalities

Arab municipalities are widely discriminated against in the distribution of the state's resources (Razin, 2000; Al-Haj & Rosenfeld, 1988). To make matters worse, most Arab municipalities are managed inefficiently because of internal political strife and the politics of family patronage (Ghanem & Azaiza, 2008). Many Arab municipalities were in a situation in which they could no longer provide decent social services for citizens residing under their jurisdictions, such as garbage collection, water circulation, sewage system, and so forth. Thus, many young activists have taken the initiative to establish local or regional associations, which take responsibility for many of the services in their towns and villages, such as education, sports, health, and welfare. Many CSOs took it upon themselves to assist underprivileged families, especially toward the beginning of the school year and before the important holidays. These initiatives were developed and even politicized, mainly by the Islamic Movement, which sees philanthropy as a main pillar of Islamic belief and culture. Therefore, many CSOs that provide basic social services, like education funding or financial support for underprivileged families, are linked to the Islamic Movement, which thus reinforces it as a source of power and influence in Arab society. The prominence of charities like Al-Saqka Al-Jariya (the overarching Islamic organization that coordinates the *zakat*) is a good example of the voluntary financial and organizational patterns that govern Arab society.[6] Dozens of initiatives like these exist in every Arab town or village, and they are mostly based on traditional-religious patterns of fundraising. Such data reflect intensive civic activity in the field of basic social services, which are provided independently of the local and national administration. A similar process occurs within Christian communities; however, associations of this kind were also active prior to the establishment of Israel. The network of Christian charities is very widespread, but because the services provided are either done discretely or are provided on a nonpartisan basis in the entire Arab society, such as schools and hospitals, they usually are not conceived as religious. Evidently, many of the most successful schools in the PCI and all prominent Arab hospitals are affiliated with Christian charities (Robson, 2011).

The financial crisis in Arab municipalities is deeply tied to the neoliberalization of the Israeli economy. This structural transformation has led to the privatization of many municipal services, which in turn has led to the transfer of many services to CSOs. This process of third-sector privatization, well known throughout the world, transformed preschool education, shelters, special education schools, daycare centers, sports, environmental services, and more with the help of CSOs funded by state resources. These CSOs aimed to provide services that the state viewed as indispensable, but also did not want to provide itself (Doron, 2003). This process thus led many associations to register as CSOs, though in fact they are merely service providers that are managed as small businesses, some of them by private owners.

This trend makes it difficult to distinguish between public voluntary associations and profitable or professional organizations that provide services. For example, hostels for the mentally disabled, the elderly, and people with special needs or various sports associations are registered as CSOs according to the 1980 CSO Law. These organizations are formally CSOs but lack the advocacy qualities of most voluntary CSOs, which emerged as an alternative to the local or national authorities and are in a constant bargaining relationship with them.

External Negative Factors

1. Inefficient political participation in the Knesset

As mentioned previously, Arab political parties are excluded from the major power centers in the Israeli government and are perceived as illegitimate coalition partners (Ghanem & Mustafa, 2009). Even in crisis situations, as in the case of Rabin's government in the early 1990s when Arabs' voices were crucial to maintaining the government, Arab political parties have never entered the coalition, but were asked to support the government from outside and prevent the opposition from shaping the government (Jamal, 2003). As opposition parties, Arab political parties cannot effectively lobby or raise support for the fundamental rights of the PCI. The suspicion against Arab parties has to do with the ideological gaps between themselves and the Zionist parties dominating the political system. This long-standing structural gap between participation in the Israeli political system, on the one hand, and the inability to influence its decisions, on the other, has led many Arab leaders, particularly those disenchanted by formal politics, to find new ways to influence Israeli society and state.

Many of these individuals view CSOs as an effective way to gain influence, one that does not require commitment to the rules of the political game dictated by the Knesset. Some of the major CSOs' sponsors and supporters provide important political and fact-finding support for Arab political parties. They empower the parties by transferring information and sharing the responsibility of pressuring the state to change its policies. Mossawa, Sikkuy, Women Against Violence, the Arab Center for Alternative Planning, the Galilee Society, I'lam, and others have conducted and still run projects that provide basic information for political parties to advocate for the equal rights of the PCI. Many Arab CSOs represent the situation of the PCI in other parts of the world. Thus, they increase the pressure on Israel to change its policies toward the Arab population from the outside. The best-known associations in this regard are Adalah, Mossawa, and the Arab Human Rights Association, which lead international advocacy programs and maintain close ties with central international organizations, including the United Nations, UNESCO, Human Rights Council, and the European Parliament.

The activity of these associations brought various international institutions, such as the OECD, the European Union, and the United Nations Human Rights Council, to investigate the status of the PCI and its discrimination by the state. This is a slow process, and CSOs have worked for many years to attract international attention to the affairs of Arab society in Israel. As a result, Israel was required to respond to the international institutions' resulting inquiries and explain its policies toward them. While the state's policy has not radically changed, the significance of this sector of civic activity is undeniable. This area of influence has not yet reached its climax, but keeps pace with the globalization of Arab civil activity and Arab society's increasing disillusionment with the state and Palestinians' desire to bypass its mechanisms in order to enforce change from outside. One of the recent examples of such CSO involvement is the leading role of Mossawa in organizing and facilitating the visit of the Joint List to the EU offices in Brussels in early September 2018 and in filing a complaint against the new Basic Law, Israel as the Nation-State of the Jewish People. PCI leadership asserts this law constitutionalizes racism and establishes an apartheid system in which Palestinians are rendered immigrants in their own homeland.[7] Strengthening ties between CSOs and the international community has become a central, strategic goal over the last few years. In the meetings of CSOs' leaders, they have expressed their determination to invest more human and financial resources in broadening their international networks.[8]

Furthermore, the basic information provided by these associations is often available for use by Arab politicians, who promote legal and political initiatives, such as new legislation. Today it is hard to imagine Arab political parties without the assistance of Arab CSOs. This is particularly true in the case of legal aid, because Arab politicians are politically persecuted by the state, and many face legal charges for their actions. Adalah was especially active in providing legal aid for key Arab leaders, as in the cases of former Knesset member Azmi Bishara and the former Knesset members Azmi Bishara and Mohammad Barakeh and current MK Heba Yazback. All were charged with misuse of their parliamentary immunity to promote illegal actions. They endured an intensive investigation, which required a professional defense and wide-scale legal assistance. Another example is the case of Al-Mezan, which represented Sheikh Raed Salah, the head of the Northern Branch of the Islamic Movement. The relationship between political parties and civil society reinforced CSOs' social and political positions in representing the interests of the PCI.

2. Insufficient social and financial services provided by the state

The State of Israel never perceived its Arab citizens as equal, and this perception has materialized in policies that translated the state's dominant, ethnic character into a social reality (Gharrah, 2016). This official policy not only discriminates against Arab citizens, but also excludes them from the possibility of receiving social and financial benefits given by the state in areas such as preschool education, social security, health services, youth education, public libraries, elderly care, tax discounts, and more (Hasson & Abu-Asba, 2004; Hasson & Karayanni, 2006). At the same time, the decline of traditional norms and solidarity mechanisms created new forms of social support by necessity. As a result of evolving state policy and social change, philanthropists and charities have become vital and thus integrated into the workings of Arab society.

3. A segregated labor market and lack of financial opportunities for educated Arabs

The Israeli labor market also maintains a pervasive policy of national segregation. Avoda Ivrit ("Hebrew Labor") was always one of the key ideals of the Zionist movement since its inception. Arab integration into the Israeli economy has thus been based historically on social disadvantage, because Arab workers were usually hired for jobs that were considered inferior (Lewin-Epstein & Semyonov, 1993). Arabs, who were mostly farmers during the 1950s and the 1960s, lost their land in a systematic process of land confiscation (Kidar & Yiftachel, 2006). This policy led to a proletarianization of Arab society and their complete dependency on the Jewish economy as a labor supplier (Lewin-Epstein & Semyonov, 1993). Arab towns did not have a strong employment infrastructure, and most Jewish employers preferred Jewish laborers; thus, income gaps, inequality, and marked differences in living standards between the two communities developed. The liberalization of the labor market during the 1980s and 1990s again highlighted the structural inferiority of the Arab labor force in Israel. The expanding job opportunities in science, academia, and service sectors, coupled with the decrease in the number of manual laborers, including the agricultural sector, further increased Israelis' discrimination and the growing divide between the skilled and professional workforce and the nonprofessional workforce dominated by Arab society. Most Arab academics work as teachers and principals in

Arab schools. Despite the increasing number of Palestinian academics in the medical services in hospitals and in public and private pharmacies, Palestinian citizens are still missing from profitable fields like technology, informatics, aviation, and media. A brief look at the Israeli labor market demonstrates that it is ethnically stratified and characterized by structural inequality on a nationwide scale. This reality pushes PCI academics to search for job opportunities that guarantee them good income, respect, and equality. The marginality or complete absence of skilled Arab workers in most government offices and companies like the Israeli Electric Corporation, Mekorot, Bezeq, Solel Boneh, Amidar, and so forth and their low presence in high-tech companies have created widespread frustration among the educated Arab elite. Among the 59,938 employees in the civil service on January 2000, only 2,835 (5%) were Arabs, most of them employed by the Ministries of Education or Health (Abu-Baker & Patir, 2000). These numbers have not significantly changed since then. The data of the parliamentary committee that investigated the integration of Arabs in public services in 2008 and the latest reports by Sikkuy prove that there is no real change in the policy of employing Arabs in the civil service and in the state's institutions.[9] The number of Arab employees reached 4,245 of a total of 60,882 (6.97%) in 2009 (*Sikkuy Report*, 2010). This percentage is much lower than the target percentage set by the government for 2012.

The employment situation in Arab society has also caused many educated Arabs to look for independent job opportunities in trading or as freelance workers. Many Arab parents who are able to fund their children's education encourage them to study medicine, law, civil engineering, or other freelance professions. These professions are considered prestigious and independent, and they carry high income potential. Many PCI academics, especially those who did not want to work as freelancers and were highly politically conscious, saw CSOs as a way to combine at least three desired professional qualities: respect, independence, and the capacity to contribute to Arab society. It should be noted here that many of the educated elite joined the CSO sector as volunteers. An analysis of the educational data of 159 board members in 20 CSOs demonstrates the high education level of Arab associations' board members. According to these data, 2% are professors, 12% hold a doctoral degree, 19% hold a master's degree, 49% hold a bachelor's degree, and 10% have other postsecondary education diplomas. Among them, 60% studied in Israeli academic institutions, while 12% studied in Europe or in the United States. They all saw the civil sector as a channel for protest and struggle, as well as challenging the state's politics.

They also considered their activity as a form of civic engagement that is not subordinated to the formal Israeli political game and can still influence the situation of Arab citizens and empower them against discriminating and biased state offices.

Positive Internal Factors

I. Rise of individual autonomy in Arab society

As mentioned earlier, the PCI has undergone tremendous structural changes. The extended family structure is in constant decline and has been replaced by the nuclear family (Abu-Baker, 2003; Sharabi, 1988). Though this process is not homogeneous, it is well-known and anticipated throughout Arab society, and this carries widespread structural implications, especially in the PCI, which is characterized by a relatively level of high mobility (Rikaz, 2018). This mobility is created by the environmental circumstances of the PCI, especially because it is dependent on the Israeli labor market and has almost no internal self-generating capital. While land ownership was their main source of income in the past, a source that united the family and preserved a strong patrimonial structure, the confiscation of Arab lands by the state absent local industrial infrastructures created a complete dependency of Arab citizens on Jewish sources of income (Gharrah, 2016). As a result, the family patriarchal authority declined steadily, and individual autonomy has increased. The financial independence of family members encouraged individualization on many levels, including the independent decision making of young men and women regarding their future and life course. This process is very important when it comes to economic independence of a growing number of women, who entered the labor market and are now earning their own income. The increasing number of educated women is creating deep social changes whose consequences are still not yet clear in the PCI (Rikaz, 2018). This individualization process is reflected in other areas of life, including the younger generations' expansion into new and different residences, especially into large, mixed cities like Haifa, Jerusalem, Jaffa, Acre, and so forth.

While the individualization process is not universal or widespread, it has resulted in the emergence of a large social class of highly educated Arabs who seek patterns of life that free them from their families' desires and direct supervision. Greater individual autonomy has enabled Arab individualists to search for their future beyond the scope of their traditions, norms, and the family realm. Higher education, which is referred to separately, has played an important role in augmenting Arabs' human capital in the form of education, as well as in expanding the autonomous horizons for a growing number of Arab youth. The university experience of young men and women further increased their desire to develop a new lifestyle apart from society's common patterns of traditional, familial social structures. One of the possible paths for such mobilization that has emerged is the joining of CSOs, which are usually based on volunteerism and individual decision making. CSOs persist beyond the family's boundaries without being a part of the state and promote a wide space of personal freedom (Hegel, 1952; Keane, 1998; Rosenblum & Post, 2002). These organizations enable young people to escape from the family's limit on activity without falling into the commercial world, which is controlled by competition, supply, and demand; or into the state's sphere, which is controlled by political and ideological discipline that educated Arabs usually refuse to accept. A considerable number of educated Arabs who find their place in various positions in CSOs or join their boards find in this activity a path to self-realization, as noted in our personal interviews with activists in chapter 9.

2. The increase in university-educated Arabs and the improvement in professional skills

The development of individual autonomy encouraged constant growth in the numbers of university-educated Arabs and the members of the educated Arab elite in Israel. While the growth rate of university-educated Arabs is still low compared to the Jewish population in Israel, this increase is steady. According to the data provided by the Central Bureau of Statistics and analyzed by Gharrah (2018), the number of Palestinian students in Israeli universities was 22,881 in 2015 and 17,804 in colleges and other institutions of higher education. Of the 22,881 students, 15,521 were females and 7,360 were males. And of the 17,804 students in colleges, 12,378 were females and 5,426 were males. In 2013, the numbers were 19,700 and 15,053, respectively. Of the university students in 2013, 12,984 were females and 6,716 males, and of the students in colleges, 10,626 were females and 4,427 males. These numbers mirror the rapid transformations and stratification taking place in the PCI, especially the increasing number of educated females who seek to find their way in the job market, including in civil society. Among the major advocacy and social change CSOs in the PCI, we find a high proportion of females in leading positions, such as in I'lam, Women Against Violence, Kayan, Arab Cultural Association, Baladna, Al-Qaws, Aswat, and others.

This development is translated into major changes in the labor market, and civil society is one of the domains that benefited greatly from this development. Though CSOs cannot feasibly employ a large number of scholars, many academy-educated Arabs found their place in them and together comprise a large number of people who might otherwise have encountered difficulties in finding jobs if this autonomous sector were not available.

3. The development of a sociopolitical awareness among Arabs and their demand for equal citizenship

The growing number of university-educated Arabs and the expansion of the cultural elite resulted in an increase in the general Arab population's awareness of its rights and how to struggle for achieving better treatment from the state. Much of this can be attributed to the new educated elite's significant gains in cultural and social capital. This group helps to raise the Arab populations' awareness of their limited possibilities compared to their Jewish-Israeli counterparts or the educated elite members in the Arab world who are able to access more paths for mobilization and advancement. Despite their education and social status, many graduates face restrictions in their integration into the job market. For many, CSOs became a default solution. Regardless of the motivations for individuals' recruitment, it seems that the structural opportunities available for the average educated Arab, and the fact that their national obligations cannot be translated into patriotic feelings toward the state, led this group to seek a civil pathway, where they can combine a personal career with national responsibility toward their community.

One of the most obvious expressions of this fact is the number of CSOs that promote the interests of and higher living standards for the PCI. Three examples are the Galilee Society, which promotes health issues and environmental safety and raises awareness for environmental hazards; Al Sadaqah Al Jariya, which provides financial aid for the underprivileged; and I'lam, which promotes the media rights of the PCI and promotes projects of strategic thinking, producing strategic documents and policy papers for the entire PCI.

4. THE DEVELOPMENT OF SOCIAL INGENUITY AMONG YOUNG ARAB LEADERS AND THE SUCCESS OF ARAB CSOs

The success of some CSOs reflects a broader social process that is inclusive of an increase in initiatives that promote new models for political and social thinking and behavior. While these initiatives were not implemented in the business world, they adopted many thinking and behavior patterns that are common in it. The founders of these initiatives had to be completely aware of the Israeli political realm of opportunities within the global CSO sector, as well as have their ability to compete for scarce resources granted by foreign donors. The global and local CSOization process was an easy and useful role model. The initial success of certain social initiatives, especially associations that gained a central position in the Arab public sphere because of their ability to promote and highlight their associations both socially and politically, caused many other Arab activists to follow in their footsteps. Successful CSOs like the Galilee Society, Adalah, and Al-Aqsa Association, as well as their leaders, became local, regional, and worldwide role models. Many new CSOs were founded by people previously employed in this sector and decided to establish new organizations, or by initiatives led by well-established CSOs, which wanted to cultivate a specific activity or encourage the adoption of new civil activities. In many cases, the new CSOs' founders knew what they must do to promote their projects and make them successful. Here, the existing networking level within the various associations was constructive and nourished the emergence of new CSOs. In many cases, the boards of successful CSOs decided to expand their range of activity by establishing a new association that would handle a certain aspect in particular. That was how Adalah was established, by encouragement from the Galilee Society, and I'lam was established, by activists in Mossawa.[10]

Positive External Factors

1. GLOBALIZATION AND THE RISE OF SOCIAL MOVEMENTS AROUND THE WORLD

One of the major factors for the rise in the Arab CSO sector was a similar rise in other parts of the world (Colas, 2002). The successful pressure of CSOs on the authoritarian regimes in Eastern Europe during the 1970s and the 1980s inspired many politicians, civil activists, and scholars and made them believe in a civil society that empowers society (Touraine, 1983; Diamond, 1994; Feldman, 1997). As Tsutsui (2004) wrote: "Linkage to global civil society gives rise to ethnic mobilization because it diffuses models of claim-making based on human rights ideas" (Tsutsui 2004).

Since civil society was perceived as promoting democratization processes, CSOs were established in many countries throughout the world. Among the main groups that saw CSOs as a viable path for promoting their interests were national minorities and indigenous peoples (Fischer, 2009). CSOs were perceived as empowerment and development agents, and therefore were viewed positively by underprivileged groups that sought to establish CSOs to assist in promoting their interests (Tsosie, 2003). This belief in the power of CSOs to create political democratization, empowerment, and development inspired PCI leaders. The rise of CSOs in the occupied Palestinian territories (OPTs) further increased this process. Social or political activists, reluctant to join political parties or the state's agents, started establishing their own CSOs. This process was intensified during the 1990s and 2000s, when the Arab civil leadership class succeeded in penetrating the financial support networks and international organizations like the European Union, the UN, and international legal organizations.

2. The expansion of Israel's CSO sector and its active presence in the public domain

The international trend of an active and dynamic civil society was evident in Jewish Israeli society, when thousands of organizations were established following the enactment of the CSO Law in 1980. CSOs in Israel were established mainly by Jewish activists and handled issues of the Jewish population in the country. Therefore, they were considered to be nationalistic (Ben-eliezer, 1999; Yishai, 1997). Despite attempts to integrate Arabs into some Israeli CSOs, and despite the existence of many Jewish-Arab associations that were established to advance the relationships between these two communities or provide services that were needed in both, Arab social entrepreneurs refused to remain in the margins of Israeli civil society after being excluded from Israeli society, politics, and economy. Arab social entrepreneurs adopted the model of Israeli CSOs for themselves and started establishing separate Arab associations of the same type. The establishment of Adalah is the perfect example of such a process: An Arab lawyer who was employed by the Association of Human Rights in Israel (ACRI) decided to establish a separate Arab legal association that would be dedicated to Arab society and its rights, not merely as individuals but also as a collective.

3. ACCESS TO EXTERNAL FINANCIAL RESOURCES

Another crucial factor that explains the rapid increase in the number of Arab CSOs in Israel is its access to foreign funds. It is hard to assess how much money is transferred into the Arab civil sector in Israel (Haklai, 2008), yet it definitely includes a few million dollars, which are split between a few dozen CSOs. The first and principle funding source is Western countries—Europe, the United States, and Canada. The second source is Arab countries. Most of the funds from Western sources are dedicated to secular CSOs, while most of the money from Arab sources is given to religious CSOs, which belong to the Islamic Movement. Based on the data provided in June 2018 by the state Registrar in the Justice Ministry, only a small number of Arab CSOs, 25.2%, receive small state funds. According to the same data, only 1.7% of the Palestinian CSOs have shared projects with state institutions.

Among the 829 active Palestinian CSOs, only 35 (3.7%) receive funds from foreign entities. This is a relatively very small number, but it reflects the heavy dependency of the large CSOs, such as Adalah, Mossawa, I'lam, Women Against Violence, Human Rights Association, the Galilee Society, and so forth, on foreign donations. Such data show that the PCI civil society is relatively poor. Parts of it function with low funding received from the community, such as the Islamic CSOs or services provided by the CSOs. Furthermore, these data raise the fear, which is evident in the literature, that associations' ideas are derived from the donors' agendas (Hulme & Edwards, 1997). The suspicious response by American donors to the publication of the aforementioned Future Vision Documents is a good example of the inherent relationship between the donors' agenda and the policy adopted by CSOs (Jamal, 2008). The attitudes of various funders, like the New Israel Fund and Ford Foundation, toward Mada Al-Carmel in Haifa—the association that published the Haifa Declaration—illustrate the dilemma of funds versus political and ideological positions. Mada Al-Carmel is considered the avant-garde of Arab CSOs, that openly object Israel's Jewish identity. This fact was the indirect cause for the reduction of the support by funds that are influenced by state policy after the state exercised indirect pressure to block the association's funding sources. The same policy line was adopted toward I'lam two years later. The organizations that do not submit to the "two state for two peoples" formula for the resolution of the Israeli-Palestinian conflict were pushed out of the support policies by Jewish foundations. The European Union, for instance, does not support organizations that support the BDS against Israel.

The attitude toward the Islamic Movements' associations is another example of the relationship between funding and ideology. This relationship has been tightening in recent years, with supporting organizations openly declaring that they refused to support activities that did not fall within the limits of the political status quo.

Furthermore, foreign support organizations prefer to endorse activities that address public policy and social change, thus demanding an interaction between the CSOs and the state's institutions. This type of support reiterates the backing the funders extend to the Israeli state as Jewish and democratic within the green line borders. Most funders oppose the BDS and the boycott of the Israeli elections by Arab citizens and therefore tend to favor organizations that submit to the spaces of political maneuvering legitimated by the state. Moreover, there is an obvious bias toward what is called by support funds "shared society." This is a euphemism for Jewish-Arab coexistence, which takes Jewish hegemony in Israel for granted and views Palestinian citizens as individuals that belong to a minority that has no collective standing. Thus, this bias frames the CSOs' activity within the formal definition of Israeli citizenship, thereby establishing a substantial differentiation between the PCI and Palestinians in the West Bank and Gaza Strip and discourages the former from establishing common associational networks with the latter.

Notwithstanding these policies, CSOs in the PCI have learned how to deal with these limitations. Despite the withdrawal of two large American foundations, namely the Ford Foundation and the Open Society Foundation, Palestinian CSOs in Israel managed to survive. Although they function in poor conditions and under severe financial strain, they still manage to raise funds and keep providing services they see necessary for their community.

4. The digital revolution and the use of electronic tools

The growth of digital media has also led to a significant change in patterns of media activity among the PCI and thus civil society. There is a marked decrease in the consumption of print media in favor of new media types such as satellite TV stations from the Arab world. Despite this increase in consumption, it is important to note that the PCI has no effect on this content (Jamal, 2009). Therefore, the internet and local sites have become a major source of basic information on developments in the political, social, and cultural spheres in their environment.

The penetration of the internet in the PCI was a strong resource for business and political media entrepreneurs, who quickly jumped on the bandwagon. A notable example is Panet, which managed to replicate the newspaper *Panorama* into a variety of successful internet services, attracting young people and adults through the combination of entertainment and news content. Other entrepreneurs, especially entrepreneurs in print media, followed its lead. Political parties and political leaders use the internet to promote their goals. Internet penetration has closed the gap between the PCI and the external world, making information that was not available on TV more accessible and thus the strength of Arab political leaders more viable. Thus the ability to actively respond and feed contents by average citizens and young entrepreneurs reinforced the movement from traditional media to digital media, resulting in the growth of new social agents.

The internet has not yet replaced TV. However, new consumer divisions are forming between news and information from the internet and watching news analysis and viewing series and movies on TV. There is a rapid transition of young people from the network, especially from news and entertainment sites to social networks that are used as platforms for social and cultural interaction. Although it is not expected that the traditional communication outlets, especially TV and radio, will disappear completely, they continue to adapt to new consumption patterns in order to survive.

The digital revolution also created intergenerational gaps (Ragnedda & Muschert, 2013). According to the data available from the 2016–2017 survey, the young PCI generation has managed to make the internet a central tool in everyday life, something that carries both positive and negative consequences. The older generation is still finding its way in the ever changing media scene, which is now beyond recognition and cannot always catch up. New media have enabled the younger generation to adopt global and cultural patterns that challenge the local social and cultural values of their parents. They live their lives in the depths of the internet and communicate more often with friends online than in person. Social networking exposes them to new worlds that were previously inaccessible. Whereas TV made places closer to their parents and reduced the geophysical world, the internet has made the social world even smaller and bridges cultural and linguistic gaps between youth from around the world.

Teenagers from remote villages in the Galilee, the Triangle, and the Negev have become a part of the global world and have replaced direct human contact with friends from their area in their online relationships with people from places they had never known. While the digital revolution localized the remote, it is important to note that it also distanced those who are close, in the social and cultural sense. Foreign patterns of thought and foreign values systems intensely permeated their life and changed their social world. Not only do many dress and behave according to patterns and values not originating in Arab culture, but many also believe in forms of life that still are not legitimated by many of the older generation in society. One of the very prominent, albeit regarding the disputation over it, is homosexuality, which is viewed by many in the young generation as a normal phenomenon, including when they do not support it or justify it.

The most interesting examples of such civic activism is the rise of several LGBTQI CSOs, such as Al-Qaws for Sexual & Gender Diversity in Palestinian Society[11] and Aswat, Palestinian Gay Women,[12] which seek to transform Palestinian society and raise awareness regarding the importance of diversity and recognition in sexual as well as other aspects of life. This type of organization, albeit not the main one, provides a clear indication of the spaces and arenas of civic activity in Palestinian society in Israel. It is important to note that these organizations not only focus on sexual aspects of life, but also assert their commitment to Palestinian national identity and contribute to the Palestinian struggle for liberation in the 1967 occupied territories and for full civic equity inside Israel. Al-Qaws states clearly that it is "a civil society organization founded in grassroots activism" and locates itself "at the forefront of vibrant Palestinian cultural and social change." Aswat states that it was established as "a home for Palestinian LBTQI women to allow safe, supportive and empowering spaces to express and address our personal, social and political struggles as a national indigenous minority living inside Israel." These statements make clear that LGBTQI organizations are among the most active organizations to promote oppositional consciousness inside Palestinian society as well as vis-à-vis the Israeli state. A major part of the activities of these organizations is conducted through online campaigns that put into creative use the available digital technology in order to penetrate all segments of society. Online campaigns such as "Difference never Justifies Violence—stand up against violence toward LGBTQs!" represent the major efforts made to influence Palestinian society and transform public consciousness toward the LGBTQI community.[13]

The development of new information and communication technologies have a great impact on society (Tufekci & Wilson, 2012; Mesch, 2006). Internet use affects social habits and relationships within the family (Al-Omoush, Yaseen, & Alma'aitah, 2012). This is especially true in traditional societies. The availability of the internet strengthens the processes of individualization and changes the nature of social involvement (Tufekci & Wilson, 2012). Compared to the television, which the whole family would watch together in the living room, in the era of the digital revolution, every family member is busy with her or his own screen outside the circle of immediate attachment. This development is weakening the basic glue that still keeps the Arab family together, namely particular altruism in the family. Parents and children suddenly live in different worlds, and parents do not always know why their children lock themselves in their rooms.

Of course, digitalization has positive aspects, such as its use in academia, school, and maintaining family memory. One cannot argue that the youth are detached from what is happening in their social, cultural, and political environments (Asseburg & Wimmen, 2016). The degree of the younger generation's involvement and their interest in social protests, such as what is happening in the Arab world, especially during the Arab Spring, demonstrate their involvement in what develops around them (Hofmann & Jamal, 2012). Broad social protest against government policies, such as the Prawer Plan, or the organization of national memorial day marches through social networking, is only illustrative of the benefits of digital activism among young people. This involvement, as reflected in the data from the 2016–2017 survey, refutes arguments that the youth have no interest in political and social issues. The same data, though, is surprising when it comes to the involvement of adults in online political participation.

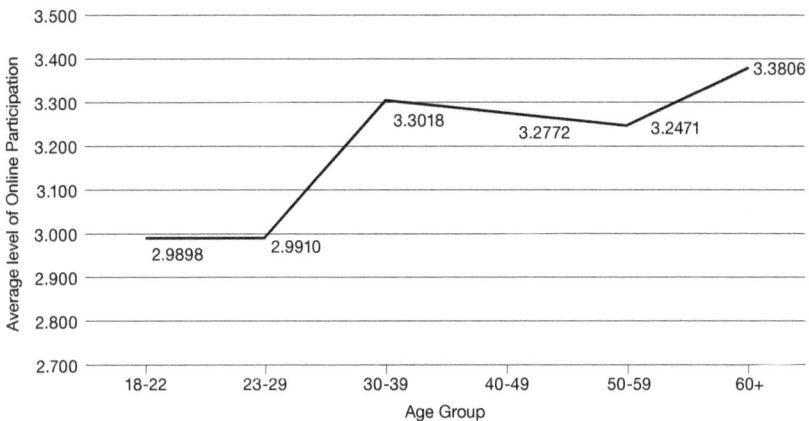

Graph 7.

The data in graph 7 show that when it comes to online political participation, we find a positive correlation between online participation and age. Despite the fact that this is a weak correlation, $p<0.05$; $r(314)$ = 0.12, older people still do not necessarily participate less online. The data are based on a sample of 350 respondents whose answers to eight questions were aggregated into a new indicator, whose internal coherence is 0.91, average = 3.16, and SD = 1.34. This indicator can help in reflecting on the broad pattern of online political participation among youth and adults in the PCI. We found that this indicator of online political participation correlates negatively with the indicator of civil satisfaction. This indicator was also developed based on 4 questions that explored the extent to which the interviewees feel at home in Israel, the extent to which they consider the political regime to be democratic, the extent to which human rights are respected by the government, and the extent to which they feel to be treated fairly by the state. The interviewees were asked to place their answer on a scale of 1 to 7 (M = 3.52; SD = 1.41). The results show clearly that the more satisfied the interviewees were, the less they participated in online political protests.

When we compare the online participation with the offline participation in political protest, we find that there is a negative correlation between participation and age. Young people tend to participate more on average than adults in offline political protest.

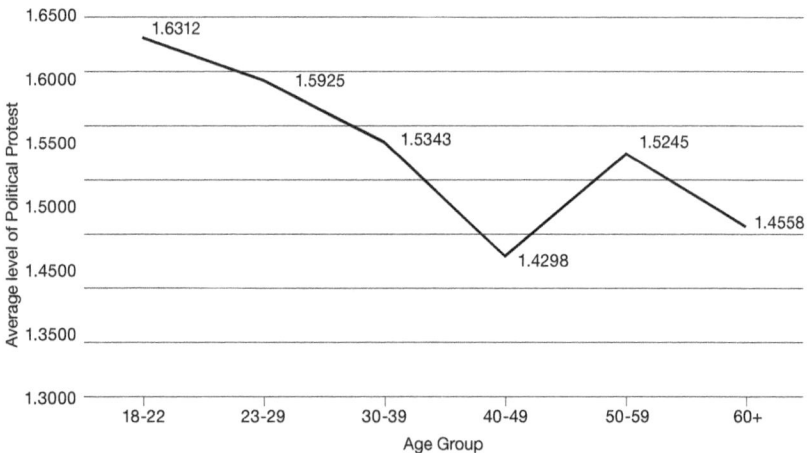

Graph 8.

As we can see from graph 8, the younger people are, the more likely they are to take part in offline political protest. This indicator was developed based on eight questions with internal coherence of 0.79 (M = 1.52; SD = 0.47). Also, here we found a negative correlation between civil satisfaction and participation in offline political protest $p < 0.01$; $r(533) = -0.19$.

It seems that age play a role in the levels and type of civil engagement and political participation. The differences between online and offline activism are surprising with regard to the first and not with regard to the second. From the data, one can learn that the older generation managed to close the gap with the younger generation when it comes to their accessibility and use of ICT. People older than 50 were in their 30s when the internet became a widespread phenomenon. Therefore, they show strong literacy in the digital world. However, when it comes to offline political protest, the youth are a more vibrant group, and they show more activism and participation than their parents' generation.

These data make the argument that the new media revolution has created a digital divide and an epistemological gap between generations into a more complex one. Whereas the older generation has managed to ride the train of technology, the perception of parental authority has been changing at lightning speed. Parents have no more effective tools to "monitor" what their children are doing, as they do not always know how to address these new challenges and cannot fully live up to their children's value system (Shen & Shakir, 2009). This situation creates a deep crisis of confidence and greatly reduces the authority of parents, but allows for greater individual autonomy, which is a basic factor for creativity. These changing patterns of authority that have been enhanced during the internet age allow youth to express themselves independently from their parents, even in defiance of them.

The digital revolution led to the rise of virtual communities that have not yet replaced the traditional community structure, but effectively reduces its presence and increases the motivations of young people to invest in the virtual world at the expense of traditional family ties, even at the level of attention and everyday interactions (Al-Omoush, Yaseen, & Alma'aitah, 2012). On a practical level, it strengthened online intimacy, particularly the willingness to be exposed to a large group of people who are not familiar due to physical or spiritual intimacy that characterized both traditional and modern societies.

The penetration of the internet and the development of digital social networks have changed and are fundamentally changing relationships in society, from the development of intergenerational gaps to the ongoing collapse of media consumption patterns and traditional media interactions. There is no doubt that the consumption of traditional media dropped dramatically in the last decade. The data from the surveys on media consumption show that there is a positive correlation between age and the intensity of watching television channels (**0.26). A similar correlation was found between age and trust in the content ones watches on television channels (**0.19).

Although online communication is characterized by short sentences and slogans that allow for a rapid evolution of a large virtual community, but make it difficult for the growth of in-depth discussions of complex issues that require a level of attention that is inconsistent with the acceleration of digital means, still the new communicative turn encourages social mobilization of a growing number of people. The ideological significance of this process depends on the worldview of the beholder, but we can say for sure that the digital revolution is empowering the individual and giving him or her the freedom of choice and opportunities that were never available in the same way in traditional societies before. The impact of this change on patterns of association is apparent, especially when examining social protests and campaigning.

Chapter 8

Public Trust and Social Capital
in Palestinian Civic Activism in Israel

This chapter explores the elitist-subaltern divide in Palestinian civic activism and the way it contributes to our understanding of the theoretical debate on the role of civil society in empowering and mobilizing subaltern groups. Thereby, the chapter contributes to our understanding of the nature of the relationship between the growth of CSOs and the rise of new social capital, as reflected in the level of public trust and strong solidarity vis-à-vis CSOs. This relationship is examined in the context of Arab public opinion and the expectations and level of trust in civic activism and its ability to face state discriminatory policies and resist its power structure. It is assumed that the general public's expectations are important in reflecting the subaltern nature of institutionalized civic activism in the eyes of the average citizen. Therefore, examining public expectations contributes to the understanding of the extent to which subaltern groups conceive the ability of CSOs to strengthen internal solidarity in society and deepen the level of trust between the different elements in it, especially between civil elites and the general public (Sosin, 2011).

Public expectations are also important in reflecting the common perceptions of civic activism and public attitudes toward the emerging civic elite in the PCI. These expectations, which begin at the level of awareness of organizations' activities, include satisfaction from the activity and trust in the organizations' intentions and capabilities and the strategies they develop, and they extend toward perceptions of their effectiveness in achieving public goals and the quality of the relationship between civil organizations. Examining these issues through public opinion may help us better understand the place of civil society, as a society with increasing levels of social capital, and the extent to which public expectations are translated into policies of the CSOs, especially the level of cooperation between them and their ability to work together to achieve common future goals.

A basic assumption in this framework is that social capital is not definite and fixed. As we have discussed earlier, social capital, as reflected in the literature in the field of political sociology and normative theory, is a complex and dynamic phenomenon that has different expressions in different contexts. Nevertheless, one can begin to pursue a practical understanding of this complex term and reveal its main characteristics through an exploration of its manifestations in society itself. Therefore, the deconstruction of social capital into its component parts and the examination of public attitudes toward these parts can become a kind of mirror image of its awareness of its social capital and individuals' willingness to contribute to it.

Public perceptions of the activities, characteristics, and effectiveness of CSOs are a partial indication of a society's social capital. Indeed, the willingness to volunteer in order to further the general public's interests and the willingness to work cooperatively to achieve these goals is another way to measure social capital. The public's level of trust in civil society and its ability to bring about change and achieve social objectives is likewise important to examining social capital.

The purpose of operationalizing the concept of social capital follows James Farr's outline of the phenomenon. Farr argues:

> In a way both compact and capacious, the concept of social capital boils down to net-works, norms, and trust. Upon inspection, networks prove dense and valuable, norms pervade individual actions and social relations, and trust appears psychologically complex . . . social capital is complexly conceptualized as the network of associations, activities, or relations that bind people together as a community via certain norms and psychological capacities, notably trust, which are essential for civil society and productive of future collective action or goods, in the manner of other forms of capital. (Farr, 2004)

Such a perspective on social capital emphasizes the importance of such capital to the existence of civil society and for collective action. When examining social capital, there are thus several options. One of these is the self-perception of society and the perceived importance of social networks and civic organizations that bear the burden of collective action, driving society to act and advocate for its needs and interests when necessary.

Analyzing the attitudes and expectations of the PCI improves our understanding of the challenges CSOs face in their own society. The level of trust of their patterns of action reflects the measure of their penetration into public consciousness and their ability not only to lead to perceptual or behavioral change in society, but also the latter's responsiveness to these efforts.

Furthermore, analyzing public opinion could help us to understand the ethical perceptions of society's value system, its dominant conception of citizenship, and the consequences of these perceptions on the patterns of civil society's collective action.

This approach to examining the elitist-subaltern relations, social capital, and public trust does carry some risks and caveats. For example, examining public attitudes toward civic activism in isolation from its organizational environment might create a distorted and misleading picture of its activities, efficacy, and relationship to the rest of society.

Therefore, it is important to note that the following analysis is based on two different but interrelated public opinion surveys conducted in two different time periods. Whereas the first was conducted in 2006–2007 and encompassed 807 interviewees, the second was conducted in 2016–2017 and included 586 interviewees. Each of the interviewees in both surveys was interviewed for 90 minutes each. The public opinion studies are meant to reflect general attitudes and illustrate the public's motives and the origins of its reasoning. It does not mean that what the public says regarding the activities of CSOs or parties is necessarily correct. Notwithstanding, we are talking about widespread attitudes and perceptions that cannot be ignored and that ought to be positively considered by CSOs when planning their actions. The importance of such an approach is deeply related to CSOs' leaders, who show high level of interest in meeting the expectations of the general public, as manifested in the personal interviews with them

Voluntarism as Civic Engagement and Social Capital

This section explores voluntarism in the PCI from a theoretical and a practical perspective. This is done through reflecting on the respondents' conceptions of voluntarism and subsequently their level of commitment toward voluntarism, as well as their understanding of who should assume the burden of volunteering, according to the respondents.

The active citizenship outlook, which in this context means a profound attachment to the immediate affiliated group rather than the state, is based on the assumption that individuals' well-doing depends on their efforts; therefore, activism and contribution to the social surroundings can improve living conditions and promote society as a whole. Volunteering within society, especially social organizations or institutions in general, can influence the course of social development (Carpenter & Myers, 2010; Musick, 1997). Moreover, volunteering in this state of mind can induce self-fulfillment and strengthen feelings of affiliation and commitment to society (Martiz & McMullin, 2004). In other words, those who believe in their ability to affect their destiny are those who are willing to volunteer and act within CSOs for the benefit of the public (ibid).

Based on this understanding, the relationship between the public's willingness to volunteer and the practices of CSOs is examined and reflected upon based on the data provided in the two surveys. One of the main subjects explored is the level of volunteering in society and the ability to establish an active civil society that can gain public trust and cooperation. In this regard, voluntarism patterns within the PCI and the implications of these patterns on the characteristics of the civil society are also explored.

It is important to note that the data on volunteering are partially affected by the fact that the volunteering activity, which the sample participants were asked about, referred to activity within CSOs or other establishments with no family ties to the volunteer. The significance lies in the fact that this kind of volunteering is not part of customary behavior patterns within the traditional Arab family unit as part of the family cultural obligation. Activities of this sort, such as assisting in family weddings or with household chores, were not regarded as volunteer activity according to the research question. Another reason for our choice to focus on voluntarism as an activity outside the family unit is to reflect the measure of public trust in CSOs and public institutions, and the average Palestinian citizen's measure of willingness to work for the general population's causes with no direct personal or familial connection and no financial gain for his or her activity. This definition of voluntarism relates to the definition of civil engagement as presented in the theoretical background (Berger, 2009). The definition is based on a general benefit that drives individuals' engagement and desire to affect any area that is not limited to personal interest only, even if the personal interest affects the decision to participate in this behavior.

The examination of volunteerism is divided into two levels: ethical and practical. To assess society's ideological perspectives, respondents were asked how they perceive the value and importance of voluntarism. In the survey of 2006–2007, 45% of the respondents said that voluntary activity for social objectives is highly important, 37.9% said it is important, 15.3% regarded volunteering as being of low importance, and 1.7% said it has no importance at all. Hence, the vast majority of respondents (83%) support voluntary activity to some extent, whereas fewer than 2% do not support it at all. In the 2016 survey, 51.9% of the respondents said volunteering is very highly important, 27.4% said that it is highly important, 12.9% said that it is somewhat important, and 6.9% argued that volunteering is not important. The data from both surveys are impressive, because a total majority (more than 80%) indicate that volunteering is an important value. Yet these data are not surprising because the question is of a theoretical nature, which allows the respondents to demonstrate their high morals without having to translate this declaration into the behavioral level.

To examine the level of congruence between the respondents' theoretical perceptions and their actual voluntary activity, the two surveys asked the participants if they volunteer or have volunteered in an association or in any other communal activity.

The responses received in the surveys varied. In the 2006–2007 survey, only 5.4% of the respondents admitted that they have actually volunteered in an association or in another public activity, while 94.6% do not. In the 2016 survey, the percentage who stated they have volunteered went up to 35.7%. The number of hours volunteered is not equal among all respondents. Nonetheless, the percentage remains much higher than in the previous survey, something that requires us to look for a reasonable explanation. When analyzing the data of those volunteering in order to understand the nature of the positive change, we found that there is a clear relationship between volunteering and gender, education, and age. It is clear that more women volunteer than men (53.4% and 46.6%, respectively). It is also clear that there is a positive correlation between education and volunteering up to a certain level. From the 2016 survey data, one sees clearly that going up the ladder of education from elementary education up to a first degree of higher education increases the percentage of volunteering from 3.9% to 17.2%. However, people who have a second university degree and above show less commitment to volunteering (5.4%). A similar positive correlation has been found when it comes to age. The younger generation is more willing to volunteer than the generation of their parents. Despite the fact that there was no attempt to establish a causal relationship between these variables, they are certainly interconnected.

As we have shown in earlier chapters, Palestinian society is becoming a more educated one. The percentage of women at higher education institutions is on the rise and their percentage has exceeded those of males.[1] This means that the younger generation is more educated than their parents and that women, who are becoming increasingly more educated, are more willing to volunteer. This broader social trend can provide some explanation as to the rise in the percentage of people involved in volunteering compared to a decade ago.

There are a few possible factors that can be linked to respondents' broader theoretical responses concerning volunteering. The data show a significant relationship between the levels of political interest and religiosity and the level of volunteering. When the levels of political interest rise, the levels of volunteering rise as well; the data show a significant relationship between these factors. Moreover, high levels of religiosity are also connected to high levels of volunteering, and there is a significant relationship between the two. Hence, greater political awareness or religiosity causes many people to shift their perceptions of volunteering from theory to practice.

In this context, political interest means an active citizenship outlook, based on a strong social commitment and the deep belief that social activity can bring change. In the 2016 survey, 55% of the respondents expressed interest in politics, 25.8% stated that they support a political party but were not active in it, and 7% stated that they are active in a specific political party. The data show clearly that those interested in politics tend to translate their positive ethical commitment to volunteerism into practice. The same argument could be made concerning religiosity. The more religious people are, the more they translate their positive ethical perception of volunteerism into practice. It seems that there is a clear positive correlation between the rising number of people who define themselves as religious and the rising number of people volunteering. Despite the fact that from a civic point of view volunteering is considered to be a positive ethical civic value, the religionization of civil activism has repercussions for many aspects of the social fabric. The positive correlation between religionization and voluntarism reflects not only the growing impact of religious values in society, but also the belief that people have to take responsibility for their environment if they wish to change it. Notwithstanding this trend, one has to take into consideration that it reflects the growing split within society between its religious segments and secular ones, something that has major implications for personal freedoms, especially of women and the LGBTQ community.

Civil Society Relations with Political Society

As indicated earlier, there is a sharp distinction in the literature between civil society and political society (Linz & Stepan, 1996). This distinction is based primarily on the claim that political society strives to accumulate political power and capture official positions of influence in the state, and civil society does not. This distinction is based on problematic normative assumptions and is not universally valid, especially when it comes to illiberal states. First, civil society has always had a deeply political facet, even those civic organizations that do not seek to conquer government. Second, political society, reflected in political parties and political movements that seek to accumulate power, has not always aspired to or been able to govern. Minority parties are a clear example of political society that does not always seek to govern, especially in the context of ethno-national conflicts such as the Israeli case, where the Jewish majority has guaranteed constitutional power to maintain and protect its domination (Jamal, 2011). In such cases, even though they operate in different arenas, political society and civil society are not strictly separated, especially when it comes to their efforts to represent the interests of their constituency and lead to policy change. This lack of ability to distinguish the two spheres is particularly true when civil society operates under the auspices of or in deep cooperation with political movements with clear ideological orientations. In this context, it is important to distinguish between many secular CSOs and their relationship with political parties, such as Hadash and Balad, and CSOs that are affiliated with the Islamic Movement, whether the outlawed Northern Branch or the more pragmatic Southern Branch. The secular CSOs that are affiliated with or that have close ties to political parties are fully independent and autonomous in their decision-making mechanisms. They have their own boards that determine the policies of the CSO and confirm its allocation of resources. The cooperation between CSOs and political parties is done on a voluntary basis. In contrast, CSOs affiliated with the Islamic Movement are part of the movement, and their personnel and resources are fully submitted to priorities determined by the movement's leadership.[2] This symbiosis raises many questions regarding our ability to conceive of these CSOs as civil society, let alone their very conservative values that clash with individual autonomy, personal liberty, and gender equality. The dilemma of how to conceive of these CSOs deepens when we consider their strong social services that with certainty empower the community and close a vacuum that the state has left open.

This dilemma mirrors one of the most important aspects of civic activism in the PCI, according to which CSOs may manifest civic patriotism on the one hand but counter civic values by promoting illiberal and antidemocratic values on the other.

As indicated in previous chapters, CSOs that were established in the last two decades were formed to address the culminating social needs of the PCI in a context in which the state became more reluctant to address these needs. This perception was reflected in the personal interviews with the directors of the various CSOs.[3] Many of them maintained that CSOs are not isolated from their social and political environment and that they assume great responsibility for any issue related to changing the living conditions of the Palestinian public they represent. Therefore, many of them, being social activists, took it upon themselves to find alternative solutions to answer the basic needs of the population. Because the increase in the number of CSOs is not a default development, the respondents in the surveys were asked to comment on the increase in the number of CSOs over recent years and the rise in their activity. Most of the respondents of the 2006–2007 survey (57.7% who were familiar with CSOs), said that the emergence of more CSOs is a positive development; another 33.5% said it was a very positive development, while only 7.1% said it was not a positive development, and 1.7% said it is not positive at all.

In the 2006–2007 survey, the respondents were asked to characterize their attitude toward CSOs and to the Arab parties in six parameters: respect, appreciation, solidarity, trust, suspicion, and criticism. Their answers were gathered according to a scale divided into positive attitudes—respect, appreciation, solidarity and trust—and negative attitudes—suspicion and criticism. This scale ranged from 1 (least negative/positive attitude) to 10 (most negative/positive).

From these responses given, we can generally say that the CSOs were awarded more positive and less negative attitudes compared to those of political parties. The average positive attitude to the CSOs was 7.22, whereas the average positive attitude to the political parties was 5.03. Regarding negative attitudes, the average negative attitude to the CSOs was 3.94, whereas the average negative attitude to the parties was 5.5. The negative appraisals are consistent with the results of the positive appraisals of CSOs. There is an increase in positive attitudes and at the same time a decline in negative attitudes. From this, we can infer that there is more suspicion toward the parties than toward the CSOs, or a low level of trust in partisan politics.

This trend also aligns with the common perception among the public that CSOs are professional organizations rather than political ones.

When looking at results from the 2016 survey, one notices similar trends. When comparing the level of trust of CSOs and political parties, we find that the gap is very telling. Whereas only 38.2% of the respondents showed above-average trust in political parties, 72.5% stated that they trust CSOs. When asked about feminist CSOs in the 2016 survey, the average dropped to 62%.

The gaps in the trust between political parties and civil associations reveal a serious difference that could be related to the basic expectation the public has from civil associations compared to political parties. The latter are expected to be representative of and to achieve practical results for its citizens. The fact that a large part of the public's expectations are not realized because the parties are in the opposition and are not part of the state's decision-making results in a structural disappointment. This structural distinction does not exist in the relationship between the public and the CSOs, although there is some suspicion toward them too. In other words, it may be that the parties' ineffectiveness results in greater disappointment and deeper criticism toward them compared to the CSOs. A speculative explanation of the lower level of disappointment in CSOs could be that while there are great expectations from the parties and therefore the level of criticism is high, the level of expectations from the CSOs is low and criticism is therefore milder. The lower level of expectations from CSOs therefore has to do with the fact that the parties are elected and are better known than the CSOs, whose leaders are not elected by the public.

In the 2006–2007 survey, participants were asked about the relationship between the CSOs and the political parties. According to the data, 21.7% of the respondents were wholly discontented with the kind of relationship between these organizations, 38.2% were discontented with this relationship, 32.4% were rather content, and 7.6% of them were very content with the relationship between the CSOs and the parties. The data indicate that those who are discontented with the relationship between the CSOs and the parties are the majority. This discontent can be interpreted in two ways. The first is that the public prefers separation between the CSOs and the parties and a clear functional division between them. The second is that the public, which is supportive of the affiliation of CSOs with parties, thinks that this relationship is not translated well or satisfactorily into the achievement of their joint objectives. The fact that a large group is indifferent to the affiliation between CSOs and parties can be interpreted in two ways: On the one hand, it reinforces the argument of discontent. On the other hand, it is a clear statement that they do not really care, which can be attributed to ineffectiveness on the part of both the CSOs and the parties.

Another important issue that arises from the data of both surveys is that socioeconomic factors greatly impact the attitudes of the public toward CSOs and their status compared to political parties and the traditional family. The more educated people are and the higher their income, the more positive and liberal their positions toward CSOs are. It is important to note that, in this context, there is no distinction between secular and religious CSOs. However, it is also important to note that most of the public perceives the CSOs as secular, and religious CSOs have not quite been perceived as part of civil society. The reason is that these associations are closely attached to the Islamic Movement, and their activities are related to fields that are considered an organic part of the society. Furthermore, socioeconomic factors turn out to be more influential than religious and cultural ones on the attitudes of the participants regarding CSOs. Of course, these data do not nullify culture as an important factor in the judgment and attitude of the average citizen in relation to her or his organic environment, as is shown by attitudes to family and family support. However, according to the data regarding volunteering and common attitudes toward CSOs, it can be seen that socioeconomic status is an accurate predictor of the public opinion of CSOs, including political parties.

The public's contact with political parties, the state, and the municipalities, as it emerges from the surveys, is an important indicator of public opinion, and it shows that the average Arab is not satisfied with her or his organizational and institutional environment. The 2016 survey demonstrates that 79% of the respondents expressed less than average satisfaction with the conduct of their local municipalities. Almost 67% expressed less than average satisfaction with their religious institutions. 94.8% expressed less than average satisfaction with political parties. 81.8% expressed the same attitude toward governmental offices, and 75.8% from the banks. By contrast, 62.5% expressed satisfaction with the conduct of the institutions of higher education. This means that the democratic gap is very high in the PCI. Citizens expect to receive better services and treatment from state institutions, including the municipalities, and are deeply disappointed by its lack of responsiveness to their needs. Simultaneously, people are aware of the limitations that CSOs have in supplying their needs and therefore cannot depend on these associations. Interestingly, the survey data show that the PCI feels abandoned by the state institutions, but have no better alternatives to rely on. CSOs with all due respect do not seem to be able to provide a sense of security to the public, especially in circumstances when they are the first to be attacked by Jewish nationalist political leaders and CSOs. The constant attacks on Palestinian CSOs are part of the general attempts of the right-wing conservative government to intimidate the PCI, its critical leadership, and its organizations. These attacks aim at creating a caveat between the PCI and the political and civil elite that speaks the language of human rights and demands civic equality and historical justice.

Summary

One of the obvious conclusions that emerge from the analysis of the survey data is that there is a large overlap between political and civil areas of activity, and that the surveys' participants did not always make a clear distinction between them. According to the data, the public does not seem to differentiate between the political and the civic spheres; this is deduced from many indications and the data, such as a major trend of people desiring that CSOs be active internationally in order to exert pressure on the Israeli government and challenge its policies. The 2006–2007 survey demonstrated that most of the respondents accept a high level of affiliation between the political parties and CSOs.

Another important conclusion is that the importance of CSOs in the eyes of the general public depends on the extent to which these associations respond to the public's needs. The further these associations are from meeting the public's basic needs, the lower their level of importance is in the eyes of the public. The data indicated that CSOs and political parties can improve in this regard. The data also indicated a low rate of public satisfaction with CSOs. Respondents related a sense of disappointment and bitterness at the ineffectiveness of CSOs. At the same time, there is no less disappointment in official state institutions, including municipalities. This paints a grim, problematic picture regarding future developments between state and society.

Another important conclusion that emerges from the surveys is the public's lack of deep familiarity with CSOs and their fields of activity. This is an important indicator of the quality of the relationship between the CSOs and the public. However, in light of this new knowledge, we can also gather that strengthening the ties between the public and the CSOs can lead to a stronger commitment by the public to volunteering of all kinds, as well as financial obligations and other contributions, especially because on the declarative level there is a high level of willingness to volunteer.

Chapter 9

Civil Engagement, Social Responsibility, and Political Empowerment

This chapter explores the behavioral patterns of the Palestinian civil elite and how it copes with the needs of Palestinian society. In doing so, it examines the self-perceptions and behavior of the civil elite through two research methods: focus groups and individual interviews (Litoselliti, 2003; Krueger, 1998). Several research questions related to the way civic activists perceive PCI civic activism were presented to a randomly chosen group of civic activists—heads of organizations and prominent figures in them—from CSOs in different regional areas. The participants in the focus groups were chosen according to snowballing. Each person chosen led to at least another civic activist. The personal interviews were based on previous knowledge or personal relationships with the author. The heads of the most prominent CSOs were interviewed. Furthermore, later meetings with them reiterated the ideas and perceptions that were raised in the interviews. This form of choice necessitated caution and the need to differentiate between the personal experiences of the author and those of other CSOs' leaders. The involvement of the author in the CSOs' world and the interactions with various CSOs' heads has turned the data presented in the upcoming two chapters into rigorous knowledge on the topic.

The participants in the focus groups, six in number, were given an explanation regarding the research, and it was made clear that they were not only allowed but actually were bidden to express their own opinions on the topic raised. They were clearly promised that when requested their identity will not be disclosed. Surprisingly, except for very limited occasions, no requests were made to keep the interviews or the information presented in them confidential.

The data were collected using a recorder while the author wrote his own notes. Afterward, the data were coded and organized based on common themes. Second, regarding reliability, the analysis of the contents made sure that different assistants reached similar conclusions based on the same data. Third, the analysis was limited to certain parameters, especially because the scope of the data collected was too wide to be presented in its entirety within the current text. Therefore, thematic analytical methods were used to organize the major themes raised during the discussions. Thematic analysis "is a method for identifying, analysing and reporting patterns (themes) within data. It minimally organizes and describes your data set in (rich) detail" (Braun & Clarke, 2006). Next, regarding data interpretation, it was decided to use a method called the Analysis Continuum. According to this method, the researcher uses a continuum of analysis starting from the collection of the raw materials, through a description of the data, and ending with data interpretation. It began by creating a general picture of the raw materials and gaining a general perspective on the process. Then, of the four main analytical strategies mentioned in the literature, Transcript-Based Analysis was used (Krueger, 1994).

Semi-structured, in-depth interviews with 85 central leaders of the CSOs were conducted. These interviews are actually conversations based on a small number of leading questions, which led to more questions according to the nature of the discussion between the interviewer and the interviewee. In such interviews, the interviewer and the interviewee jointly develop the subjects ensuing from the conversation (Shkedi, 2003, p. 71). The interviewer followed the conversation's directions taken by the interviewee and organized the order of the topics discussed and transitions between them, leaving leeway for the interviewee to bring up details or issues that are important to him or her (Shore & Sabar Ben-Yehoshua, 2010, p. 200; Shkedi, 2003, p. 71).

It is important, as we relate to the primary data obtained from these methodological approaches, to keep in mind that the context of these data is crucial for understanding and reaching broader conclusions as to their meaning. Therefore, in some cases, almost complete dialogues between the participants are presented to reveal the extent of the differences between the various interviewees regarding civil society and its objectives, motives, and relationship with its environment. While this presentation may seem burdensome to some readers, this approach helps them understand the discussion's atmosphere and the extent of agreement or dispute regarding various aspects of the issue at hand. The analysis is subdivided into major themes to facilitate the reader's understanding. This division is not conclusive, and was not always made by the participants themselves, something that has led to some repetition in the data presented.

The Relationship between Civil Society and the General Population

A trend emerged in our analysis of several interviews in which many leaders of CSOs attribute the emergence of CSOs in Palestinian society to the state's failure to perform its duties as expected. Generally, they believe that the organizations emerged to fill the vacuum created by the state's negligent policy.[1] This negligence has two aspects, each resulting in the establishment of different types of organizations that respond to different needs. The first presented by interviewees is material and relates to services that should have been provided by the state. They established a relationship between this reality and the growing neoliberal economy and privatization trends that encourage the state to retreat from its position as a service provider (Ben-Bassat & Dahan, 2009). In their view, these policies severely affected the PCI and presented new obstacles that made it even more difficult for it to survive the Israeli reality, financially and legally. Being aware of the fact that the PCI is found in the three lower segments of the socioeconomic index and cannot rely on official institutions in facing new challenges, they expressed their views that CSOs seek to either provide some of the services that make it easier for the PCI to survive, or advocate for equality in the allocation of resources by state institutions. These efforts are deeply related to the retreat in the ability of the municipalities to provide basic services compared to what they have provided in the past, especially in consideration of the growing public's needs.

The second aspect of the politics of negligence is related to psychological dimensions, namely the citizens' disenchantment with the state and formal politics, including the ability of Arab parties represented in the Knesset to have any serious impact on the prevalent policies of the state. CSO leaders agreed that the Palestinian populations' growing awareness as to their rights motivated them to act in order to demand these rights. In their view, there was and still is a need for social empowerment of the PCI, and thus civil activity was enhanced to fulfill this need. Accordingly, CSOs took it upon themselves to lead struggles against the state to protect the basic rights of the PCI. CSOs serve as mechanisms for social solidarity in the PCI. These took the shape of popular committees, which handle basic rights such as land rights in the Negev or construction and development rights in towns in central and northern Israel. These efforts explain the CSOs' lobbying efforts for promoting essential interests and causes in the Knesset, in courts, and in international forums. Several participants declared that CSOs engage in politics and attempt to influence the PCI's political ambitions both theoretically and practically by drafting visionary or strategic documents or attempting to influence Palestinian education's policies and curriculum.

The data from the personal interviews and the focus groups also suggest that the demand for basic services is conceived as fundamental social challenge, leading many to conclude that service-providing associations are more organic and better connected to the population. Notwithstanding, several civic activists who were either interviewed or took part in the focus groups indicated that by providing services, CSOs are tempted to invest their time and resources in positions that should be filled by the state, and by doing so they hinder the population's efforts toward social empowerment and social change. Accordingly, because advocacy and lobbying organizations represent a fair share of the Palestinian civil sphere, most of their efforts are directed toward challenging the state, resulting in investing most of their energies to change its policies instead of being in stronger contact with the population.

The discussion of CSO leaders brought up the notion that this strategy of many CSOs, focusing mainly on advocacy and lobby vis-à-vis the state, detach them from the population, weakening their position when they need to mobilize people to support certain activities. They also agreed that this strategy weakens their efforts to raise awareness of the population to its own rights. Two cases that exemplify this point occurred recently, namely, when the government decided to evacuate the village of Umm Al-Hirran in the Negev area (January 18, 2017) and demolished eleven houses in the village of Qalansawa in the triangle area (January 10, 2017). Several CSO leaders expressed frustration due to the populations' level of commitment to civic activism. They also argued that the distance between CSOs and the general public is behind why religious CSOs are better able to mobilize underprivileged segments of society in favor of activities that they organize, which are also exploited to preserve social conservatism and promote patriarchal values in society.[2]

According to the focus groups' data, the processes of identifying the vacuums left by the state, setting goals. and forming CSOs are dominated by a few common traits. One of these traits is that the CSOs' founders and activists, like political parties, are elitist. Their main failings are similar in this regard—their primary cause is to challenge the state, not to influence Palestinian society. Hence, CSOs' leadership is not characterized by dialogue with its environment. This disconnect is consistent with respondents' answers to the public opinion survey presented in the previous chapter.

One of the focus groups' participants made an interesting distinction between the causes for the formation of different associations:

> OMAR: We should divide the CSOs. Some promote a specific cause, lobby for a social project, improve a specific process and so on . . . for example—the recently established women organizations are not the result of the State's negligence. They were formed for a specific cause. At the same time, some CSOs were established to fill the gap that was left by the government. The failure of the municipalities created the need to establish certain service-providing CSOs. (Baqa Al-Garbiyye, February 24, 2009)

This statement goes along the argument made by one of the interviewees, who said that the PCI tends to be passive and oblivious. People are unwilling to take risks because the state is intolerant and reacts harshly to any wave of collective protest.[3]

Even when activists try to engage others in the process of defining needs and setting goals, these attempts usually fail, and eventually the CSOs design their own agenda by themselves. Therefore, it is hard for them to evaluate themselves and their activities' alignment with the populations' needs and demands. The weak interaction between CSOs and the population forces them to choose the easiest route, which is working vis-à-vis the state and paying less attention to activities within Palestinian society itself. This pattern of action is viewed as raising doubts as to CSOs' capacity to increase society's social capital, especially in light of its weak networking skills.

The data collected from the focus groups, the observations, and the interviews also show no uniformity in the relationship between CSOs and the PCI. Some argued passionately that civil society had stopped its interaction with the PCI because CSOs are reluctant to assume full responsibility for many of their challenges. Others argued that there is no distance between CSOs and the general population, though they seem to be a minority. However, in this context, the interviewees distinguished between advocacy activities, which do not always lead to direct contact with the community, and empowerment and development, which are based on direct contact with the community.

Many of the focus group participants expressed the view that many CSOs were formed without sufficient examination of the population's needs. The emergence of CSOs was spontaneous and elitist, and many of them were formed by a personal rather than group initiative, without extensive consultations. Another insight was that many CSOs lack clearly defined goals and work plans; while some CSOs do have long-term strategic plans in specific areas, other CSOs lack a plan and therefore intrude into specialty fields of other CSOs. This overlap causes a waste of resources and feeds internal competition between CSOs at the expense of cooperation and networking—and social capital.

The data of the interviews and contents from the focus group data demonstrate that there is a widespread opinion that the identity of the leadership in the CSOs forms a central factor in the success or failure of any CSO. A few interviewees said that the lack of effective leadership, especially that which acts according to preset goals, might cause the organization to fail. Of course, the opposite is also true in their opinion: The success of the CSO is dependent on a good leadership. Most interviewees and focus group participants seem to agree that CSOs' leadership should share and delegate responsibilities to prevent contradictions between the essence of civil activity, which is horizontal, and the dominant authority patterns, which are vertical, within associations. Many of the interviewees agreed that there is a wide gap between theory and practice regarding leadership and also pointed out the personalization problem of many associations.

One of the female interviewees argued that personalization is a common phenomenon in a patriarchal society, where people are used to looking for a key personality at the top of the pyramid.[4] She argued that it has nothing to do with the CSOs' leadership pattern per se. Another participant supported this statement, emphasizing the importance of the relationship between stable organizational leadership and continuity in these CSOs, and the great contribution to the association's stability made by a long-term leading figure. On the other hand, another interviewee mentioned a negative effect of personalization; some CSOs are identified with specific figures, to the extent that the CSO cannot exist without them.[5] The dissatisfaction with the personalization and the connection between personalization and the extent of the association's success in improving and developing Palestinian society are evident in the following quote:

> What do we do to make a change? Can we do anything to change this reality and improve our work as CSOs? I see two main reasons regarding this issue: First, CSOs' personalization—this is a very basic and important issue. In several CSOs there is one or more activists that are more important than the CSO itself. In other CSOs, the idea is more important than the people. In the Islamic Movement, for instance, the idea still comes before the activists. (Nazareth, June 6, 2008)

Later in the same session, another participant complained about the nature of the relationship between civil society and the population, pointing out a large extent of alienation and distance between them:

> Concerning the issue of alienation and distance from the population, the CSOs are not interested in publishing their activities, because they do not consider the public as their source of income, and subsequently use English in their literature and websites. (Nazareth, June 6, 2008)

Another position came up in the same session when we discussed the issue of criticism toward CSOs. Some of the participants tried to avoid this question while stating that the problem lies with the fact that the expectations for the CSOs are too high. They believe that the public has an unrealistic image of CSOs' activities, while in reality their contribution is minor and cannot substitute for the state as the principle service provider.

We can generally say that, according to the focus groups' data, the participants try to evade responsibility concerning the low level of public trust in CSOs. In one of the sessions, a dispute developed between two positions regarding public trust: While the first pinned the blame on the associations, which failed to prove their ability to influence Palestinian citizens' lifestyle and standard of living, the alternative or even opposing view suggested that the blame lies with a critical social worldview unrelated to CSOs.[6]

This elitist discourse was also expressed in participants' criticism of Palestinian society, which is distanced from civil society because of its tribal, clan, and undemocratic nature.[7] In response to the researcher's argument that CSOs weaken social activism (demonstrations), many of the focus groups' participants argued that generally, CSOs empower society, and that the PCI was not very active even before these associations were formed.

Subsequently, some said that the lack of civil society causes educated Palestinians to be marginalized, and thus the clan traditions remain a highly important influence on society's structure and preferences. They also argued that the CSOs emerged as a response to crisis and that crisis remains their main narrative. When the crisis feeling decreases, it is difficult to mobilize the population into action, and society sinks into a state of passivity and with little initiative.

When faced with the argument that the emergence of CSOs might have been a tool for creating a new labor market of educated Palestinians, many focus group participants rejected it, claiming that civil society and its associations should not be seen as opportunists. They responded that these elites lead organizational processes and that it is only natural that CSOs would be formed by educated people. A different, technical argument was brought up regarding the fact that CSOs can only employ a small number of educated people and therefore cannot be seen merely as a source of employment. The participants said that CSOs must develop for a long time before they can employ people, and even then, their employees' number is limited. Yet when the participants were asked about the reasons for the lack of public trust in CSOs, some said there is a feeling that certain CSOs were formed for personal rather than collective interests. In this regard, one participant said:

> Some of the people here came from political parties and their objectives have to do with the parties. Therefore, it is not about finding a job. No. Some people could have been Knesset Members today, but they chose not to. Some people plan to be Knesset Members. It has to do with the parties. We must pay attention to this issue and shouldn't ignore it, because it is related to values and ideology. (Tel Aviv, December 5, 2007)

Relationships with the Political Parties

This previous quote leads us to another key issue brought up in the interviews and focus groups regarding the relationship between CSOs and political parties. In the focus groups, we identified an explicit position claiming that most of the big, nation-wide CSOs are tied to political parties, and therefore there is little distinction between civil and political society. Some of these CSOs are identified with the Islamic Movement, Hadash, or Balad, though there are a few exceptions with no partisan affiliation.

The flow of personnel between CSOs and the political system runs both ways. Some CSOs founders are ex–party members who abandoned the party platform because it was insufficient to their desired level of political engagement. At the same time, some CSOs' activists use their activity as a stepping stone into politics. The discussions in the focus groups demonstrated that there is also a lively debate concerning the limits between civil and political activity. Some said that partisan activities should be detached from civil activities, but at the same time not ignore the political aspect of civil activity.[8] Supporters of this position are well aware of the deeply embedded political dimensions in civil activity, stemming from the very fact that this activity is meant to affect society and its internal power relations. Yet the political aspect cannot sum up the entirety of these activities. Civil activity can also be detached from partisan interests and even challenge them when parties mobilize people based on a narrow ideological basis.

Regarding the expectations of CSOs and the connections between them and parties, the leaders warned that the Palestinian public's expectations are too high compared to the associations' actual abilities:

> There's a kind of optimism, or unrealistic expectations from the CSOs. CSOs are expected to be different from the parties, as if they are really disconnected from society and politics. This is not true. CSOs suffer from the same "diseases" as society as a whole. Many of the successful CSOs in Israel today are led by ex-party members. They are the ones who formed the CSOs. They might have done it because they felt alienated by the party, because they identified new needs, because they felt the party is dysfunctional or because they didn't find their place there anymore. The reason doesn't really matter. They still come from a partisan background. (Nazareth, June 6, 2008)

The importance of setting boundaries between parties and CSOs' roles in national issues, like the constitution, was also brought up during the focus groups' sessions. Yet some argued that the model of distinguishing between political and civil activity is irrelevant for the PCI, because Arab parties are not part of the government and therefore function as an integral part of civil society. Some stressed the legitimacy of realizing the partisan ideology through CSOs. One female participant said, in that regard:

> If the subject of this focus group is civil society, we should include representatives from political parties. (Nazareth, June 6, 2008)

At the same time, others felt it is very exaggerated to claim that the CSOs' political activity minimizes or weakens the parties. They believe that the CSOs' involvement in various issues (like the future vision documents) is in fact an intrusion into the parties' responsibility. This intrusion thus assists the state and the financing foundations in their effort to weaken the parties by highlighting the roles of the CSOs. The following discussion puts things in perspective:

> JABAR: First, in the long run, who is threatened by the relationship between the parties and the CSOs? Only the parties, not the CSOs. Look at the West Bank, for example. There are parties there, which invested in an CSO, and both collapsed. When the political movement was weakened, they had to submit to the wishes of the financing funds. Our position might be better in this context, since we don't get a lot of funds. We are a society like any other: we have political cultures, we need politicians, but there are many nationalist parties; they have different strategies, and the variance between them is clear and might even increase. The question regarding diversification is not about variance, it's about the managing of variance. The question is how do we deal with diversification; we must find the common ground and the difference, and to find a way to manage variance. This is impossible without legitimate authority sources. Everyone can exist side by side, if there is a suitable formula, and I think this is the biggest challenge.

> HANAN: We have to examine the sources of authority of CSOs and the drafting of the Future Vision Documents by CSOs is a good example. It might be dangerous that CSOs write a political convention, similar to a constitution. How can the future vision for Arab society be written by CSOs leaders? I find it very odd! This is not their job. When the EU representatives want to meet Arab representatives, they request a meeting with CSOs' leaders! They don't meet Knesset Members or parties; this is an odd and dangerous phenomenon. (Tel Aviv, December 5, 2007)

In direct relation to this discussion, during another focus group discussion, a heavy debate broke out between one of the CSOs' leaders, who blamed other CSOs of being party affiliated and committed to party considerations. In response, several CSOs leaders responded, arguing that all advocacy and lobbying CSOs are somehow related or affiliated with political parties or movements, because each of them has either an ideological commitment or personal ties that disclose their loyalty to one party or another.[9]

Many participants in various focus groups and interviews argued that because CSOs often replace the state as a service provider, they are empowered compared to political parties. The latter, which under normal conditions are supposed to have a strong impact on decision making of the states, have no influence in the case of the Arab parties in Israel. Therefore, parties cannot help in providing services to the community because they are never part of the government; they have no impact on policy making, and therefore there shouldn't be any conflicts between parties and CSOs' activities.

> MOHAMAD: In the Triangle (in the center of Israel) no one trusts the State or the Knesset; this distrust is spread to the Knesset's Arab parties, to the national leadership, and in recent years, the local parties and municipalities have also lost the public's trust. There is a problem with the leadership and its relationship with the public. Particularly the Knesset Members and their relationships with the voters. I feel alone: I live in one state and the Knesset Member lives in a different one. (Baqa Al-Garbiyye, February 24, 2009)

> SABBER: I see the gain in the maturing process. The operation through CSOs were enforced on the PCI; it was born out of individual needs and a mature vision of several people that worked with the parties, as well as a result of pressure on unemployed intellectuals at the time. These two elements have created this sphere. Now we have to ask: Does this sphere encourage social change or not? Another question is: what kind of society do we want? And later—is there a definition of the civil society institutions we need in order to build this society? Is there any general vision? (Nazareth, June 6, 2008)

This argument concerning trust has been examined in the 2016–2017 survey. The data of the survey reveal that the argument made by Mohamad, which was made by many others in the focus groups and the personal interviews, is highly valid. Only 8.2% of the interviewees stated that they highly trust political parties. By contrast, 61.8% stated that they have low or no trust in political parties.

In one of the interviews conducted with an activist in one of the leading CSOs, he argued that CSOs are a part of society and have the same diseases as society and its institutions.[10] The CSOs, he said, are similar to the parties, especially because the CSOs' activists were raised in the parties. They carry the same values and problems that exist in parties, like competition and lack of cooperation. While civil society expanded the population's activity in the public sphere, it also lowered the "political ceiling"—weakened the political participation through the parties.

Regarding the question of ideological and/or partisan affiliation of CSOs, some said that there are CSOs that hide behind a veil of inexplicit ideological affiliation, as is the case with the Islamic Movement's associations. Others argued that the ideological affiliation of CSOs, especially their leaders, is public knowledge.

> MOHAMAD: The big CSOs are related to political parties: some belong to the Islamic Movement, some belong to Hadash and some to Balad. These are the three parties that formed CSOs. (Baqa Al-Garbiyye, February 24, 2009)

Some said that it is legitimate for a CSO to present itself as a continuation of a party's ideology or paradigm, as well as a nonpartisan ideology; at the same time, there will always be CSOs that will manage to reflect a general ideology that includes everyone, and this approach is also legitimate. Some also said that the CSOs have the courage sometimes to raise social issues that the parties refuse or are afraid to address, and that the CSOs open the possibility of political and legal translation of the consensus by creating a nonpartisan political and legal discourse. This means that CSOs help define the nature of the public sphere and the contents and forms of deliberating public matters, especially those disputed between different parts of the community.

> HANAN: No CSO publicly declare: "I belong to a party," yet we all know its political-ideological affiliation.

> JABAR: I think there are two different spheres here. There is an important sphere, though we ignore its importance, of inclusive CSOs, which can serve the Arab collective as a whole, connect

the Islamic Movement, Hadash, Balad and Abnaa Al-Balad, and work with everybody everywhere. It is legitimate, and it must be. However, CSOs can also work in the service of a specific ideological vision. Ideological, not necessarily partisan. (Tel Aviv, December 5, 2007)

When discussing the relationships between parties and CSOs, whereas some argued that there is no competition between the two, others claimed that the lack of coordination between them creates a competitive atmosphere. This conversation led to another topic concerning the relationship between the level of collaboration between CSOs and their social contribution. Several participants in different focus groups argued that political parties hardly collaborate within themselves. The fierce competition between politicians and parties has negative implications for the possibility of collaborations between other parties and CSOs. This argument has been reiterated even after the establishment of the Joint List toward the 2015 Knesset elections. CSOs' leaders who were interviewed claimed that the Joint List has not been established as a result of a willful strategic decision of the Arab parties. It has been imposed on the parties by the political circumstances, especially raising the threshold to 3.25%, something that put all Arab parties in danger of not passing it. Therefore, mutual suspicion still characterizes the work of the elected leaders in the Joint List, something that is reflected in the dissatisfaction of the PCI with the conduct of the List. The 2016–2017 survey revealed that only 16% were satisfied with the functioning of the List. A total of 35.3% expressed their dissatisfaction with the List, and 36.3% expressed an in-between position. When asked about the extent to which Palestinian politicians take into consideration their preferences, a majority of 51.7% claimed they don't care, and 25% claimed that they do care. When asked if they—the Palestinian public—have any influence on determining the agenda of Arab parties, 61% claimed that they have no influence, and only 16.2% claimed they do have some influence. But when asked about the extent to which Arab parties are essential for protecting the rights of the PCI, 58.4% answered that they are. These data reflect the ambivalent position of the PCI toward Arab parties. They don't trust them very much and do not think that they are effective, but simultaneously the same public would like to see the parties continue their efforts and think they are essential for demanding equal civic rights.

One focus group participant elaborated on the CSOs' contribution while emphasizing their political role, which complements the role of the parties:

HANAN: I think CSOs contribute in a few principal areas: Their first is bringing society closer to the public sphere. The CSOs have reached population segments that the parties were unable to penetrate, because [of] their partisan nature. The second is creating political agreement among various segments of society, translated into common documents, such as the Haifa Declaration or the Future Vision Document. The third is providing a legal hope for the minority. The fourth contribution has to do with defending liberal civil values, such as women's rights. CSOs have demonstrated that they are more courageous than political parties when it comes to women's rights. A fifth contribution is their ability to organize and mobilize certain segments of society, such as farmers and journalists. Notwithstanding these contributions, CSOs are limited for financial considerations and seek to protect their relationship with the donors and for political calculations, such as not clashing with state authorities. CSOs are treated like political parties in that regard. Therefore, CSOs would benefit from cooperating with the parties; this collaboration gives them the credibility they need, for they are not elected institutions. (Tel Aviv, December 5, 2007)

An important point raised in personal interviews has been that political-partisan diversification within a civil society is important because it makes it easier for the CSOs to serve different segments of society. Accordingly, diversity encourages tolerance. Partisan affiliation should not be considered negative or wrong as long as society benefits from it. A partisan affiliation, or lack thereof, is not the main factor granting legitimacy to CSOs' activities. Their legitimacy litmus test is their voice: political, social, religious, and so forth.

When summarizing all data related to the relationship between civil and political societies, it becomes clear that the leaders of the CSOs are aware of the fact that their lack of mutual trust and cooperation is a major problem contributing to the public's distrust in their CSOs. It has also become clear that CSOs' leaders are aware of the energies invested in the competition between them. They made clear that whereas diversity is constructive and normal, there should be a difference between pluralism and factionalism. Whereas the former enables better representation of the variety of worldviews and ideologies in society, the latter mirrors a culture of animosity, lack of maturity, and mutual respect and the inability to bridge the differences to achieve common goals. This culture is problematic when looked at from the prism of social capital, as based on trust, networking, and constructive communication. It is also problematic when viewed from the vantage point of the state, which tends to classify Palestinian CSOs based on their loyalty to the hegemonic political order and separates moderates from extremists—a classification that determines their support or lack thereof. The interviewed made clear that competition between CSOs should be perceived as positive and important, but that it is dangerous when it enables the state to exploit the differences to promote its policy of divide and conquer.

It was made clear that there is a need to find ways to enhance the cooperation between CSOs, especially between those of different ideological backgrounds, if bridging and bonding is a strategy to empower the PCI in the face of state discriminatory policies. The fact that this awareness is not successfully realized means that CSOs are a mirror image of the political parties, albeit with some differences.

The Distinction between Civic Secular and Islamic Associations

One of the major debates that arose during the personal interviews as well as the focus groups is the connection between religious and secular associations and the similarities and differences between them. The participants argued that the distinction between those two types of associations is institutional, behavioral, and valuational. Before relating to this topic, it is important to make two important clarifications. The first has to do with the outlawing of the Northern Branch of the Islamic Movement and 13 CSOs affiliated with it in November 2015. This extreme measure made by the Cabinet came to eliminate the institutional pillars of the movement and hinder its deep engagement in society. Although the movement found a way to bypass this extreme measure, it is not possible to ignore the implications of such a decision on a very central movement in the PCI and the chilling effect it has on the activity of other CSOs in the community.

What also has to be noted is the fact that the Cabinet's decision passed without much protest in the community. The events organized by the Islamic Movement to protest the decision were relatively minor and quiet, demonstrating the recognition that it is a sort of provocation that ought not draw the supporters of the movement into a confrontation with the state's security forces. Furthermore, it seems that the movement was able to transfer its activities to new organizations that had and still have to operate under a new banner. The impact of the movement and the services it provides have never stopped, something that reflects the mutual understanding between state authorities and the movement that the measure taken has symbolic and public relations effects more than practical ones.

The second note has to do with the establishment of the Joint List, which, as already mentioned, eased the tensions between the political parties, especially between Hadash and Balad and the former and the Southern Branch of the Islamic Movement. The importance of these events is undisputable for any analysis of PCI politics and civic activism. Part of the interviews and the focus groups were conducted before these events took place, and therefore part of the data presented does not relate to them.

Activists from the Islamic Movement (the Northern Branch) argued that, unlike secular CSOs, the activities of CSOs affiliated with the movement are based on strict ideological beliefs. These activities are rooted in and derive from religious thought and culture, which are based on the individual's duty to assume social responsibilities. This is a very important factor, turning CSOs affiliated with the movement into purely grassroots organizations related to the basic habitus of the Islamic society. The organizational abilities of these CSOs and their popular (communal) leadership base make them able to reach out to the community and communicate with its members based on a common language missing from the activities of many secular CSOs. Accordingly, activists from the movement's CSOs argued that this character of their organization makes them more trusted by the public.

> SULEIMAN: Regarding financial support, today, when I give a donation to an association like *al-zakat* or *al-Igatha* (charity organizations that are based on collecting donations according to the Islamic religious duty), I don't expect anything in return. I assume the money will be dispersed to all segments of society, not just among Muslims, because not all the donors belong to the Islamic Movement. The Islamic Movement includes more than 15 associations. The public trust these associations. (Nazareth, June 6, 2008)

Furthermore, activists from the movement made it clear that Islamic associations are in fact a natural continuation of society and its history, because Arab society is a religious society. Hence, it is easier for them to succeed in organizing and mobilizing the public. In view of these activists, secular CSOs are influenced by Western ideas, and therefore they are not authentic to society and as such are intrusive. This explains for them the focusing of secular CSOs on the relationship with the state, emphasizing lobbying and advocacy activities, which turn the state not only into the main legitimate authority, but also submits to a politics of compliance that renders the PCI fully dependent on the state and awaits its responsiveness. Activists in Islamic CSOs showed some understanding of secular CSOs' activism, arguing that the latter do not have to be as authentic or deeply connected to the community, because their activism is fully instrumental. However, they argued that such activities familiarize society with the secular discourse, something that is unacceptable to them. In this context, they expressed their opposition to feminist organizations that are funded by Western sources and import values that are alien to the Arab Islamic culture.

> SULEIMAN: I don't want to compare Islamic and non-Islamic associations, but as far as I know, in Islamic associations the volunteers come from all the segments of society—people who belong to the Movement and people who are not part of it. For example, in the event "empowering the Negev" on Land Day, when the Imam in the Mosque calls for cooperation, even people who don't pray and hear about the event, cooperate. (Nazareth, June 6, 2008)

The tension and differences between secular and religious civic activists came up several times and was translated into debates concerning the centrality of funding for civil society and its ability to be authentic and independent. In one of the focus groups, the following discussion took place:

> MOHAMMAD: The Islamic Movement receives only local funds.

> HASSAN: True. Local funds. It is not like other institutions, which are supported by outside sources.

> NIBAL: Yes, this is part of what we talked about. This is an independent society.

> HASSAN: Indeed. Moreover, there are groups today in Islamic countries, in Europe and in Arab countries, which work like the EU. The projects make the world a more open space, and when the EU cannot support certain needs, you can find a different

source. There are legal restrictions on fundraising of the Islamic movement. The police investigate dozen of young people, asks about the Islamic movement civil activities, and where the Islamic project intends to develop. There were always restrictions and harassments to our activists, which become very dominant today. There is a difference between turning off the air-conditioner and taking off the jacket. This is the funds' policy: they push slowly, without using violence. But when it comes to the law, the attitude is tougher and more oppressive towards religious activists. (Nazareth, June 6, 2008)

During the discussion about the distinction between secular and religious CSOs, the difference between the two on the basis of the connection between service provision and the existence of political and social visions was emphasized. In this context, it was argued that the Islamic Movement doesn't only answer social needs but rather tries to build an independent political, economic, and social society. Religious activists argued that religious CSOs concentrate mainly on empowerment rather than purely addressing social needs. The transformation of people's consciousness is very central in order to make them independent subjects. Accordingly, such engagement is the only guarantee to resist state policies and liberate society from being totally dependent on its services. In the view of Islamic activists, the secular CSOs speak the language of rights, expecting the state to answer their demands. But they actually legitimate the state and institutionalize the dependence of the PCI on state institutions.[11] Only building an autarkic society, according to which the community relies on its own sources, can empower society and return its feeling of pride.

One of the secular activists claimed in one of the focus groups in this regard that:

BAKER: The cultural-intellectual aspect exists in the Islamic Movement's institutions. They know how to organize things. They have a leadership that grew out of the field work, and this is the reason for their success. (Baqa Al-Garbiyye, February 24, 2009)

Another activist questioned the existence of a vision or a common desire for social change among secular civic organization.

> SABBER: There are several CSOs that were formed based on a social vision and a need to build and promote a certain social idea. A social vision can have different principles, some are related to identity. The other vision that guides CSOs is the process of social change. Civil secular organizations respond and react but do not initiate. There is no common vision regarding the desired change. (Nazareth, June 6, 2008)

Secular activist criticized the fundraising policy of the CSOs affiliated with the Islamic Movement. Some claimed that these organizations exploit religion, especially fear and people's dependence on receiving services to raise money from society. Notwithstanding, they praised the authenticity of the civic activism of the Islamic Movement, which is also guaranteed through the financial sources of Islamic CSOs. They added that CSOs of the Islamic Movement raise money from the community and do not extend their hands to the EU or American funds, rendering themselves totally dependent on the free will of these foreign entities. Such dependence on these latter sources is not without a price. Islamic CSOs look for external funding, but address only other Arab or Islamic countries.[12] The main logic behind this behavior is their unwillingness to exchange their authentic culture for financial support. In the view of Islamic activists, adopting the discourse of Western fundraising endangers the Islamic faith, as indicated by the following:

> OMAR: Islamic association are often not supported by external sources but rather by internal ones—charity and *zakat* money. CSOs that are supported by external sources tend to collapse or suffer from internal disputes.

> MUHAMMAD: The external funds have demands that impact the CSOs' policies.

> OMAR: Do we want to build a society where Islamic principles are under attack due to the policy of a foreign funding?

> SAKER: We need to learn the politics of funding. There are some funds and institutions I refuse to cooperate with on principle.

MOHAMMAD: Our society is religious in nature, and it is normal that associations established on the basis of religion are closer to people and that they are trusted more because they are part of history. Secular associations are built on a secular basis, which originates from Europe. So, normally a secular association is an external entity. Secularism as culture or as a way of thinking is not based in Arabic societies' norms, its roots aren't deep and strong.

MARZUK: There's a growing awareness of the need to establish institutions. It might be a result of the disappointment with the State, which doesn't fulfill its duties regarding services; it might be the result of the disappointment with political activity and its use. I think that we, as a society, live in chaos. (Baqa Al-Garbiyye, February 24, 2009)

The Relationships between CSOs and Social Capital

The nature of the relationship between CSOs as an indicator of the dynamic nature of social capital has been a central topic in the personal interviews and the focus groups. One of the main indicators of social capital is networking and cooperation between CSOs on topics of central importance for society. Another indicator is mutual trust, manifested by the willingness to bridge differences and cooperate. A third indicator of social capital is the intensity of communication and the channels used to facilitate a homogenizing process on the procedural level in order to regulate the differences on the substantial ideological and valuational levels.

Focus group discussions revealed heavy critique of the lack of sufficient cooperation between CSOs. Activists differentiated in their aspirations for cooperation, the discourse on cooperation, and the practical level of cooperation in reality. Almost all people who were interviewed and who participated in the focus groups expressed the view that cooperation based on mutual trust and respect is a very important value and wished-for policy. They also emphasized the common discourse on trust and cooperation. However, when it comes to the practical level, most activists expressed their dissatisfaction and skepticism. The data gathered mirror a split reality based on several factors. Activists differentiated between healthy competition and complete mistrust that leads to wars between CSOs. They also differentiated between imposed cooperation, enforced by donors that encourage CSOs to cooperate on projects to save resources, and voluntary cooperation based on substantial agreements and constructive communication. Interviewees and participants in focus groups pointed out that when looking at cooperation between Palestinian CSOs, it is possible to notice a process of maturity. Nevertheless, cooperation is usually made based on ideological affiliation or personal ties. It is more likely that CSOs affiliated with the same ideological camp cooperate than CSOs across ideological camps. Personal ties between heads of CSOs are also a very central factor in determining the nature and intensity of cooperation between CSOs.

One of the important observations made by many activists is that more cooperation between CSOs enables them to better contribute to society and win its trust. By contrast, lack of cooperation was depicted as one of the main sources of weakness in the PCI's civil activism. Furthermore, the growing numbers of CSOs is another source of competition that leads to the dwindling of the resources available for CSOs to be able to strongly intervene in society. The existence of a large number of CSOs working separately in the same field weakens them and society as a whole. Participants in focus groups agreed that some CSOs should join forces so they can pool their resources and empower their activities.

Some of them suggested that CSOs are unable to positively translate the structural and ideological pluralism of Palestinian civil society into a strategic venture. Many CSO, it has been argued, enhance competition to gain more salience and as a result more influence in society. One of the interviewed argued:

> There is a diversity, but we haven't used it for our benefit. The lack of positive competition distanced the CSOs from their target audience. CSOs have lost the public's trust. Today everything is a routine. Everyone forms their own CSOs and operates within their own routine.[13]

An activist participating in one of the focus groups suggested that one should distinguish between the level of pluralism between the local and the national levels. In his view, this differentiation should be overcome through mutual agreements. CSOs should work between these two levels, depending on the issue or activity at hand. Accordingly, there must be an agreement on the national level, and pluralism should be limited. In issues that are not national, CSOs can act based on the existing pluralism. Yet it appears that this distinction is more theoretical than practical.

NAHED: I think there is a need in collaborations on political issues as well. I believe in diversity; each of us has a specific policy and ideology, even if our political agenda is the same. Even within Feminism there is more than one way of thought. You can see we are disputed on the issue of women's representation. Some believe in direct elections while others boycott it. The diversity is a source of strength, not weakness.

MUSTAFA: I don't understand why there is a dispute and why there are different ideologies to different parties. Democracy is based on diversity, but there is a ceiling to the diversity. This is the thing that unites us as a national minority in Israel. If we manage to combine both ceilings of diversity and national affiliation, we can work together despite our differences. (Tel Aviv, December 5, 2007)

The idea of distinguishing between two levels brought up the need for a consensus on national issues. One example of such a consensus mentioned in one of the focus groups is the one achieved during the elections to determine the head of the Follow-Up Committee on October 24, 2015.[14] It has been argued that, despite the competition between different factions and camps, at the end of the day all parties agreed to support one candidate. Another example that led to heavy debates between participants of focus groups is the Future Vision Documents, which represent various political worldviews. One group of the participants indicated that one should differ between issues related to the need to cooperate between various CSOs in order to fundraise for a project and cooperation in order to promote social solidarity, a strategic goal, or a common substantial belief. The example used was the inability of CSOs to cooperate in 2005–2006 to issue one future vision document. The issuing of three documents, it was argued, demonstrates the deep mistrust between CSOs from different ideological backgrounds. Other participants in focus groups argued that the fact that different groups of CSOs issued different documents is an indication of the normality of the PCI, which is split over ideological and political matters. The problem in their view is the way the differences are regulated and whether the different groups are able to communicate and discuss the similarities and differences to promote the agreed-upon goals together.

Based on these debates, several activists suggested that CSOs should try to find common ground in every issue discussed. Accordingly, CSOs should coordinate their activities, as in the case of the commemoration of the Nakba Day or the agreement on the March of Return, which form social consensus in which CSOs work together to mark a broad agreement on these topics. Notwithstanding, participants in focus groups flagged the lack of trust on issues that are not a matter of consensus in society. They reiterated that CSOs fear not cooperating only when they know that the public will not forgive those who break the consensus. When the public itself is split on the matter discussed, CSOs allow themselves to differ. A more current example used in one of the focus groups is the opposition to the Prawer Plan and the emergency meeting of political parties and CSOs in the Negev on September 26, 2016.[15] By contrast, others said that in every issue, there will always be disagreements. Some offered the idea that cooperation is usually harder on issues that are not related to women, but the presence of women may encourage cooperation. One of the interviewees argued:

> TAMIM: I think there is a collision between CSOs, not a competition. Sometimes, when we organize an activity, we feel there is someone trying to fail us because of our party affiliation. (Baqa Al-Garbiyye, March 18, 2012)

The Relationship between CSOs and the State

The nature of the relationship between Palestinian civil society in Israel and the state was raised in all focus groups and interviews. A general observation that came through is the atmosphere of alienation and mistrust vis-à-vis the state, especially since Benjamin Netanyahu became prime minister in 1996 and returned to power in 2009. This mistrust reflects the general feelings of the Palestinian citizens, as expressed in the survey of 2016–2017. In this survey, people were asked to express their degree of trust in various institutions of the state. Graph 9 on the next page mirrors the prevailing attitudes in the PCI.

When confronted with arguments regarding the state's interest in expanding Palestinian civil society to enforce fragmentation and impose control, many participants in various focus groups disagreed. Some said that the state is not always antagonistic to Palestinian civil society. Others argued that the state tries to control civil society by dictating which CSOs will continue to exist and which will not, as the case of outlawing the CSOs affiliated with the Islamic Movement demonstrates. Another position expressed by participants was that the state is interested in empowering CSOs because

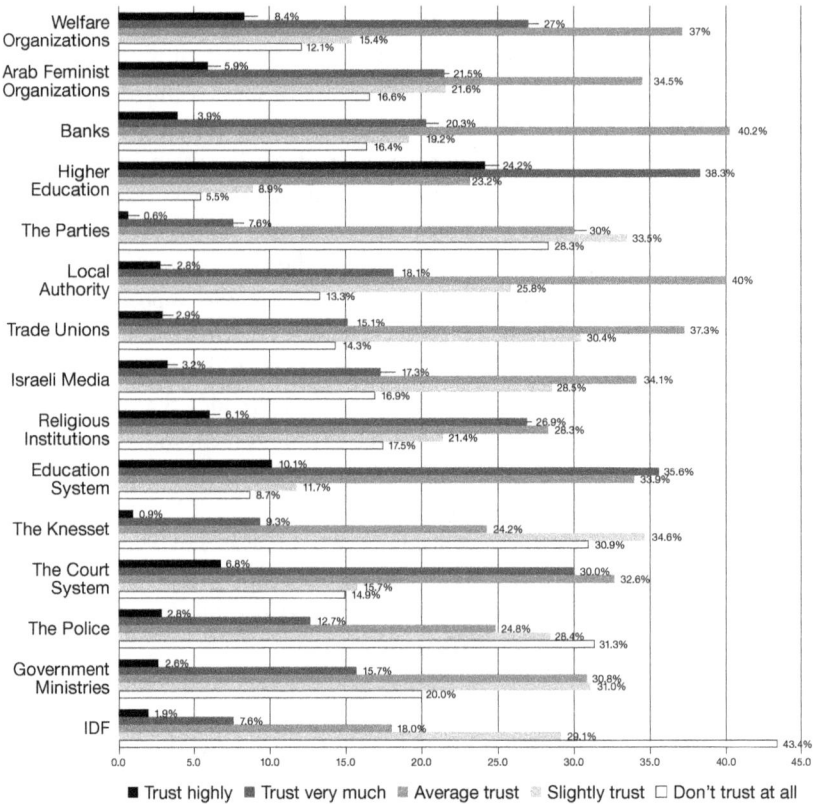

Welfare Organizations — 8.4% | 27% | 37% | 12.1% | 15.4%
Arab Feminist Organizations — 5.9% | 21.5% | 21.6% | 34.5% | 16.6%
Banks — 3.9% | 20.3% | 19.2% | 16.4% | 40.2%
Higher Education — 24.2% | 23.2% | 38.3% | 5.5% | 8.9%
The Parties — 0.6% | 7.6% | 30% | 33.5% | 28.3%
Local Authority — 2.8% | 18.1% | 25.8% | 40% | 13.3%
Trade Unions — 2.9% | 15.1% | 14.3% | 30.4% | 37.3%
Israeli Media — 3.2% | 17.3% | 16.9% | 28.5% | 34.1%
Religious Institutions — 6.1% | 26.9% | 28.3% | 21.4% | 17.5%
Education System — 10.1% | 11.7% | 8.7% | 35.6% | 33.9%
The Knesset — 0.9% | 9.3% | 24.2% | 30.9% | 34.6%
The Court System — 6.8% | 15.7% | 14.9% | 30.0% | 32.6%
The Police — 2.8% | 12.7% | 24.8% | 28.4% | 31.3%
Government Ministries — 2.6% | 15.7% | 20.0% | 30.8% | 31.0%
IDF — 1.9% | 7.6% | 18.0% | 29.1% | 43.4%

■ Trust highly ■ Trust very much ■ Average trust ▨ Slightly trust □ Don't trust at all

Graph 9.

the state itself is interested in shifting part of its responsibilities to civil society without losing the ability to determine the rules of the game and the limits of legitimate civic engagement. One of the interesting arguments made by several activists is that the state encourages the formation of CSOs to encourage society to engage in its own internal affairs.

When discussing the CSOs' role in the struggle against state policies toward the PCI, many activists questioned the CSOs' ability to effectively influence the state and change its policies. Some of the activists made this argument based on the exclusive and narrow ethnic identity of the state and the automatic majority guaranteed in all its institutions. Others made the argument that the PCI civil society lack a common strategy to deal with its challenges, and therefore it is always on the defense when it comes to dealing with state policies in various fields. These reiterated the need to develop a more strategic national plan with regard to all challenges facing the PCI. One of the activists in a focus group argued that one should be aware of the fact that large parts of the CSOs actually participate in the privatization process supporting the state's retreat and its policy of neglect.[16]

One of the interviewees expressed his fear that relying on the state means its involvement in the cultural affairs of the PCI. He argued that if the PCI prefers that the state not be involved in determining its values, it should not rely on the state for resources.[17] The example that was raised to illustrate that point is the Al-Midan theater affair. According to him, the policy of budget cuts of the Ministry of Culture based on what the theater produces is a clear illustration of the deep affinity between content and money. The ministry has always tied the budgets to a clear line of tolerance of the contents presented in the theater. When this line was passed, as in the case of the "Parallel Time" play,[18] as the ministry interpreted it, the financial support has been cut completely.[19] The state's financial support is fully tied to meeting clear conditions of loyalty and submission, as the case of the film director Suha Arraf with her film *Villa Tuma* demonstrates.[20] One of the interviewees argued that when the financial support provided by the ministry to Palestinian artists and filmmakers stipulates loyalty and deep intervention in the cultural contents produced, it becomes censorship, something that CSOs have to be aware of.[21] In this regard, participants in one of the focus groups ran this discussion:

> NAHED: The state's policy is to transform us into service providers, like women and girls' shelters. We have to compete against companies in the state's tenders. It turns us into assistance centers for girls in trouble. The state must provide these services, but it privatizes them to CSOs or companies that are listed as profitable associations. Some CSOs support, unintentionally, the state's avoidance of responsibility regarding the citizens' rights.

> SANAA: I see people who try to form CSOs in the field of art without the state's support. They don't ask for the state's support, to prevent government interference with contents. Some complain when the state supports a project—it seems to answer our demands, but in practice it's done against our will. The state distorts our needs according to its interests. I don't want the state to interfere in my business as long as it has interests of its own. (Tel Aviv, December 5, 2007)

We can see in this conversation that the discourse vis-à-vis the state is unequivocal and not ambivalent. The positions regarding the state are clear: Participants focus on the fact that the PCI is a deprived, discriminated against, and neglected minority; and an assumption that civic activism should, among other things, promote a political, financial, and social civil struggle in order to change reality. Yet there is no one voice concerning the relationship with the state.

Summary

This chapter reflects the central dilemmas faced by activists in Palestinian CSOs. It points out the complexity of the political, social, and organizational reality that these activists face. On the structural level, activists point to the legal, institutional, social, and cultural constraints that limit their ability to influence their environment. The common perception of activists is that CSOs possess a strong potential to impact the environment. This potential is not fully implemented because of the structural constraints in which they operate. There is a very high level of disappointment in state policies that not only violate the basic rights of Palestinian citizens, but also limit CSOs' ability to influence the shaping of society in which it emerged and operates. The examples used to illustrate this point are the outlawing of the CSOs affiliated with the Islamic Movement in November 2015 and the budget freeze for Al-Midan theater, also in 2015.

The social capital accumulated through the growth of civil society and the establishment of corporate networks characterized by organizational and human abilities has encountered strong legal, political, and social barriers. From the activists' point of view, one sees that there are internal limitations that have to do with the ability of civil organizations from different ideological streams to cooperate. CSOs fail to facilitate these relationships for several reasons. The organizational culture, which leads to deep personalization of CSOs, results in cooperation based on personal relations rather than common thematic issues. The phenomenon of the "founding father" of the organizations and those individuals' control of their organizations makes cooperation more of a personal matter than an organizational need, something that further drains their potential.

Chapter 10

Civic Engagement and
the Democratic Argument

To deepen our understanding of the complexities of Palestinian civil activity and to improve our insights regarding the considerations that guide the activities of those involved in this field, we carried out an opinion survey based on a questionnaire that was given to 97 civic activists who were active participants in two major consultation meetings of CSOs' leaders and activists. The purpose of these two methods was to clarify a number of issues pertaining to the personal and organizational traits of these activists and to explore the motives and considerations that guide them. As part of this endeavor, we sought to examine the level of internal democracy in their associations and the extent to which civic activism in them is consistent with what they seek to reach and demand from the state. Furthermore, we sought to explore the extent of the activists' satisfaction from their involvement in the development of society, its empowerment, and the extent to which their civic engagement is effective.

Between January and April 2008, a large number of middle-management–level activists in various CSOs were asked to fill out the opinion survey regarding the nature of their work in their associations, the nature of their associations' activities, the extent of their satisfaction, the extent to which they participate in the associations' decision-making processes, and the ways in which decisions are made in the association. The sample included a total of 97 respondents from 20 organizations (28 men, 69 women)[1] whose age ranged from 21 to 63. A total of 75.6% have an academic education, and 16% have post–high school education, such as a professional diploma or partial academic studies. The average number of years of study of the participants was 15.77. This level of education is not typical of a population in which the percentage of university graduates within it is relatively low, as we showed before. This gap reflects the elitism that characterizes civic society and that makes it something of a social, cultural, and political avant-garde. These data demonstrate the growth of the middle-class Arab elite, which has been developing in recent decades and which is having increasing effects on the cultural and political behavior of the PCI.

The participants in the consultation meetings, which took place on January 29 and March 18, 2016, were of the same social and cultural fabric. Five participants attended the two meetings. The rest of the two groups—in each group—were different people who attended either meeting. The two groups were gender diverse and included nine men and 15 women. The topics discussed during the meetings were the nationalization of Israeli politics and its impact on the activities of Palestinian CSOs and the attack on sources of CSOs funding, which threatens their mere existence.

Almost 17% of the survey participants were the original founders of their associations, whereas 81.3% were not a part of their CSOs' establishment. On average, participants began working in their associations four and a half years ago. This fact is important because it indicates the stability of the CSOs and the fact that the intergeneration handover does not impair them. Nearly 47% of the respondents work in CSOs with a secular orientation; 38.5% work in CSOs that maintain neutrality regarding religious orientation, while 14.6% work in CSOs that define themselves as religious in orientation. At this point, it is important to point out that it was difficult to interview activists of religious CSOs. This pattern repeated itself when speaking of the consultation meetings in which only secular organizations took part, despite the fact that religious organizations were invited and the challenges related to them were discussed, especially after the declaring of the Northern Branch of the Islamic Movement and the CSOs affiliated with it defined as illegal associations by the Israeli cabinet in November 2015. The main reason for this difficulty was their high level of suspicion toward any external agent collecting information about them, even if only by Palestinian scholarship. This is especially true regarding CSOs belonging to the Islamic Movement's Northern Branch. These CSOs were the victims of suspicious state policy, which carried a high price for organizations, including, for some, closure.

In order for us to carry out the survey back in 2008 among activists and associations affiliated with the Northern Branch of the Islamic Movement, we had to receive authorization from the movement's leaders. To this end, the author met with one of the leading figures in the movement to explain the research objectives.[2] Only when these were understood was limited consent given for a small number of activists to fill out the questionnaire. Any attempts to conduct personal interviews with more activists were encountered with refusal. Given these restrictions and the fact that no religious organizations participated in the two consultation meetings, most of the conclusions expressed in this chapter reflect the reality of nonreligious associations.

Nonetheless, nearly 80% of the respondents of the survey work in national associations, 13.5% in regional associations, and 7.3% in local associations operating in a specific city or village. These figures were concluded from the activists' testimonies, though all the associations selected for this study officially define themselves as national and all-inclusive.

Reasons for Participation in CSOs

One of the main points of interest in the civil society scholarship is the pattern of social mobilization and the motivations behind civilians' civic activism. In this regard, as mentioned in the theoretical framework earlier, political participation can take various forms, especially in the digital age. People can participate and be active while hiding in their air-conditioned rooms. This reality has great impact on the theory of active citizenship, which refers to the involvement of citizens in determining their fate through physical and virtual involvement in political and social processes. This means that civic engagement is a form of resistance, especially in contexts in which the constitutional order entails unequal citizenship. In such realities, civic activism means challenging the core values of the state and introducing a counter-hegemonic discourse that seeks to transform the reality in which one lives.

To examine the nature of Palestinian civic engagement in Israel, we developed several hypotheses, which are linked to the stratification and the ethnic segmentation of the Israeli labor market, to the structural barriers that prevent the integration of educated Palestinian citizens in the Israeli market or state institutions, and also to the alienation and separatism among educated Arabs and their refusal to become dependent on Jewish employers or on a state that is viewed by them as ethnically biased. In addition, we developed hypotheses concerning the desire of educated Arabs to affect change in Palestinian society or to serve as lobbyists or advocates against state institutions. An additional research hypothesis involves the issue of social capital and its impact on the characteristics of involvement of educated citizens in civic activity.

To evaluate the research hypotheses and to map the reality of the PCI, participants were presented with questions aimed at understanding the logic that motivates the activity from the activists' perspective. The research questions were divided into different topics to examine various aspects of CSOs' activities. One of the major issues that was examined was the motives for participating in civil activity. According to our interpretation, engagement in civil society associations stems from different considerations that can be divided into two main categories: pragmatic reasons related to the labor market and difficulties encountered by educated individuals in finding jobs in state institutions or with Jewish employers; and ideological considerations, which deal with the desire to contribute to the advancement of Palestinian society, defend its rights, and provide for its needs in fields where the state does not. Additionally, the drive to influence Palestinian society and to shape its image is an important consideration among civil society activists—a fact that gives more weight to the ideological consideration against the pragmatic one.

When examining the motivation behind civic activism using statistical means, including factor analysis[3] to verify the validity of the data, we found that a majority of respondents (73.4%) refused to consider pragmatic reasoning, such as lack of opportunities in the Israeli labor market as the main reason behind their civic engagement. Nonetheless, more than 50% of the respondents to the survey questions claimed that one of the motivations behind their engagement in civil associations is their avoidance of having to work for a state institution or a Jewish employer. When posing ideological considerations, such as improving the status and protecting of the rights of the PCI or the striving for the reshaping of Palestinian identity, as the main motivation behind civic activism, more than 90% of respondents affirmed that their activity comes from such considerations to a large extent or to a very large extent.

These data strongly indicate that activists in Palestinian civil society prefer occupational autonomy and independence of Jewish employers or the state, as it enables wider freedom of action. Although this inclination does not signify a desire for complete autonomy, especially in light of the fact that a large part of CSOs' financial resources are related to Jewish funds, there is still a clear desire to maintain separate spheres of civic activism. This inclination is fully asserted in the consultation meetings in which the author participated as an active observant and in the personal interviews conducted with leaders of the CSOs. Many of the participants in the meetings stated clearly that the needs and interests of the Palestinian CSOs are fundamentally different from those of Jewish CSOs. Accordingly, they stood behind the widely accepted argument that Palestinian CSOs should maintain their separate spheres of activism, despite the fact that many of them agree that this should and does not mean total separation from Israeli civil society activists. Several of the Palestinian CSOs leaders went further to argue that their commitment is fully national and they are not willing to contribute to the whitewashing efforts of many of the Israeli CSOs, which put some pressure on the Israeli state to change its policies, yet still comply with the constitutional definition of the Israeli state as Jewish and thereby indirectly commit to unequal civic status inside the Israeli power structure.

That said, it seems that many of the PCI's civil activists not only seek occupational autonomy, but also express their resistance to the normalization of their civic activism under the banner of the broader Israeli civil society. When taking into account that respondents are an educated group that, for the most part, studied in Israeli academic institutions, we can conclude that the processes of academic and professional specialization seem to reinforce their alienation from Israeli reality, which does not provide amenable conditions for integration. When looking at these data through the prism of the social capital theory, one may confidently say that as this capital increases as a resource, reflected in the ability to establish social and communicative networks, so society's willingness to resist dependency on Jewish society increases. The Palestinian civic elite seeks to promote civic networks as a form of resistance against subordination and compliance.

The opinions expressed by Palestinian civic activists in Israel reflect strong patriotic feelings and loyalty to their society. Civic activists strongly express their identification with their society, despite their dissatisfaction with many of the dominant social norms and their strong desire to reshape its character. They see themselves as leaders or agents of change, which is mirrored in their obvious day-to-day. The volume of seminars and conferences that CSOs hold is immense, as are the number of publications, reports, and petitions, which has increased over time. This development, which is clear over the last two decades, includes an obvious political dimension of their output, such as the publication of the Future Vision Documents in 2006–2007 or the Strategic Reports (I and II), published in 2016 and 2018, respectively. Whereas the Future Vision Documents sidestepped the political parties and excluded them from drafting these unmistakably ideological-political documents (Jamal, 2010), the Strategic Reports provided very thorough mapping of the possible future scenarios the PCI may have to face and the main challenges it deals with. Furthermore, one of the most pronounced manifestations of the political engagement of CSOs is their involvement in organizing national commemoration days (Sorek, 2015), particularly "Land Day,"[4] "Nakba Day,"[5] "the Marches of Return,"[6] and the memorial day for October 2000 events.[7]

Another issue that arises from the data is the desire of civil society activists to circumvent the state's direct influence on shaping the character of the PCI and to deal with day-to-day challenges independently. In fact, this is an indirect expression of disappointment and distrust in the intentions and desire of Jewish society and the state to develop Palestinian society.

Pluralization or Fragmentation— The Cooperation between CSOs

It is important to note that CSOs do not operate in a vacuum. They develop and operate within a social and a cultural environment, which has an impact on their formation and possible means of action. The affinity between CSOs, their social environment, and the relationships within it comprise an important index, which enables an understanding of its attributes and much of its social capital. A key argument in social capital theory relates to the mediating role of CSOs and their ability to create new and active service-providing networks, which are formed as a result of investing society's resources and effort. The gathering of resources to form long-term networks of contacts built on mutual social recognition is an important dimension of social capital theory (Bourdieu, 1985). Accordingly, civil-social networks do not develop naturally, but require strategic investment of society's human and material resources in order to establish relationships that did not exist previously. These are social networks, founded not on the family or the clan. This distinction between local and external fundraising in creating these new networks is an important dimension to look at.

To map the relationships between CSOs and the complex, dynamic environment in which they operate, three spheres of collaboration were addressed in the survey, the consultation meetings, and in the personal interviews; namely collaboration between and among CSOs, between CSOs and Arab political parties, and between CSOs and government institutions.[8]

A decisive majority of the survey participants (96.9%) clarified that there is collaboration between the association in which they work and other Palestinian CSOs. Most of them defined the relationship between their CSOs and other ones as either good or very good. However, a high percentage of the activists are not satisfied with the quality of the collaboration between Palestinian CSOs. That is to say, there is a strong desire to strengthen the working together of CSOs in order to have greater impact on shaping the consciousness and practices of the PCI and to mobilize it in order to protect its rights. The reasons behind the dissatisfaction with the quality of collaboration between CSOs vary. The first reason is related to the simple attitude that collaboration is not always necessary, especially if it complicates associations' activities. A second reason mentioned is the lack of sufficient womanpower and resources available to facilitate intensive cooperation. Collaboration between associations often requires setting up coordination teams to handle communication and common activities; this requires special effort. This reasoning emerged in the personal interviews and the consultative meetings. Many participants argued that because most Palestinian CSOs are small organizations, they cannot afford to allocate significant resources for this purpose. The projectal nature of CSOs' work and the total dependency on external funds that pressure them to see how the financial aid is translated into particular activities make devoting resources to invest in establishing cooperation networks a big challenge. Activists clearly stated that whereas donors encourage submitting projects in common between several CSOs, this is done for the sake of efficiency rather than genuine effort to assist in promoting networking among CSOs. This means that the limited resources provided to CSOs encourage formal cooperation, but do not necessarily lead to overcoming the competition caused by the same limited resources. One of the central points that came up in the data and explains the dissatisfaction with the quality of cooperation between CSOs has to do with the high level of personalization in the various CSOs. Thus, collaboration between CSOs is not determined by the objectives of the projects or according to the functional needs to have an impact on the environment. It is based more on the personal relationship between the individuals at the head of the organizations. Therefore, the level of cooperation is deeply impacted by personal relations, a factor that may be mixed with the personal ties known from social capital theory, but actually differs, because the entire organizational structure is submitted to relations between specific leaders. This reasoning was firmly confirmed by participants in the consultative meetings and in the personal interviews, in which leaders of CSOs stated clearly that their personal relationships play an important role in their networking policies. Furthermore, the personal tension between leaders of CSOs, including feminist ones, manifested itself during the consultation meetings, where participants criticized each other's personalizing practices.[9]

The previous reasons for explaining the level of cooperation between Palestinian CSOs are strengthened further by their political or party identity. As clarified in previous chapters, many of the Palestinian CSOs are affiliated or at least identified with political parties. Therefore, many CSO leaders admit that joint projects or initiatives are deeply influenced by this factor. This means that in cases where relations between the leaders of CSOs are good and there is a common political identity, the chance of collaboration increases. Many activists and leaders testified to this logic in the personal interviews and the consultation meetings. Even in cases where this is not stated outright, many of the CSOs' leaders and activists still admit that it is more convenient and natural to collaborate with associations with similar ideological beliefs or at least similar political background than with others.

In view of these findings, one could say generally that CSOs' activists would like to see more collaboration between the various associations. Many have regarded interorganizational collaboration as both functional and ethical. It is perceived as functional because it increases the associations' chances of success in realizing their aims and objectives. It is also functional because it provides a positive model for other social agents to follow. It is also viewed as ethical, for there is an added value in its existence, because it brings up the need to deliberate the justifications for the various actions taken by CSOs. These deliberations resonate in establishing new norms that either differ from the traditional ones or adapt the latter to the new circumstances under which the PCI has to live. Many argued that collaborating reinforces the feeling of belonging and the common fate of the associations in particular and of the PCI in general. There is an identity-cultural notion, derived from much of the data extracted from the personal interviews and the consultative meetings. The raising of social cohesion is a value in itself in the eyes of leaders and activists with relatively high social and political awareness, something that begs the gap elaborated by Sharabi (1988) between the external structure of social organizations in Arab societies and their internal cultural norms and habits, which sustain old traditional culture that stands in contrast to the impression made by the external structure. Whereas CSOs are modern organizations that function based on formal rules and have to meet clear legal formalities, the internal dynamics and the forms of communication inside them are still deeply influenced by cultural habits that characterize family ties and clan commitments.

Practicing Democracy and the Challenging of Social and State Authority

Another important issue that has occupied researchers in the field of civic activism is the intraorganizational environment of CSOs, particularly the degree of democracy practiced within them and its implications on their practices and achievements. This interest is based on the widespread theory that CSOs contribute to society's democratization and are a major sociopolitical agent for greater civic engagement in the public sphere. Tocquevillian ideas characterize most of the writing on CSOs and their contribution to maintaining the citizens' sovereignty over their own lives (de Tocqueville, 1961). Many CSOs studies assume the importance of social capital theory, which views CSOs as capital invested in promoting society's democracy and in addressing social needs (Portes, 1998). It follows that alongside the representative and pluralistic dimension of CSOs' existence there is a practical dimension, which is reflected in the social capital invested in promoting society's needs and democracy. That said, one can add the contribution made by postcolonial scholars concerning the oppositional dimension of CSOs and their resistance to the dominant political structure (Kaviraj & Khilnani, 2001). According to this understanding, it becomes crucial that CSOs restructure social and political relations when seeking to resist the distribution of authority in their environment. Along the lines presented in the theoretical framework, in which civil society in the postcolonial context is understood in political terms, it becomes crucial to follow the modes of engagement and practices envisaged by civic activists when seeking to transform their social environment as well as challenge state authority.

For the sake of clarifying the practices of civic activists and the outcomes of their resistance to state authority, our surveys, meetings, and personal interviews with CSOs and the PCI provide data on the patterns of organizational conduct within CSOs and in their relationship with their environment. One can make the distinction between two kinds of organizational democracy—internal and external. The first kind relates to the degree of the activists' involvement in managing the association and its activities, and the second relates to the relationship between the CSOs and their target audience.

It is possible to speak of a number of indicators to measure the degree of internal democracy within CSOs, including the degree of cooperative management, the accessibility of the associations' leaders to activists, the latter's familiarity with the activities of their CSO, and their degree of involvement in the decision-making processes in their association. The survey data present a clear picture of the high degree of involvement, accessibility, and power sharing in Palestinian CSOs. That said, it is important to note that the data show an important difference between the degree of involvement and accessibility to information by activists and the degree of power sharing in decision making. The gap between these indicators is significant. Whereas 94.8% of respondents said that their association is managed cooperatively, 96.8% state that they have direct access to the association's leader, 99% said that they are familiar with all the activities taking place in their association, and only 68.4% of the respondents answered positively when asked about the degree of their involvement in determining policy-making decisions in their CSO. An non-negligible percent (30.6%) of civic activists in the survey testified that they are involved only to a small extent or not at all in decision making in their CSO. These data may lead to the distinction made by activists between the availability of information to all members of the association and the decision-making procedures. One may argue that these procedures are set, at least in part, by the CSO Law, according to which policy decisions are made by the association's management. Nonetheless, one cannot ignore the significant gap between the flow of information and activists' familiarity with the activities of their CSOs. Whereas activists participate in CSOs to demand their social, political, and legal rights from the state, these same rights are not granted to them within their own organizations. One of the interviewees stated clearly that in her organization, the gap between the external discourse and the internal practices is tremendous.[10] This topic was discussed in one of the focus groups and was also reflected in much of the survey data.

One of our most important findings is that civic activists see a strong correlation between the degree of internal democracy in their CSOs and the ability of these civic organizations to achieve their objectives. Thus, the more highly the activists evaluate the level of internal democracy in their CSOs, the more highly they evaluate the success of their association in achieving its objectives.[11] What is puzzling in this context is that no significant differences were found between secular and religious civil activists when it came to their evaluation of the relationship between internal organizational democracy and the effectiveness of CSOs in achieving their goals. The aspirations of civic activists and their opinions of their CSOs' intraorganizational democracy are important indications that the degree of power sharing in CSOs is not fully satisfactory, something that harms the ability of CSOs to achieve their objectives.

In other words, it seems that intraorganizational democratic practices, especially when it comes to decision making, have not only an ethical significance, but also a practical and even utilitarian importance. A more democratic association increases the chances that activists contribute more to its success and the achievement of its objectives. Hierarchical organizational structures and inflexible management disempower civic activists and CSOs' ability to achieve their objectives.

This conclusion was supported by our survey of the civic activists. In it, activists attribute a high level of significance to the broader public's degree of involvement in determining the fields and degrees of CSOs' civic activism. As such, three-quarters of the respondents testified that their association develops special tools to examine the needs of its social environment and to adapt itself accordingly, and that it has indeed changed its objectives, aims, or policy in view of its examination of the environment's needs. Activists attached a high level of importance to responding to the demands and needs of their associations' target audience. This responsiveness to the preferences of the social environment is an important variant in understanding CSOs democratic aspirations and the way they treat the public's needs and demands as representative of a public will.

Summary

This chapter identifies a significant gap between the desire and the ability of civic activists to change and influence their environment and the options granted to them to do so. There is a desire and willingness among civic activists to be involved in influencing their environment. There is also strong organizational patriotism and thus a sense of citizenship in the sense that individuals are willing to contribute to improving the quality of life of society. This patriotism is countered by the hostility of the state, and hence the degree of their willingness to cooperate with state institutions is particularly low. There is also a suspicion toward the external environment, particularly toward the state and its institutions. Civic activists demonstrate that organizations have structural difficulties, which are expressed not only in relations with the state, but also with funding sources and their own society. They also testify to the importance of a positive correlation between internal organizational democracy and the ethical power they have to resist state policies of discrimination and repression.

Chapter 11

CSOization, Democratization, Empowerment, and Development

CSOization—Image and Reality

The basic hypothesis of liberal literature, particularly the literature based on the Tocquevillian legacy, is that voluntary organizations support civil society because of their ideals and their democratic and cooperative attitude (Kaviraj & Khilnani, 2001). According to this theory, we must defend the strong and pluralist civil society against the state's power. CSOs are the avant-garde of defending civil society, as they legitimize and promote a diversity of lifestyles and worldviews. Civic organizations are considered a major agent of social mobilization and political change. Civil society as a whole is thus considered an important tool for preventing the state from exploiting its power for negative purposes and preventing authoritarian forces from gaining control of the political system. It is also important for encouraging citizens' participation and turning the state's behavior into a subject for public debate. CSOs, as part of civil society, strengthen the institutional sphere, providing opportunities for various social groups to speak out and serving as a "watchdog" against the state. Moreover, these organizations can lead a unified revolution, where one or more organizations will engage in public interests' issues. The networking process of CSOs encourages the pluralization of civil society by enlarging its number of active voices versus the state and creating a buffer between the state and its citizens. This buffer is important for the individual's autonomy in her search for a better life.

According to the CSO Registrar, there are 3,895 registered CSOs, of which only 829 are active. When compared to the 43,714 registered

CSOs in Israel, of which 14,810 are active, we find that the PCI's level of institutionalization is very low. Active Palestinian CSOs are only 0.055% of Israel's total active CSOs. Given that the PCI is 20% of the Israeli population, one can say with confidence that this number of Palestinian CSOs supports the argument that CSOization is not really valid in the case of the PCI. These data counter the impression that many large CSOs have managed to create, which is that they are many and central to the PCI. This insight is even more true when we consider that many of these organizations are in fact businesses, which provide services or address society's needs, as the state has since privatized services like daycare centers, housing for people with special needs, sports association, and others. It is correct that the existing CSOs reflect an important trend of institutionalization, which might have significant implications on Palestinian society's accumulation of social capital and its social and political culture. Notwithstanding this fact, most Palestinian CSOs are small and operate with very low budgets that do not allow them to seriously impact their environment. However, it seems that many CSOs, especially the advocacy, lobbying, and human rights organizations, are successful in capturing the attention of the media or more accurately portraying themselves as political. As a result, they have garnered the attention of the government and many radical Zionist political parties. This attention creates an image that is much stronger than the real presence of the CSOs on the ground. It is important to note that these insights are not intended to belittle the contribution of CSOs, but to correct the exaggerated impression they have made in the media and to provide a realistic view of their presence, activities, and impact.

CSOs and Democratization

CSOs are formed to address the needs and interests of citizens' groups and increase the number of voices that pressure the government to acknowledge these needs. The rise in the number of Palestinian CSOs since the early 1990s marked Palestinian society's pluralization. The variety of mandates, tasks, and strategic objectives cultivated by these organizations is vast. Some CSOs work in development, advocacy, social mobilization, and service provision. There are also many specialized CSOs in the fields of welfare, education, law, housing, public health, and religion. The ideological and political orientations of these organizations vary widely. Their diversity undoubtedly contributes to the legitimacy of various social, cultural, and political causes in society.

Furthermore, the increasing number of CSOs, especially secular organizations like human rights and women's organizations, contributes greatly to Palestinian society's internal democratization. The growing number of Palestinian CSOs, especially advocacy organizations, encourages tolerance and internal dialogue between each other and the social groups they represent. Despites their differences, Palestinian CSOs have managed to present social, political, and cultural patterns of behavior that reinforce and emphasize this diversity. Different organizations collaborate on a number of projects, despite their differences. These patterns are vastly different from the organization of tribal society typical of the PCI and from the relationships common between leading Arab political parties.

CSOs provide a number of services, among which is informal democratic socialization. The number of conferences, which has grown substantially over the last several years, is a reflection of CSOs' prominence in this area. In general, we can say that there is at least one public event held by a Palestinian CSO in Israel almost every week, whether it address housing, health, media, art, or music. Conferences and cultural events are held most often in the larger cities in the Galilee, the Triangle, and the Naqab, though some occur in smaller villages and towns. Through these events, Palestinian CSOs open new frontiers of debate among the Palestinian public. One of the examples that illustrates these efforts is the set of 12 roundtables organized by I'lam Center in 2017, in which experts and the public were invited to discuss the PCI's challenges and the strategies needed to address them. Tens of people participated in these discussions, which culminated in the publication of the Second Strategic Report in August 2018. Another example is the highly attended yearly conference of the Arab Center for Alternative Planning. This CSO tackles the issue of planning and housing in the PCI. These events enable many sectors of the Palestinian population to engage in discussions of public interest vis-à-vis the state or within Palestinian society. One of the most prominent issues currently being debated in the PCI is women's status in society and culture, as well as changes in gender relations. These issues are also deeply entrenched in debates between community associations with religious tendencies, as well as many secular organizations.

This debate also reflects the large gaps between the lifestyles of different Palestinian communities. Underprivileged groups, such as the elderly, children, and people with disabilities, are also discussed. For example, Al-Manarah, which addresses the needs and advocacy of people with special needs, hosts many conferences on topics relating to state and society. These discussions open the door for collective thinking and reflection regarding society's priorities for facing these populations' challenges, as well as discussions regarding their basic needs like health, education, housing, and so forth. By arranging these debates and presenting different positions regarding their social and cultural challenges, these CSOs automatically rule out conservative and absolute concepts regarding the nature of the ideal social order and raise various alternatives. This is an important step in revealing the relativity of truth, the common good, or the desired social order. Such discussions challenge the patriarchal, conservative social structure in Palestinian towns and villages and bring about initiatives that have a transformative impact on society, even if is not necessarily observed in the short term.

Moreover, the variety of Palestinian CSOs reflects a rise in the number and range of attempts to examine state policy and challenge official decisions that hurt the PCI. At the same time, these CSOs and their activities come to replace the areas of need that are neglected by the state, such as childcare, health, religion, and so forth. CSOs have created a fundamental associative transformation, connected groups of intellectuals and social-political activists from different backgrounds, and thus join new social energies by empowering the PCI in its various social and political positions. These associations increased the number of voices speaking out against the state's negligence and promoted sophisticated and well-organized public expression. The amount of knowledge and data provided by CSOs regarding Palestinian society and the state's policy in different areas like education, health, welfare, infrastructure, planning, construction, and so forth is enormous. These data are published and disseminated widely in books, journals, leaflets, and other publications. Many CSOs' websites provide the public with information that was previously inaccessible; together these data empower organizations and support their ability to argue against the state and demand more rights. Even if these efforts do not lead to an immediate change in state policies or even draw a negative reaction by the state, this is an impact that cannot be ignored.

These voices together unite in protest and apply significant pressure to decision makers. Furthermore, these CSOs create a buffer zone between the state and its Palestinian citizens and prevent unfair and disproportionate treatment. Palestinian CSOs raise the PCI's awareness of the state's abuse of power, place these issues on national and international agendas, and confront decision makers who are obliged to consider this population when developing new policy. These particular actions of CSOs have gained prominence in public discourse over the last few years. The best evidence of this reputation is the information brought to the EU headquarters in Brussels or the OECD institutions. Both organizations have leverage and can influence Israel's policy toward its Palestinian minority and are well aware of Israel's activities because of it.

To illustrate this point, we note Adalah's work in the High Court that led to a groundbreaking ruling. On February 27, 2006, seven judges ruled unanimously that the state's decision regarding "national priority areas" should be changed,[1] because this decision discriminates against Israel's Palestinian citizens based on race and national affiliation. The High Court ruled that the definition of "national priority areas" should be canceled, particularly with regard to educational resources, because no clear and systematic criteria were set for allocating resources, thus leading to its discrimination against Palestinian citizens (Decision no. 2288). The High Court gave the Ministry of Education one year to change its policy and deemed it unconstitutional in its present state. This victory is an indicator of CSOs' influence in many arenas, even those most inhospitable to the PCI. Adalah's success in eradicating a widespread government policy is only one such example of the role of Palestinian CSOs and their influence on the state's democratization. Another example of the influence of CSOs on the state's democratization has to do with the issue of planning and development. The Arab Center for Alternative Planning managed to change the state's plans for the development of Road 6 in northeast Israel. These plans would have significantly infringed on Arab landowners' rights. In this case, the impact of their work was substantial, as it forced the state to approve an outline and new development plans for Palestinian villages after stalling for many years.

Another example is I'lam's and Adalah's success in 2015 to stop the Second Broadcasting Authority for TV and Radio from limiting the broadcasts of the Arab radio station Ashams. In this case, the Israeli government asserted that Ashams may not broadcast its regular programming on the Yom Kippur Jewish holiday. The two organizations argued that because Ashams's audience is the Arab population and because Jewish citizens do not listen to the radio on this holiday, the order to silence Ashams, based on the argument that it should respect the sentiment of Jewish citizens, is unconstitutional. Both I'lam and Adalah argued that such an order violates the collective rights of the Arab community—and they won.

Yet, as described in the theoretical background, we must be cautious when exploring CSOs' contribution to the state's democratization. Socially, we witness a prolonged struggle between secular and religious associations. We also acknowledge the trend of religiosity and social conservatism, which have been common in Palestinian society in recent decades. These trends are not necessarily undemocratic, but they have a serious impact on the pluralistic fabric of society and can promote intolerance toward and denigrate women's status (Abu-Baker, 2009). There have been efforts made by many religious CSOs to mobilize the public against activities they considered unacceptable to their community's social norms. One such examples is the letter sent by Mirsad and the Al-Fahmawi Initiative to the Ministry of Culture to stop screening the film *In Between*. In their view, the film, which dealt with internal affairs and relationships between youth of both sexes in Arab society, harmed the feelings of the Arabs and Muslims.[2]

Statewise, we witness anticivic and antidemocratic tendencies leading to policies that damage Palestinian citizens' status and strive to limit their political leeway. Laws like the Boycott Law, the amendments to the Defamation Law, the Citizenship Law, the Civil Organizations Law, the Nakba Law, and the Nation-State Law, all enacted in the last decade, are a clear indication of their undemocratic tendencies. Furthermore, there has been no significant or real change in resource distribution and the state's policy toward its Palestinian citizens.[3] Even when public statements are made to this effect, the general trend is to continue the policy of discrimination and negligence. Even when the Court's judgment, as in the case of the "Priority Areas," has been favorable, we know that the government's policy has not been seriously changed, and other ways were found to continue the same policy of discrimination despite court orders.

Regarding civil engagement, we identify a trend of regression in the rate of Palestinian citizens' participation in civic activities, which are designed to increase their influence on decision-making processes. Generally, we can say that CSOs' advances have indirectly decreased citizens' willingness to engage in social issues, particularly regarding the distribution of public resources and in defining their lifestyle. This trend correlates with Yishai's (2008) argument presented earlier in this book: that everyday citizens retreat from taking responsibility for their future not because of the ineffectiveness of their engagement but because they rely on CSOs to do the work for them.

One of the questions that comes to mind in this context is why CSOs are not always successful in raising support. To clarify this matter and to attempt to explain the limitations of CSOs in influencing democratization processes, five related issues are discussed.

A. When it comes to creating political change that leads to democratization, the intentions of the state are important for assessing the CSO's contribution to democratization. The State of Israel is an ethnic national state, which angles for ways to diffuse the demands of CSOs using an equal allocation policy and, in addition, bypassing requests to integrate more Arabs into the decision-making process. While the state does negotiate with Palestinian CSOs and considers their requests on the formal level, these considerations are characterized by self-justifications for preserving or even expanding its discriminatory policy. In an attempt to avoid dealing with the challenges or demands of the Palestinian CSOs in various fields, many state institutions respond unreasonably and even mistreat CSOs that force them to seek creative solutions. The attitudes of relevant government agencies to the policies of development, planning, and construction; media policies; allocation of resources to development areas determined by the state, and more reflect Israel's unresponsiveness to demands raised by Palestinian CSOs such as Adalah, the Arab Center for Alternate Planning, Mossawa, I'lam, the Follow-Up Committee for Arab Education, and others.

The government's policy in relation to Palestinian CSOs is reflected best in the policy adopted to circumvent and bypass court rulings in cases where these rulings promote equal rights for Palestinian citizens, as in the case known as the *Qa'adan* Family case.[4] Even though Palestinian CSOs can always appeal to the Supreme Court, the state's reaction tells us how the government seeks to override court rulings. Another example of state policies towards Palestinian CSOs is the state's attempt to block the activity of the National Committee for the Rights of the Internally Displaced Palestinians in Israel, which seeks to promote the rights of the 300,000 internal refugees who are still fighting for their property since the passage of the Absentee Law.[5] Another example is the declaration made by the state of many traditional and religious sites, such as mosques and cemeteries from the pre-1948 era, as closed military zones, thereby preventing efforts to preserve them. Al-Aqsa Association is one such organization that has been unable to fulfill its mission in this regard. These examples illustrate that while civic activity raises awareness of issues and antidemocratic tendencies, they do not necessarily manage to change state policies. And, in states with clear ethnic characteristics, the government is likely to view CSOs as an existential threat, which reinforces the state's policy of discrimination and strengthens antidemocratic trends, as we have witnessed in recent years. In such cases, state institutions run an all-out battle against human rights organizations and consider them a threat to its position. This phenomenon has led to legislation aimed at limiting the leeway of those CSOs that promote human rights, while strengthening CSOs with political tendencies or nationalist worldviews, like the Kohelet Policy Forum, Institute for Zionist Strategies, NGO Monitor, and others.

B. Another aspect of this explanation deals with the influence of CSOs on democratization, which are in turn influenced by donors. Although Palestinian CSOs were not founded as a result of an external schema and are in fact associations that operate separately from the main political arena out of necessity, this does not necessarily mean that they are immune to falling into this "trap." Given that a significant amount of financial support for Palestinian CSOs, except for Islamic ones, comes from Western countries, the relationship between the political agenda of these sources and the government's policy must be taken into account. The support afforded to Palestinian CSOs falls within the stipulations of what is allowed and what is forbidden by the state, which are set by the state's objectives. In recent years, the issue of external support has become a policy challenge of the Israeli government, and many proclaim that the limits and conditions allowed for outside agencies to provide funding for CSOs in Israel is too extensive. The amendments to the Civil Organizations Law, presented earlier in this book, came to restrict this support and establish political and ethical criteria for it, in clear contrast with the declarations made by the government about its commitment to civil society and freedoms.

Regardless of this development, external support for CSOs does allow Israel to evade responsibility for the Palestinian community without forcing the state to pay the price for sacrificing its tolerance and its democratic advantage. The government's detachment from its responsibilities toward the PCI is compensated for by CSOs. The government thus profits twice, first because it is "exempted" from providing services and, secondly, that even when doing so, it is not considered to be abandoning its civilians. Moreover, the state also uses the fact that these services are provided by the CSOs to emphasize its level of democracy and tolerance, and even to showcase its support for the empowerment of its citizens. This position exempts the state from its responsibility for its citizens and puts it into the hands of the CSOs that are legally dependent on the state yet do not receive any financial support, for only 1.7% of Arab CSOs are contracted by governmental offices to conduct projects in the PCI, and only 25.2% receive some funding from the state.

This is a control pattern that illustrates the fundamental idea behind the concept of "governmentality," as coined by French philosopher Michel Foucault, when he spoke about control through increased supervision by state institutions in the ever-growing areas of civic life (Foucault, 1991). Foucault (2003) explains the complexity of control and power:

> If power were never anything but repressive, if it never did any-thing but say no, do you really think one would be brought to obey it? What makes power hold good, what makes it accepted, is simply the fact that it doesn't only weigh on us a force that says no; it also traverses and produces things, it induces pleasure, forms knowledge, produces discourse. It needs to be considered as a productive network that runs through the whole social body, much more than as a negative instance whose function is repression. (307)

According to this perception, the citizens' sense of freedom to act, espe-cially if they are active in a civic association, legitimizes the state's ability to monitor their activities and to become a "benefactor" looking out for their interests and saving them from themselves.

C. In their classic book *The Civic Culture*, Gabriel Almond and Sidney Verba claim that "pluralism, even if not explicitly political pluralism, may indeed be one of the most important foundations of political democracy" (Almond & Verba, 1963, 319–320). Despite this assertion, society's pluralization and diversification can actually reveal fragmentation that can become fertile ground for devastating competition, especially when the state views internal division as a tool for control. As can be seen with Palestinian CSOs, there is considerable division between secular and Islamic CSOs. Each of these sectors operates separately and even boycotts the other in some cases, either on an individual basis or on the basis of affiliation.

Many prominent Palestinian CSOs are affiliated with political parties, a fact that is usually accompanied by pressures that often impair their abilities to promote change in their community. And while internal competition between Palestinian CSOs can be constructive, it can also have negative consequences: More energy and resources are invested in managing these internal conflicts than in developing a pluralistic civil society. Thus, the relationship between CSOs is one based on constructive competition on the one hand, but on the philosophy of boycott on the other. Collaboration between CSOs tends to go hand in hand with the CSOs' political-ideological affiliation whenever such collaboration exists.

Such combinations indeed allow for the development of structured pluralism, but they do not necessarily simultaneously allow for the devel-opment of civil and cultural pluralism as part of standard norms. If we accept Almond and Verba's concepts for judging Palestinian civic reality in Israel, we can say that these are the beginnings of civic culture, but it is not necessarily resistant to competitive pressures, especially ideological ones. The spread of religious political culture that is committed to stringent religious norms and values is contrary to the culture of debate and pluralistic diversity and creates a clear barrier to interorganizational collaboration due to normative and ideological disputes. As a result, one can generalize that structured pluralism in Palestinian civil society cannot circumvent or diminish the power of the tribal political culture that is inherent in the PCI. This is not to dismiss the contribution that many Palestinian CSOs make to the development of forums for the discussion and deliberation of topics that were previously considered taboo, such as the status of women, sexuality, and single-parent families. The contributions of women's organizations to the dialogue regarding the status of women and their rights, or to the rights of the handicapped, are important and fundamental. There is no doubt that these new areas of discussion exhibit a profound change compared to the past, and compared to societies in many other Arab countries. However, there remains a large gap between debate and real change. New trends in society pose new challenges that make it more difficult for CSOs to promote the normalization of human rights, which neutralizes gender in civil status. The strengthening religious movement represents a solid, conservative worldview that makes it difficult to promote pluralism, tolerance, and the autonomy of the individual, especially when that individual is a woman.

D. The personalization of CSOs is another important phenomenon that impairs their role as democratization agents. As Hadenius and Uggla (1996) claimed: "Traditional norms, rituals and patterns of authority are part of the reason why a strong and viable civil society is absent in many Third World Countries" (1625). Although one should not expect that rooted social norms, behavior, and sociocultural values will absolutely change for the development of civil society, some features and communication norms have been developed so that civil society can promote tolerance, compromise, and respect for opposing opinions (Diamond, 1994).

When considering Palestinian civil society in Israel, one can perceive how traditional norms still control many CSOs, such as the personalization of the CSO itself. Personalization of institutions and leadership roles is not unique to Palestinian society. This trend has persisted throughout history and continues to exist at different levels in different parts of the world, including Israel. However, in general, its importance in shaping politics, especially that of public institutions, began to fade in modern times with the spread of democratic forms of government and the influence of modern media (Deutsch, 1966; Mutz, 1998). Despite the fact that this process partly took place in Palestinian society, the identification of public institutions, such as political parties and CSOs, with certain leaders is still widespread.

The personal imprint of leadership in Palestinian CSOs is still a common phenomenon. When examining large, dynamic CSOs in the PCI, we can see that most associations' leaders have been in their role for an extended time and, in some cases, a decade or more. If the leader of an association is part of its establishment, a guardianship phenomenon develops, the centrality of which in decision-making processes and organizational activity is hard to ignore. On another level, another common pattern can be identified, whereby leaders control the decision-making process and impose their will on the association.

This pattern is true for some of the feminist organizations and is especially prominent in religiously oriented associations. In some of the feminist organizations, the identification of the director of the organization with a leading figurehead in society is reflected in the total dependence of the organization on that figure and the inability of activists in it to acquire any autonomy themselves. This reality restricts the contribution of CSOs in establishing civic culture and harms their ability to fight against patriarchal patterns of authority. In such cases, internal debate is muted, and the gap between discourse and action becomes evident. In some cases, this gap can lead to the fragmentation of the CSO and to a loss of its legitimacy in the public's eyes. Indeed, it is impossible to make a general argument that all CSOs are managed in this fashion, but this leadership pattern exists in many, including those that ostensibly speak for human rights, law, and justice.

There is no doubt that this pattern can be attributed to the establishment stage and the culture of the founding fathers that characterize enterprises of various forms, including states. The ability of CSOs to overcome this pattern and produce an administrative model and a power structure that can serve as a role model to society and bring about its democratization is a crucial indicator. A lack of open and transparent internal discourse in CSOs is expressed in religious organizations belonging to the Islamic Movement, where decision making is rigid and based on a clear, authoritative hierarchy; every pronouncement or decision made by the highest echelons of the movement must be accepted and pervades its various associations.[6]

Alongside this phenomenon, we also identify the existence of extensive discourse in many CSOs on matters regarding their internal democracy and patterns of control and leadership. Personal interviews have indicated that many leaders are well aware of this challenge and invest much effort in dealing with the personalization of their organization. In some associations, new organizational and power-sharing dynamics are being developed, not only allowing the functional division of roles and responsibilities within the organization, but also establishing consultation circles that allow employees at various levels to be an integral part of the decision-making processes.

E. The patriarchal social structure of society is another factor that must be considered when examining the role of CSOs in the democratization of society (Kandiyoti, 1991). This factor is especially important regarding the influence of feminist CSOs on women's rights in society. Although some feminist CSOs seek to promote women's rights and change traditional behavior patterns, their influence on Palestinian society is not very profound, and there is a large gap between the discourse and the debate on these issues. It is important to note that some feminist CSOs are traditional and operate according to the Islamic *shari'ah*. Other secular CSOs knowingly avoid dealing directly with any conflict regarding prevailing social and cultural norms. Furthermore, there is considerable social resistance to the efforts made by women's organizations, especially when it involves women in key social roles or who defend their autonomy as individuals and their right for free movement. The waves of Islamization, which have characterized Palestinian society over the past two decades, have limited feminists' efforts in creating a more liberal society, to the point that these efforts are only symbolic (Shalhoub-Kevorkian, 2007).

Nonetheless, it is important to point out that the contribution of feminist CSOs in embedding norms and behavioral patterns into society is in stark contrast to the usual patterns in Palestinian society. The importance of battered women's shelters, for example, and despite their very small numbers, stems from the fact that the responsibility for the care of these women has been removed from the family sphere, and an alternative has been introduced that challenges patriarchal authority.

Additionally, it is important to mention the insistence of feminist organizations that women fully participate in the public sphere, ranging from demonstrations and protests, or in the job market. Feminist CSOs are working for women's integration into the labor market, based on the idea that the financial independence of the woman is an important factor in her personal emancipation and her ability to cope with her subjugation to traditional social structures and norms. In recent years, there has been a growing number of such projects. Concurrently, these organizations and initiatives encourage the development and strengthening of business culture among CSOs in particular and society in general. The activity of these organizations serves a neoliberal policy that is tested by measuring production power, labor market involvement, and productivity. Many CSOs contribute to what Yael Yishai (2008) termed "the separation of civil society from its basic values."

CSOs and Empowerment

Empowerment is perceived as one of civil society's major contributions. When reading the literature on CSOs, we see that there is a basic assumption that these organizations expand the individual's or collective's choices and enable them to translate their choice into effective actions (Mercer, 2002). CSOs are required to provide information for those who are interested in them—information that is necessary to expand their political opportunities, both socially and geographically. CSOs are also required to provide missing information in order to expose a discriminating governmental policy and to increase the personal and organizational engagement in the public sphere. They are also expected to increase the representation of marginalized social segments in the public sphere and lead campaigns in favor of the marginalized groups and try to influence the public policy toward them. CSOs are also expected to challenge the state's power by developing a string of alternative political concepts and supervising the state's activities. These roles of CSOs empower civil society by increasing the number of mediating organizations between the citizens and the state (Fisher, 1998).

When looking at the Palestinian CSOs in Israel, we can see that most of the roles described in the literature are only their aspirations. Yet some CSOs do empower individuals and groups within Palestinian society and improve their decision-making processes by providing them with necessary information. Many CSOs have developed special skills for investigating their field of action. Women Against Violence, for instance, is a feminist CSO that provided shelters for abused women in the past and still provides help for women who face social problems, such as domestic violence and repression. The CSO has extensively researched Palestinian society's attitudes toward women and their social roles in order to provide useful information that can then facilitate change (Ghanim, 2005). I'lam researched the issue of media consumption in Palestinian society (Jamal, 2006c) and provided two Strategic Reports that address the main challenges facing the PCI. Mada Al-Carmel writes on Palestinians' attitudes to a variety of social and political issues (Mada Al-Carmel, 2004; Rouhana, 2007). The Galilee Society created a social index that provided extensive information regarding the characteristics and limited development of Palestinian society. The Society provides extensive information on two central topics: health and the environment. This information is not made available by any other source, including government institutions. Mossawa Center published widely regarding budget issues and discrimination and racism against Palestinian citizens (Mossawa, 2009). The Arab Center for Alternative Planning published studies on issues of planning and construction, as well as the policy of expropriation of land. It became a very central source of information, empowerment, and mobilization in the field of housing. Adalah continuously publishes items about various legal issues, from civil and political rights to land and employment rights. The CSO Baladna published an extensive study about Palestinian youth, providing information that was never before available.

These and other CSOs maintain their own mailing lists and publish pamphlets, booklets, and more. This information published by Palestinian CSOs became vitally important for Palestinian citizens, as well as Arab political parties, in pressuring the political system to change its public policy on key issues. One of the best examples is Mossawa's coverage of the government's budget and its implications for Palestinian society. Another example is the information provided by the Arab Center for Alternative Planning regarding housing and the state's planning policy and its implication for Palestinian society; for instance, the plan to expand the residence area in the Jewish city of Nazareth (Nof Hagalil) in order to stop the development of the Arab village of Ein Mahel (*Kul al-Arab*, October 25, 2007).

An important example of the key role of Palestinian CSOs in empowering society is the extended educational programs developed by Arab human rights CSOs for Arab schools. As part of HRA's programming, elementary and secondary school students are familiarized with human rights discourse and develop an awareness of their fundamental rights as human beings and citizens. The program's objective is to empower students and increase their awareness of the gaps between reality and notions of basic human and civil rights. This kind of mission reflects the desire to promote a more just community and empowers growing parts of society not only by teaching them their rights, but also by presenting ways for them to achieve those rights.

This program teaches human ideals like freedom, equality, and individual autonomy. Thus, students are more aware of the rights owed to them by the state and also of oppressive ideals within conservative Palestinian society.

Another educational program was developed by the outlawed Islamic association Iqraa, which developed special centers designed to assist Palestinian students to prepare for their exams (Agbaria & Mustafa, 2012). These centers offer special courses, preparing high school students for their university studies. The association was also active on university campuses, trying to assist students. These kinds of activities are designed to empower Palestinian youth and create what Rabinowitz (2001) described as a special model of civil society, developed by the Islamic Movement.

However, cooperation between Islamic and secular associations is rather limited (ibid.). The empowerment and development activities of Islamic CSOs are meant to increase the movement's political and ideological power. Both branches of the Islamic Movement desire to create an ideal society, which might contradict the norms of liberal freedom and equality. In interviews with activists in the Islamic Movement, many expressed their satisfaction with the fact that the state does not fulfill its duties in areas like education. The state thereby enables the movement to establish its own education system. The fundamental link between development and conservative, nonliberal ideology opposes the objectives and interests of many secular CSOs, especially those involved in human rights and feminist issues.

The competition over resources is much fiercer between secular CSOs, as they are all supported by the same European and U.S. funds. According to some activists, this tension led to cases of "industrial espionage," when some CSOs caused others to lose their funding sources by leaking false information or "stealing" ideas and programs, which were presented as original ideas. This competition creates segregation among CSOs, thus blocking the possibility for positive and constructive communication. Because every association does its own fundraising and creates its own projects, each focuses on its own interests, and the result is a narcissistic, competitive culture. Instead of networking, which does exist between some organizations, we witness an atomization of civil society; thus, Palestinian civil society often obeys the rules of a competitive market, even in cases when each association has its own positive civic objective.

We also discovered fragmentation in the aspect of geography. Palestinian society resides in three areas that are almost completely separate from each other—the Galilee, the Triangle, and the Negev. The most developed CSOs are centered in the Galilee, especially in the three large cities—Haifa,

Nazareth, and Shfar'am—and their surroundings in which we find 62% of all Palestinian CSOs in Israel. Only 14% of Palestinian CSOs are located in the Triangle, 5.5% in the Negev, 17.5% in mixed cities, and 1.1% in other places in the center of the country.

The gap between the number, size, and activity scale of CSOs in these three areas is huge. Almost all Palestinian CSOs in Israel are centered in Galilee, except for those affiliated with the Islamic Movement, whose center is in Umm Al-Fahm, one of the largest Arab towns in the north part of the Triangle. These gaps lead to a certain tension and competition between the different areas, as well as to pluralization of some and negligence of others. The gaps between the Galilee and the Negev are enormous. In fact, most nationwide CSOs, which established offices or expanded their activities to the Negev, had to close their offices or retreat from their activities in this area. The only association left with an office in the Negev is Adalah, which also faces tense relationships with local associations and activists. The Regional Council of Unrecognized Villages (RCUV) has repeatedly accused Northern CSOs of ignoring the authentic needs of the local Bedouin population and promoting their own interests instead.[7] In recent years, there has been a change in this area; Northern and Southern CSOs now collaborate in certain cases. However, the gaps between the different regions are still vast, and nationwide associations' involvement in different regions is still unequal.

CSOs, Rights, and Development

Any discussion of the contribution of Palestinian CSOs to the development of the PCI has to be done in light of the state's neoliberal economic tendencies. This part is limited to two issues: wage differentials and preschool education. In both, Palestinian society shares similar traits with other societies in developing countries.

Generally, Palestinian society is positioned in the lower part of Israel's economic scale. The data analyzed by the Adva Center regarding equality suggest that the average wage of Arab employees is much lower than the average wage of urban employees in Israel (Swirski, Connor-Attias, & Lieberman, 2019).

The data provided by the National Insurance Institute demonstrate that the rate of Palestinian citizens living below the poverty line is much larger than their proportion of the population. The number of poor Palestinian families increased from 47.6% (112,300 families) of the total number of

Palestinian families in 2002, to 48.4% (119,700) of the total number in 2003, while in the general population in Israel the rate of poor families was 18.1% in 2002 and 19.3% in 2003. The rate of Jewish poor families was 13.9% in 2002 and 14.9% in 2003. According to the data from recent years, the situation continues to deteriorate: According to the National Insurance Institution, the rate of poverty among the Palestinian population has grown steadily between 1997 and 2006 (Abu-Bader & Gottlieb, 2009). The rate of poor Arab children in the north has grown from 36% in 1997 to 60% in 2006. A similar trend was spotted in the Bedouin communities of the South (ibid.). The average gross income of an Arab household in 2005 was 7,414 NIS, and in 2006 it reached 7,590 NIS (compared to 12,643 NIS and 13,245 NIS, respectively, in Jewish households).[8] In 2008, the average gross income per household reached 8,151 NIS in Arab households, while Jewish households were making 14,157 NIS.[9] These data suggest that the gap between household incomes in Arab and Jewish communities has maintained or even increased in size. This trend continues to this day, according to the Central Bureau of Statistics.[10] In 2010, the Arab families living under poverty line amounted to 53.2%. In 2011, it went up to 53.5%. In 2015 it was 53.3%, and in 2016 it dropped to 49.2%. These data mean that low-income Arab families comprise about the 40% of all low-income families in Israel, despite the fact that the PCI is 20% of the population.

For these reasons, CSOs' projects should carry a significant contribution to society's welfare. Palestinian CSOs offer various kinds of activities that support different segments of society. Many of these welfare and development activities were previously carried out by religious associations. These welfare associations adopted special functioning models that suit the needs of Palestinian society (Rabinowitz, 2001). Religious associations provide basic food supplies to low-income families, especially during the holidays. Another services grants a small but fixed monthly sum to families who were harmed by the amendment to the Citizenship Law in 2003. These associations raise funds with almost no help from their society or, sometimes, from outside sources.

Furthermore, in many cities and villages, religious associations have been providing preschool education services—a basic service that the state fails to provide for all (Filc & Ram, 2004). For example, the outlawed Iqraa set a goal of preparing high-school students for university and established kindergartens in more than 20 Palestinian cities and communities. This CSO operated 21 centers for after-school programs. This is a rather impressive scale, considering the fact that its financial resources are limited. The association's funds are raised by its members from the Palestinian public. Many of the activities are performed by volunteers. We can say for sure that there is no secular CSO that executes a voluntary educational activity on such a scale. Iqraa's pattern of behavior reflects the attempt of CSOs, especially religious ones, to find internal solutions to problems that Palestinian citizens face on a daily basis. This pattern of voluntarism reflects the religious ideals of collective action and civil engagement and also demonstrates that the presence of CSOs is not necessarily correlated with social liberty and democracy.

The ability to prioritize social change is one of the important traits of religious CSOs, especially regarding educational development programs. Religious associations play an important role in establishing a religious society with modern awareness. Therefore, the Islamic Movement's leaders declare that, despite the state's discriminating policy, they are happy to be given the chance to assist their society and promote education in the spirit of Islamic tradition.

Palestinian society has always suffered discrimination in education. The state does not merely refrain from assisting in establishing an alternative and independent education system, but it also fails to create new initiatives because of its intention to maintain direct control of the Arab education system as a whole. The experiences of Masar in Nazareth and Hiwar in Haifa and their contacts with the Ministry of Education are good examples of the difficulties Palestinian CSOs must deal with when trying to challenge the state's unitary control over the Arab education system. In both cases, the Ministry of Education tried to enforce teaching programs and enlist specific educators for these independent education systems. The struggle of the board and the parents caused financial losses and a split in Hiwar's school in Haifa. The same can be said about the preschool systems opened by various CSOs in different areas. In most cases, the state refused to extend its assistance to these institutions, leaving the CSOs to address Palestinian society's needs on their own.

The initiatives led by a growing network of associations, both religious and secular, play an increasingly large role in providing social services. They empower civil society and established what was called by Clarke (1998) "a parallel virtual state" or what could be called, in the case of Palestinian society in Israel, "a cultural autonomy by default." The state's retreat to provide social services and its refusal to assist in finding educational alternatives for preschools allows the CSO sector to establish a sphere of influence in education and other social services, detached from the state's direct control. Another example is the legal department of Kayan—a department that provides free counseling and advocacy for Arab women in issues relating to their status in the family, in society, and in the state.

The State of Israel has decided to gradually reduce its social services, leaving thousands of people with no basic assistance (Barak-Erez, 2012; Filc & Ram, 2004). The decline of the Israeli welfare state illustrates the importance of CSOs, which provide services for those who were marginalized financially. They are even more important in recent years, in light of the policy of privatization and neoliberalization declared by the Israeli government. Welfare associations distribute thousands of meals to the underprivileged every year.[11] This food distribution, which testifies to the declining socioeconomic status of a growing segment of Jewish society, often doesn't reach the poorest population in Israel, the PCI. The food is distributed according to national and religious background, and therefore this activity is often limited solely to Jewish communities. While Palestinian society has a tradition of philanthropy and assistance based on religious ideals, most of them Muslim, those working in the name of these causes get no serious support from government ministries or external sources.

When exploring Palestinian CSOs and their resources, we can see that they are not sufficient. CSOs cannot offer a suitable alternative to the state's funds. The best proof of this is the decline in living standards of a growing number of Arab families and the growing numbers of people living below the poverty line and its relationship with the level of services provided by the CSO community; the rates of each do not compare. The economic crisis that broke at the end of 2008 and was reinforced in 2011 negatively affected civil society as a whole, particularly Palestinian civil society. Because most Palestinian CSOs' resources are supported from abroad, the global financial decline that led to budget cuts and the outbreak of the social upheavals in Arab countries in 2011 initially damaged what was considered to be altruistic luxury. Many CSOs struggle to raise funds, a fact that impairs their ability to deal with the growing number of challenges in the PCI.

Conclusions

A number of conclusions can be deduced from this chapter. First, Palestinian society in Israel has witnessed an institutionalization process or the creation of a large number of active CSOs. This process increased Palestinian society's engagement in an effort to raise support for its interests and needs. The growing number of Palestinian CSOs created a diversified civil society with no singular political ideal, yet the organizations work together—to some extent—toward improving the status of Palestinian citizens in Israel and enabling them to exercise their rights. These Palestinian CSOs try to limit the state's hegemonic power and change its identity in an attempt to spread the idea of joint citizenship and democratic culture.

The rising number of Palestinian CSOs also illustrates the restructuring of Arab politics: from complementing formal means, like elections, where the party is the main political agent, to bolstering informal politics, where CSOs are used as a new and significant tool for mobilization. This change is particularly important because CSOs provide services for Palestinian society that the parties failed to extract from the state. When examining the agenda of the Israeli public, it is hard to miss the dominant role of CSOs in bringing Arab issues to attention and expressing Arab interests. While pushing the state's institutions to change their policy, Palestinian CSOs also provide services in many areas neglected by the state. Therefore, Palestinian civil society plays an antihegemonic role in its work vis-à-vis the state and assists political parties in improving their position in the political arena. Yet we cannot simply say that Palestinian civil society has managed to truly implement democratization processes in the State of Israel. The 2009, 2013, 2015, and 2019 elections and the rise of radical right-wing parties indicate a strengthening chauvinist trend in Israeli society and politics.

Nevertheless, Palestinian CSOs create an autonomous sphere in the field of the state's direct and harsh auspices of power, a sphere that is used as a legal and cultural buffer zone between the state and deprived Palestinian citizens. Despite the state's unwillingness to consider delegation of authorities—beside local councils and welfare services—the Palestinian CSOs, which rely mostly on foreign funds, manages to remain relatively autonomous. Palestinian CSOs lead a large number of activities that enrich Palestinian society and its culture and address material and symbolic needs that would not have been met otherwise.

In addition, Palestinian CSOs have managed to formulate the Arab Future Vision Documents, which are highly significant both historically and politically. CSOs have drafted society's vision for the future and defined the nature of their relationships with their Israeli, Palestinian, and Arab environment. The Future Vision Documents are in fact an ideal and political master plan that cannot be ignored by any future Arab power in Israel. This is a considerable achievement, which probably couldn't have been reached by the Palestinian fragmented society without the involvement of Palestinian CSOs (Jamal, 2009).

In spite of their contra-hegemonic role, we must draw our attention to the gap between CSOs' influence on democratization and their influence in the field of empowerment and development. As demonstrated here, Palestinian CSOs are not very successful in promoting the democratization of the State of Israel, especially regarding its Palestinian citizens. On the contrary, the more this sector is active, the more the state resorts to exclusive, ethnically based policies. The Citizenship Law and the Nation-State Law are two examples, demonstrating the state's desire to take racist steps in order to avoid giving its Palestinian citizens full and equal rights. Generally, we can say that, despite the rise in power of Palestinian CSOs in recent years and their significant efforts in raising support, they did not successfully equip Palestinians in Israel with the ability to fully exercise their citizenship. As the state took steps to reinforce its ethnic and national policy, Palestinian citizenship was robbed of its substantive meaning, and the citizens were robbed of their ability to effectively impact policy and decision making processes, even in issues relevant to Palestinian society itself (Jamal, 2011; Peled, 2005).

However, the fact that Palestinian CSOs couldn't change the state's policy is not due to their lack of efforts and cannot undercut their considerable achievement in other areas. Palestinian CSOs' failure to influence Israel's political nature and ethnic-cultural identity is, in fact, not their fault. The state has refrained from acknowledging any effort to change its policy toward Palestinian society. Palestinian CSOs couldn't convince or "force" the state to change its policy and identity in order to include Palestinian identity and the basic rights of Palestinians as equal Israeli citizens. Furthermore, the impact of the Palestinian CSOs on the state cannot be limited to positive change. The fact that the state has been reacting aggressively leads it to unveil its true ethno-nationalist and racial character, something that the CSOs could use in the struggle in the international arena. The shrinking of the freedom spaces and the establishing of a racialized stratification regime that differentiates between citizens based on their national affiliation is a reaction that is fully used by Palestinian CSOs in order to demonstrate the real policies that the PCI faces in Israel.

Furthermore, when looking at the achievements of Palestinian CSOs in empowerment and development, the picture changes a bit. Palestinian CSOs have definitely managed, through their own resources or resources extracted from external sources, to solve many problems in Palestinian society. A mere glance at what was done to promote the basic rights of the unrecognized villages gives us the feeling that the Palestinian CSOs' contributed undisputedly to the well-being of their society. While Palestinian CSOs cannot solve every problem for the public, and while they suffer from their own internal disputes, personalization, lack of institutionalization, and threat of falling into antiliberal hands, their significant contribution to empowerment and development cannot be ignored.

These goals couldn't be achieved if not for the networks connection established by CSOs over time. The campaigns dealing with social and political issues in new media are another example of the importance of the organizations' contribution to raising the awareness of social and political collective goals. Most of these campaigns challenge state policies in various areas of life, particularly planning and housing, commemoration and collective historical consciousness, opposing military and national service, and women's rights. These efforts are innovative and point to significant changes in the Palestinian civic engagement that could not be explained without the intensive activism of CSOs that were formed by young activists with new skills that allow this kind of engagement (Jamal, 2017). Based on these patterns of engagement, it is possible to argue that Palestinian youth in Israel are seizing the opportunities made available by information and communication technology in order to overcome limitations embedded in traditional forms of civic engagement and political participation. The openness and dynamic nature of the digital sphere enable many to be engaged and voice themselves via various media and in various ways. What remains to be further explored in future research is how these new patterns transform the political environment in which they act and how impactful the online activity could be to achieve such a goal.

Epilogue and Future Prospects

It is not easy to summarize this kind of research, because every chapter included its own conclusions and we wouldn't want to repeat them all here. Therefore, in this epilogue I present a number of general conclusions, both theoretical and empirical, and dedicate some attention to possible future developments.

First, regarding theory: This study demonstrates the need for a theoretical stretching of the literature on civil society and subaltern mobilization if we are to better understand the particularities of civic activism in postcolonial settings. The liberal-pluralist bias in the literature concerning civil society and social capital must be balanced by integrating insights learned from the tradition of subaltern studies. Such a balancing act enables us to better understand the motivations and patterns of mobilization among minorities at risk and their search for new modes and meanings of civility that transform the power structure in which they live. Such an effort demonstrates Balibar's conceptualization of the political, according to which emancipation from domination entails transformative civic activism and civility (Balibar, 2002). Having said that, the case of Palestinian civic activism in Israel demonstrates that transforming its political environment does not always occur in the direction intended. In ethnic states, civic activism could be effective but lead to counterdemocratic policies by the state. The Israeli case shows that the more active CSOs and human rights organizations are, the more reactive the state becomes in seeking to silence critics and delegitimize oppositional voices.

As indicated in the theoretical framework, Foley and Edwards (1996) have distinguished between civil society that challenges the state and one that is not necessarily politically motivated. This research illustrates that this distinction is irrelevant. This is due to its lack of sensitivity to the possibility of more complex realities in which the state is defined in exclusive ethnic terms, where civility is not available for all citizens. In such cases, civic activism is political by the mere fact that it seeks to reconstruct the civic sphere and transform the state. It is true that CSOs of subaltern societies are enabled by state law; however, they still act in opposition to state policies, seeking to empower, develop, and mobilize social forces that seek to transform the state and lead to its democratization.

The patterns of collective action and political mobilization discussed in the empirical chapters provide evidence of the theoretical argument that the subaltern minority's civic activism seeks to reconstruct the civic sphere and transform the state. There is enough evidence to make the argument that there is not such apolitical civic activism. Subaltern civic activism represents alternative epistemic and valuational perceptions to those at the state level and promoted by its agencies. This is especially true in postcolonial contexts in which the homeland minority struggles against repressive and marginalizing policies of an ethnically exclusive state. CSOs are political by advocating socioculturally based identities and challenging the state's power structure, seeking to instill universal democratic ideals instead of ethnically motivated principles, especially in its distribution of material and symbolic resources.

As part of their efforts to promote universal human rights values, liberal Palestinian CSOs in Israel not only try to promote the interests of their affiliated society, but also to transform the Israeli state and motivate the Jewish majority society to meet higher moral and ethical standards of political behavior. Civil society based on the civic ideals of equality and freedom must challenge the state, even if it is given a wide leeway.

As we have seen in the personal interviews and in focus groups' sessions, civic activism seeks to politicize issues of concern. Its politicizing urge is embedded in its mere role in revealing state policies in various fields and setting alternatives in universal terms. Palestinian civic activism is mainly civic. It promotes a civic conceptualization of the state, which is an alternative to its ethno-national character. It further entails challenging the control and supervision mechanisms of the majority over the minority living in its midst.

Another theoretical conclusion we make is that the concept of social capital cannot be reduced to networking processes alone, as argued by Pierre Bourdieu, and social networks cannot serve as an indication of the measure of a certain society's democratization, as Robert Putnam argued. In order to elaborate on the complexity of this phenomenon and turn the concept into a more reflective tool to be used in understanding complex social movements and collective behavior, there is a need to combine three dimensions of the phenomenon, elaborated in the theoretical framework. As this study demonstrates, social capital is an individual resource, based on networks of connections, mobilizable in promoting personal or collective objectives; it is a structural social trait that enables society to promote its common goals more effectively; and it entails communicative practices that enable open discussions between relevant organizations.

According to the findings of this study, and in light of such an inclusive definition of social capital, we argue that the social capital of Palestinian society in Israel has indeed been increasing. The network of CSOs and the awareness of its activists are a historical and significant transformation, on the social, cultural and political levels, if we take into consideration that we are speaking of a minority group that had to rebuild its basic social fabric after experiencing a disastrous destruction, facing state policies that have blocked its development and submitted its resources to the benefit of the Jewish majority society since 1948.

Palestinian CSOs in Israel have led to the rise of new patterns of social and political collaboration that are not based on purely traditional forms of sociocultural conduct. Despite the differences between various CSOs and in spite of the personalization and internal competition, Palestinian civic activism in Israel, led by and within the frames of CSOs, overcomes some of the challenges that traditional forms of collective organization used to face. CSOs work together on various issues and face challenges that turn their efforts cumulative.

There is a high level of civic activity in Palestinian society in Israel, taking the form of conferences, assemblies, publications, demonstrations, petitions, online protests, and lobbying in the state's institutions. All of these manifestations empower Palestinian society and expand its presence in the Israeli public sphere and in the international arena. While Palestinian society has no strong direct influence on state policy, we cannot ignore its rising position in the state's agenda; this rise is translated into two opposing trends. The first trend is translated into an attempt of the Jewish majority and the state to tighten control and supervision mechanisms inside the PCI and in civil society. Such a reaction reflects the impact of Palestinian civic activism and Jewish human rights organizations on the state. They manage to lead the state to reveal its "true" ethnic and discriminatory character and thereby mobilize part of the Israeli liberal elite against state policies. Simultaneously, one notices the expansion of co-optation policy in an attempt to minimize the influence of the CSOs on their social environment. Both policies of the state reveal its exclusive ethnic nature, its racialized policies, and its double moral standards, rendering it more vulnerable to critique and increasing efforts to transform, even by liberal Zionist citizens, who recognize the growing gap between the Jewish and democratic state they envision and the emerging racial state they experience.

Based on the research's findings, we argue that the social capital reflected in and created by the activity of CSOs is highly influenced by the civic gap, derived from the fact that Palestinian society is a minority that is excluded from Israeli citizenship. The meaningless citizenship status, a byproduct of government policy, makes Palestinian political participation ineffective and structures Palestinian citizenship as a mechanism of control and supervision, instead of one based on equal rights. Yet this policy, especially as exercised by the legal actions and activities of right-wing CSOs, is proof of the presence of Palestinian civil society and its success in promoting a civically and politically challenging discourse.

In practice, the strong presence of Palestinian CSOs in the Israeli public sphere is not always translated into policy, but the civic discourse promoted by Palestinian CSOs causes the state to face uneasy ideological and ethical tests on a day-to-day basis. International organizations explore the status of Palestinian citizens and the official discrimination against them; this intervention could not occur without the efforts of CSOs in local and global advocacy and lobbying. Various reports of the European Union, the OECD, the Human Rights Council of the United Nations, and others are deeply connected to the activities of CSOs in legal, financial, cultural, social, and political fields.

The issue of social capital is important not only in the context of the Israeli system, but also in the context of Palestinian society itself. We can say that the social capital of Palestinian society was increased because of the networks of many CSOs that promote Palestinian society's various interests and ideals, yet when we examine the expressions of social capital in the field of voluntarism, the networking and trust found in society itself are a bit gloomy. The level of voluntarism in Palestinian society beyond family or clan is low. As a deprived minority, we expected to find higher levels of voluntary work in the PCI. Palestinian CSOs carry much of the responsibility for the current situation. The relationship between civil society and the general population is not well established. The public's level of awareness of the organizations' activities is relatively low. The public's low level of awareness stands in contrast to the growing institutionalization of

Palestinian CSOs. This contradiction indicates the loss of important social capital, which, if it were gathered and used constructively, might be able to assist Palestinian society to better deal with some of its challenges.

When it comes to public awareness of the CSOs, the average person surveyed has a hard time answering questions about the nature and activities of CSOs without leading questions. Apparently, the efforts of some CSOs to familiarize the public with their activities are unsuccessful. This reality decreases the social capital and the scale of citizens' civic engagement in various social segments in the autonomic activity of Palestinian CSOs. Notwithstanding the social capital accumulated by establishing these CSOs, this lack of popular engagement severely damages society's prospects for translating social capital into more effective political mobilization. It should be noted here that Palestinian society is financially underprivileged and characterized by high rates of poverty and unemployment. These facts seem to impair the chances of CSOs to recruit large numbers of activists and volunteers for their ongoing activities. They also result in making the public more reluctant to protect and defend CSOs when they are financially or politically attacked by the state. The cold reaction to the closure of more than 10 CSOs connected to the Islamic movement in November 2015 demonstrates the vulnerability of liberal CSOs, who don't have the social leverage and backing of the Islamic ones. The former CSOs seem to be totally dependent on the well of the state and its "whitewashing" policies, seeking to pass as liberal and democratic vis-à-vis the international society.

Hence, if CSOs are interested in a deep and well-established relationship with their social environment—on whose behalf they work and whose rights they promote—they must make a significant change in their public relations policy and in their networking patterns with different populations and communities and invest more material and human resources in their approach. This challenge is more acute in the case of secular organizations than in religious ones. The latter are connected to clearly defined local communities by the nature of their activities, and they communicate with them constantly. This gap between secular and religious organizations is important in the context of social capital, as well as the context of creating a social backing, defending CSOs in times of need.

While we posit a decline in civic engagement in formal Israeli politics, we do note a rise in the scale of civic engagement in other realms, like forming CSOs, professional conferences, legal petitions, professional lobbying in the Knesset, and mobilization in other forms such as online and offline protests, demonstrations, charitable giving, and social media.

At the time of completing this book, there have been several large-scale media campaigns seeking to raise awareness of and support for certain positions and for social mobilization to support policies that promote basic rights for the PCI. "Prawer lan yamor" (Prawer will not pass), "Orfod, Sha'abak Bihmik" (Refuse, your people will protect you), and "Zahal Ma Bistahal" (IDF is inappropriate) are some of the more high-profile campaigns that seek to shape public opinion and support political mobilization. One of the major challenges facing these kind of online campaigns is ensuring their continuity. The example of the very well-organized and intensively motivated campaign against the prawar Plan, which almost completely disappeared after the government decided to freeze it, is a good example. If the energies and material and symbolic resources invested in the campaign are lost after a vibrant and very active period of time and if civic activists do not work hard to guarantee continuity, then the transforming of part of Palestinian civic activism from offline to online activism entails a great danger for the future of Palestinian civil society.

A serious challenge facing Palestinian civic activism stems from the fact that most activities performed by secular CSOs are financed by outside sources, especially from Europe and North America. This financial dependency is not only problematic but also mortal. The future of secular CSOs has to be guaranteed by finding the right way to fundraise from the emerging Palestinian middle class, which does not commit itself yet to philanthropy and does not act to encourage civic engagement. This shift in strategy has begun for some CSOs, but it is still in its initial stages and necessitates more daring and innovations that are still lacking.

Secular CSOs concentrate most of their energies in activities challenging state policies that discriminate against the PCI and promoting social interests through advocacy, lobbying, litigation, and social mobilization. Most of the activities that seek recruiting the public and are funded by local resources are performed by CSOs that belong to the Islamic Movement. These CSOs refrain from dealing with the state and invest most of their energy in intrasocietal activities, striving for Islamization and expanding their internal networking in order to gain more infrastructural power.

When we compare secular and religious CSOs using the terminology of social capital, we see that the latter are better able to invest their social capital using intraorganizational networking, service provision, and opening communication channels between different social and geographical segments, thus creating a "society within society" based on traditional rules, one that is well organized and orchestrated to achieve common objectives. While secular Palestinian CSOs work in various dimensions and empower and create networks, they are not part of a general common worldview that brings them together. These two parts of Palestinian civil society are ideologically differentiated, based on a fundamental gap in their worldviews. Secular organizations are based on a national identity and use civil means to challenge the state, while religious organizations are based on a religious paradigm and use educational, disciplinary, and organizational means to control society.

When comparing these two branches on the basis of civil engagement, it is possible to say that in both, the level of political awareness is a key factor in determining the level of civil engagement. Notwithstanding, the correlation between political awareness and civic engagement in the PCI is weakened even when activity in the civil sphere increases through civic association's activities; this trend goes against the common argument in the literature: that civil engagement encourages higher political awareness. A possible explanation for this conflict is the fact that Palestinian civil society is a minority society that suffers from discrimination and is excluded from the power structure and decision-making processes. The awareness of this reality, coupled with the search after informal paths of influence alongside political parties, brings many to act as part of Palestinian civil society.

Despite all that, we must turn our attention to the possible relationship between the rise of CSOs in the public sphere, as well as their activity in various fields of life, and the minimized civil engagement of the average Palestinian citizen. There is a general feeling in the PCI that civic engagement is ineffective and therefore inexpedient. This feeling is expanding alongside the emergence of CSOs, which become the central agents to act vis-à-vis the state and promote policies that impact the fair distribution of resources.

The various chapters of this book have illustrated this paradox. CSOs are an important element of the social-political existence in modern society. They are vital for creating spheres of civil freedom and autonomy, which are distanced from the state. Voluntary activity is important for creating social and political balances in society, which would have been difficult to create without CSOs. Notwithstanding, CSOs are professional organizations that invest most of their resources in implementing projects they are entrusted with or subcontracted to conduct. This type of action means that they have to be a bit detached from the public. This detachment leads to alienation, lack of knowledge, and unwillingness of the public to support CSOs in times of need. Changing the balance between projectal orientation and engagement with the public becomes a must for the survival of CSOs in the future.

We must also acknowledge the social class aspect of CSOs. The various empirical chapters provide sufficient evidence to the argument that CSOs are a bourgeois phenomenon. The rise of a Palestinian middle class that seeks to expand the spaces of maneuvering available to it and acts to promote its aspirations, mobilizing growing segments of Palestinian society and constructing new understanding of the civic, is behind the rising civic activism among Palestinians in Israel. This emerging elite draws the attention and constructs the political imagination of significant social forces, which commit to resist the rules of the political game and the values of the political culture dictated by the political regime. These characteristics are true in conflict situations and in cases where civil society belongs to an excluded minority. CSOs are related to an elite and specific social class. They are distanced from the general population, even when they provide social services and struggle on behalf of the population against the market and the state.

CSOs deal with various social and political issues and provide vital social services. Today, we can hardly imagine a society with no active CSOs. But their existence doesn't solve the challenge of the state's discriminate supervision, abuse of power, continuous infiltration into the economy and every other sphere of life, including the most intimate, and social and economic inequality. The challenge of CSOs presents a challenge to the social-political order and undermines the arbitrariness of power relations, but it doesn't undercut them completely. Palestinian civic activism manages to unveil the racial characteristics of the Israeli regime by leading it to react to its demands and reveal the extent to which the Israeli democratic procedures promote discriminatory and repressive policies toward the Palestinian minority, using the majoritarian tyranny of the majority.

An important aspect of this phenomenon is the distinction between secular CSOs that employ civic and human rights discourse, and communal organizations with religious and conservative worldviews. The behavioral patterns and discourse spheres of these organizations are different and even contradictory. While secular organizations promote the rights of Palestinian society through advocacy and lobbying strategies versus the state, based on human and civil rights discourse, religious organizations are more communal in nature and promote a mainly social-communal discourse. The latter deals with socialization and provides services autonomously through a system of local fundraising. By comparison, the secular organizations raise funds mainly from outside sources. This difference requires a distinction regarding the relationship between social capital, empowerment, and democracy. We cannot ignore the social capital of communal organizations. It serves as a major resource for promoting objectives that are in conflict with liberal and pluralist ideals. This fact implicates social capital in all its forms, suggesting that social capital cannot be perceived as democratic or liberal in essence. In fact, this kind of social capital is a communal resource, which might cause tension with major democratic ideals, especially concerning women's rights and individual autonomy. The growth of communal organizations and their close link to society, compared to the distance between secular organizations and society, and the fact that organizations of the first can raise the lion's share of their resources from within the community, raise questions regarding the ability of civic activism to empower the underprivileged segments of Palestinian society. At the same time, the state's retreat from providing vital welfare services and its policies of exclusion and repression toward Palestinian society support those who argue for the need in segregation, self-sufficiency, and delegitimization of the state.

Secular civic activists, fighting over dwindling external funds, face more and more hardships and are gradually losing their power. The state is becoming a major threat to their ability to promote their values and their impact on their environment. In this situation, communal associations are left to fill the large void in society, thus creating a growing trend of conservatism and retreat from liberal, pluralist, and democratic ideals. This means that the dialectics between the chauvinist nationalistic project promoted by the state and the religious civic activism of large segments of the Palestinian minority forces liberal and human rights organizations into an iron cage of an antagonistic value system. Palestinian liberal and human rights organizations are pushed to the corner in which they have to determine if they follow the Arabic maxim "Assist your brother whether he is a victimizer or victimized" or follow a value system that is either transcendentally universal or existentially humanitarian.

This point leads us to one of the major dilemmas that face civic activism, namely that civic activism, when challenging the existing power structure, has to use tools provided by the state. Therefore, the politics of resistance falls into the traps of the political system, reaffirming the persisting power relations and becoming instrumentalized for the legitimization needed to maintain the status quo. Notwithstanding, civic activism, in order to be effective, has to promote universal values of the civic and not limit itself to a particularistic identitarian system of rights. Overcoming the power trap of the political system demands that civic activism not be a mirror image of the ethnic character of the state. As Partha Chatterjee has illustrated, identitarian projects, even when they are anticolonial, may assert the epistemological superiority of the colonial system by demanding to replicate it in the name of the nation. This conclusion is very relevant to civic activism that has to go above and beyond narrow national or religious rights and demand the universalization of the value system under which various identities and aspirational projects can live. This point is very crucial when we compare CSOs acting under the auspices of the Islamic Movement and liberal ones. Whereas the former are a mirror image of the ethnic state, thereby legitimizing its epistemology, albeit indirectly, part of the latter, especially feminist ones, seek to promote universal values of autonomy, equality, and freedom. Thereby they set a serious challenge to the predominant epistemological order.

That said, the Israeli regime is assisted by a growing number of conservative CSOs that are subcontracted to conduct policies instead, but with the encouragement of the state in fields that violate basic rights of non-Jewish citizens and non-citizens living under the Israeli control system. This civil activity, depicted as "bad civil society," not only promotes its own interests, such as promoting Jewish settlements in Palestinian areas and the religionization of Jewish society, but also seek to delegitimize liberal CSOs and the entire human rights community, Jewish and Palestinian, stigmatizing them as enemies of the state and society and mobilizing the political system to shrink the spaces in which they act. This silencing policy is manifested in many legal and bureaucratic measures that have been promoted in the last decade.

According to our findings and despite the prevailing findings in the literature, the dichotomy between civil and political society does not exist in reality. Many aspects of CSOs' activities are carried out in the political arena. When struggling to change policies in various fields, CSOs' activity cannot be detached from politics. Of course, in some cases, the actions of political organizations may be considered damaging to the activities of CSOs. This fact is especially true with regard to minority political parties, which are not part of the government. Accordingly, minority civil society is a complex phenomenon, which holds many conflicts and tensions. These internal conflicts enable it to exist and challenge the state, but at the same time potentially serve as an indirect means of control.

It is possible to confidently assert that Palestinian CSOs—mainly secular—have managed to increase social capital in Palestinian society, but failed to create the necessary distinction between their contribution to the society's empowerment, its development in certain aspects, and the CSOs' ability to promote a political change and democratization of the state and of their own society. The mere existence of civic activism is significant, but it doesn't guarantee democratization, empowerment, or development. Greater collaboration between various CSOs with different worldviews, especially collaborations between secular and religious organizations, is required to empower Palestinian civil society and overcome many of the hardships faced by Palestinian society to challenge the power structure that excludes Palestinians from effective civic participation and prevents them from promoting civic equality ideals in Israeli society in general and in Palestinian society in particular. This means that the challenges that Palestinian civic activism face, when it comes to its ideals, are not and cannot be limited to resisting state policies of discriminations, but have to tackle internal dilemmas and face the social patterns and norms that violate basic human rights inside Palestinian society, such as women, children, the elderly, and people with special needs.

The dilemma that comes up in this context is that liberal CSOs have to face not only the state's discriminatory policies, but also the conservative worldviews of religious CSOs. Such a challenge engages them in a dual combat, a challenge that places them in a serious dilemma. Given that their resources are from outside society, namely Western countries, they become targeted by the state for being "foreign agents," interfering in in the state's internal affairs on the one hand, and by religious CSOs and political parties for being foreign agents of Western culture on the other hand, promoting values that are anathema to the Islamic history and tradition. This situation makes CSOs' activism a serious challenge that is different from the experience of liberal CSOs in Western countries. This is especially true when adding the colonial argument made by Chatterjee introduced earlier. Furthermore, these challenges bring to mind the Aristotelian concept of *philia* (civic friendship) and the ability of liberal and conservative civic activists to communicatively interact and openly deliberate social and cultural values. Arab civic activists not only have to face the discriminatory policies of the state and the cultural alienation from Israeli Jewish society, but they also have to develop new communicative language that enables them to overcome the valuational gaps within their own society. This challenge remains one of the most precarious in the PCI's civic sphere because it provides an indication as to its maturity and its sincerity when having to facilitate internal differences.

A central conclusion of this book is that the civil as not a pregiven context or value, but rather an open avenue of collective conduct in which civic activism seeks to determine the identity of society and challenge the legal and political structure of the hegemonic Jewish majority, which seeks to impose limitations on the behavior of the Palestinian community. Palestinian civic activism in Israel, especially in the cultural arena, seeks to institutionalize its relationships with the Arab world and thereby defies the limitations imposed on it by the Israeli reality. Furthermore, it seeks to influence the identity and consciousness of the Arab community, which is receptive to these efforts, as manifested in its culture of media consumption. Palestinian society in Israel is located in the Arab world through its consumption of news and entertainment programs from Arab televisions channels or via social media tools. Palestinian theaters in Israel, artists, musicians, poets, and novelists are deeply involved in Arab societies surrounding Israel, and thereby they challenge the hegemonic Israeli citizenship and counter the efforts made by the state to confine them to its horizons of identity. This type of civic activism challenges the Israeli hegemonic concept of citizenship and promotes an alternative understanding that views the civic not in terms of loyalty to the state and submitting to its value system, but rather as an open space of collective conduct, whose meaning is to be determined, but, as the horizon, never reaches an end.

The other side of this coin is that Palestinian civic activism in Israel is deeply influenced by patterns of institutionalization known in Arab culture, especially personalization. As Ahmed (2004) recommended, we should not fall into the traps of authenticity and idealization when examining one of the most vibrant and interesting phenomena in the subaltern Palestinian minority in Israel. Despite the importance of Palestinian CSOs, they still manifest patterns of behavior that are rooted in values and customs that are contradictory to basic individual freedoms, tolerance, and equality. This is especially true of CSOs identified with the Islam movement, but not only. Some secular CSOs reflect patterns of behavior that do not match basic freedoms and equality, especially when it comes to women's rights.

According to what has been said thus far, we can also conclude that when civil society fails to challenge power or is blocked from performing this role, it fails to meet its definition as such. We do not intend to assign the full responsibility for the subversion of civil society to the hegemonic power structure on the former, but only to clarify that the mere existence of civil society imposes restriction on the power structure. It also reflects a dialectical reality where civic activism seeks to limit the state's power and influence its policy and institutions, seeking to expand their authority and help to determine controversial issues.

Furthermore, it has been made evident that civic activism can adopt characteristics of dominant players in the market and instruments of rationality and logic typical to the private sector and various state institutions. Because civic activism provides ideas and political expectations that become a model to be followed by broader segments in society, solving the dilemma created by being collective agents that follow the neoliberal economic patterns of conduct on the one hand and seeking to promote humanistic values and policies on the other, becomes a very serious challenge. The commitment to alternative value systems is common in civil society, and such a reality is what grants civil society its name. However, when these alternative value systems submit to broader means of instrumental rationality and succumb to the epistemology of the market economy, they become part of the hegemonic order rather than autonomous agents that seek its transformation. Palestinian civil activism in Israel is mostly conducive to the prevailing economic system. It has submitted to it in order to survive. Notwithstanding, as long as many civil society organizations behave like subcontractors of the state in providing social services or remain dependent on the market of funds made available by political entities in Western countries, it seems that civic activism remains affirmative rather than transformative when it comes to the value system prevailing in society.

The funding for Palestinian civil organizations in Israel, mainly the secular social change and human rights ones, is a painful issue. The fact that most Palestinian secular civic organizations rely on external funding sources means not only that they lose the competition with Islamic organizations, which are funded in most cases by internal sources or the Islamic Movement, but that they are also subject to the political and cultural agendas, views, and interests dictated by the Western world. That doesn't mean that they have no autonomy or ability to manage independent policy and to promote their authentic interests, but their complete dependence on external funding creates a situation that enables the state to restrict a large part of civil society's activities through its policies toward foreign donors. The pressures exerted on the European Union or external funds, such as the Open Society Foundation by the Israeli government, make the vulnerability of liberal and human rights very existential. The withdrawal of the Ford Foundation and the Open Society Foundation from supporting liberal civic activism in Israel is an example of the dangers awaiting this entire sphere in face of the nationalizing trends in Israeli Jewish society. That is why one of the conclusions of this study is that civic activism that does not succeed in developing a culture of support and funding sources from within its own society can end up subjected to considerations that are not always consistent with the motives and ideals they were established to serve in the first place.

To end on an important epistemological note, it is good to remind the reader that this whole effort to examine the Palestinian civic activism in Israel has been instigated by the recognition that subaltern social groups should not and ought not to be studied from the prism of a paradigm of compliance. The given hegemonic political order, legally and conceptually, should not be taken as given. The civic activism of subaltern groups is formed by the given context, but also transforms it, even if the direction of the transformation is not the one wished for by the subaltern activists. The extent to which subaltern civil activism meet the hegemonic epistemic and perceptual order cannot be a good starting point for the study of subaltern groups. The study of Palestinian civic activism in Israel presents an alternative path that demonstrates the importance of theoretical self-consciousness, as recommended by central theorists from various backgrounds, whether from the pluralistic tradition, such as William Connolly (1973), or from the more critical tradition, such as Michel Foucault (2003). Civic engagement cannot be a closed concept according to which the practices of civil activists on the ground are measured. It is an open phenomenon that does not have pregiven determinants and should remain as such if we are to maintain the dynamic nature of the phenomenon. In other words, civic activism is about defining itself in ways that enable its dynamism and transformative nature. When civic activism manages to make the state responsive to it, even in directions that are not wished for, it achieves its goal. The nature of the policies of the state vis-à-vis civic activism cannot become an excuse to dismiss its importance. In the contrary, state policies vis-à-vis civic activism are a clear indication of what civic activism means.

Notes

Chapter 4

1. Personal interview with a prominent leader of the southern branch of the Islamic Movement, Nazareth, March, 18, 2016.

2. Translation by Abdullah Yusuf Ali, retrieved from http://search-the-quraan.com/search/one%20nation.

Chapter 5

1. Retrieved from http://www.haaretz.co.il/news/politics/.premium-1.2253235

2. Retrieved from http://www.hrw.org/ar/news/2010/07/23

3. Retrieved from http://www.ynet.co.il/articles/0,7340,L-4011888,00.html

4. Retrieved from https://imti.org.il/publication/goldstone/

5. Retrieved from http://oknesset.org/bill/5881/

6. The Knesset Documents, P/3140/18.

7. Retrieved from http://www.acri.org.il/he/wp-content/uploads/2011/12/amutot0612111.pdf

8. Retrieved from http://www.globes.co.il/news/article.aspx?did=1000704331

9. Retrieved from http://glz.co.il/NewsArticle.aspx?newsid=95061

10. The Knesset Documents, P/4089/18.

11. Retrieved from http://www.ynet.co.il/articles/0,7340,L-4465697,00.html

12. Retrieved from http://www.ynet.co.il/articles/0,7340,L-4011888,00.html

13. Retrieved from https://imti.org.il/wp-content/uploads/2015/02/Academic SpeechGag.pdf

14. Retrieved from http://izs.org.il/papers/PostZionismAcademia2010.pdf

15. Retrieved from https://imti.org.il/wp-content/uploads/2015/02/Academic SpeechGag.pdf http://izs.org.il/papers/PostZionismAcademia2010.pdf

16. Retrieved from http://www.knessetnow.co.il/%D7%95%D7%A2%D 7%93%D7%95%D7%AA/%D7%A4%D7%A8%D7%95%D7%98%D7%95%

257

D7%A7%D7%95%D7%9C/30183/%D7%94%D7%93%D7%A8%D7%AA-%D7%A2%D7%9E%D7%93%D7%95%D7%AA-%D7%A6%D7%99%D7%95%D7%A0%D7%99%D7%95%D7%AA-%D7%91%D7%90%D7%A7%D7%93%D7%9E%D7%99%D7%94

17. Retrieved from https://www.haaretz.co.il/news/education/.premium-1.415 9992

18. Matan Peleg, the head of *Im Tirtzu*, stated clearly that his organization supported the development of the ethical code for academia, and it came to prevent liberal leftist academics from "exploiting" their academic position to promote their worldviews, retrieved from www.davar1.co.ii/71715/

19. Retrieved from https://imti.org.il/en/publication/foreign-agents-report/

20. Retrieved from www.acri.org.il/he/36596

21. Retrieved from http://www.ngo-monitor.org/about/about-us/

22. Retrieved from http://www.ngo-monitor.org/about/who-funds-ngo-monitor/

23. Retrieved from http://www.nif.org/news-media/press-releases/nif-under-attack/

24. Retrieved from http://www.haaretz.com/israel-news/.premium-1.697566

25. Retrieved from http://www.haaretz.com/israel-news/.premium-1.697566

26. Retrieved from http://www.newsweek.com/israeli-parliament-passes-ngo-bill-opposition-warns-budding-fascism-479665

27. Retrieved from http://www.haaretz.com/israel-news/.premium-1.697566

28. Retrieved from http://www.haaretz.com/israel-news/.premium-1.703825

29. Retrieved from http://main.knesset.gov.il/News/PressReleases/Pages/press120716.aspx

30. Retrieved from https://www.theguardian.com/global-development-professionals-network/2016/may/11/israel-some-ngos-are-seen-as-the-enemy-from-the-inside

31. Ibid.

32. Retrieved from https://www.theguardian.com/global-development-professionals-network/2016/may/11/israel-some-ngos-are-seen-as-the-enemy-from-the-inside

33. See 2013 annual report of NGO Monitor, page 6, retrieved from http://www.ngo-monitor.org/pdf/annual_report2013.pdf

34. Kahana, Ariel, "The EU Stopped Funding for a Left CSO," *Yisrael Hayom*, 7.8.2018. https://www.israelhayom.co.il/article/577723

35. Retrieved from http://www.93fm.co.il/radio/478359/

Chapter 6

1. The party, which was a mixed Arab-Jewish party since its establishment in the 1920s, was split in 1943 into two parties—one Arab and one Jewish—fol-

lowing the growing conflict between the Zionist movement and the Palestinian national movement.

Chapter 7

1. Personal interview with Mohammad Miari, one of the founders of the committee, Haifa, February 26, 2009.

2. It is important to note that the data presented has been gathered from different documents of the NGOs Registrar in the Ministry of Justice. The lack of order in the provided documents at the time made it difficult to sort out the exact numbers of CSOs according to field of occupation.

3. *Sijal Magazine*, March 6, 2014, retrieved from http://www.ilam-center.org/publication.aspx?id=484

4. In a conference organized by I'lam Center on May 6, 2014, in Nazareth a special session was devoted to addressing the digital mobilization of Arab youth in Israel. Several young leaders who initiated and led digital campaigns addressed the conference and clarified the patterns of thinking and behavior behind their digital activism.

5. Personal interview with Sheikh Kamal Khatib, vice president of the Northern Branch of the Islamic Movement, Kufar Kanna, July 31, 2008.

6. Personal interview with a prominent activist in the Northern Branch of the Islamic Movement, Kufar Kassem, August 24, 2012.

7. Omar Dallashah, "The Joint List Demands from the EU to Pressure Israel," Arabs 48, retrieved from https://www.arab48.com/%D9%85%D8%AD%D9%84%D9%8A%D8%A7%D8%AA/%D8%B3%D9%8A%D8%A7%D8%B3%D8%A9/2018/09/03/%D9%88%D9%81%D8%AF-%D8%A7%D9%84%D9%82%D8%A7%D8%A6%D9%85%D8%A9-%D8%A7%D9%84%D9%85%D8%B4%D8%AA%D8%B1%D9%83%D8%A9-%D9%8A%D8%B5%D9%84-%D8%A8%D8%B1%D9%88%D9%83%D8%B3%D9%84-%D9%84%D8%B4%D8%B1%D8%AD-%D9%85%D8%AE%D8%A7%D8%B7%D8%B1-%D9%82%D8%A7%D9%86%D9%88%D9%86-%D8%A7%D9%84%D9%82%D9%88%D9%85%D9%8A%D8%A9-

8. Meeting of 15 CSO leaders in Nazareth on September 17, 2018. All participants agreed that there is a need to strengthen the ties with the international community, and one of them has been commissioned to write a concept paper on the topic. This issue was also part of I'lam's strategic thinking project in which two policy papers have been written, one on the PCI relationship with international civil society and the other on the PCI relationship with International organizations, such as the UN.

9. Retrieved from http://www.knesset.gov.il/committees/heb/docs/arab_workers17.pdf

10. A personal interview with Hassan Jabareen, founder and manager of Adalah. Shafa'amr, March 20, 2007.

11. Retrieved from http://alqaws.org/siteEn/index

12. Retrieved from http://www.aswatgroup.org/en/content/who-we-are (last visited 25 July, 2017).

13. Retrieved from http://alqaws.org/news/Difference-never-justifies-violence-New-Social-Media-Campaign?category_id=0

Chapter 8

1. Datel, lior, "Mahfach: 80 percent Rise in the Number of Arab Students in Higher Education," *The Marker*, 24 January, 2018, retrieved from https://www.themarker.com/news/education/1.5762853

2. Personal interview with a prominent activist in the Northern Branch of the Islamic Movement, Kufar Kassem, August 28, 2012.

3. A personal interview with Hassan Jabareen founder and manager of Adalah, Shafa'amr, March 20, 2007.

Chapter 9

1. Meeting with 12 CSO leaders, Nazareth, March 29, 2015.

2. A personal interview with a prominent civic activist, Nazareth, March 29, 2015.

3. A personal interview with Muhammad Zidan, head of the Arab Human Rights Association, Nazareth, April 24, 2012.

4. Personal interview with a prominent civic activist, Nazareth, March 3, 2013.

5. Personal interview with a prominent civic activist, Haifa, May 19, 2013.

6. Meeting with 15 CSO leaders, Nazareth, March 18, 2016.

7. Observation of a meeting of 12 CSO leaders, Shefa'amr, February 1, 2018.

8. Meeting with 15 CSO leaders, Nazareth, March 18, 2016.

9. Meeting with 15 CSO leaders, Nazareth, March 18, 2016.

10. Personal interview with a prominent civic activist, Nazareth, December 18, 2015.

11. Personal interview with a prominent activist in the Northern Branch of the Islamic Movement, Kufar Kassem, August 28, 2012.

12. Personal interview with a prominent activist in the Northern Branch of the Islamic Movement, Kufar Kassem, August 28, 2012.

13. Personal interview. with a prominent civic activist, Haifa, January 27, 2015.

14. Focus group in Haifa, December 5, 2017.

15. Focus group in Haifa, December 5, 2017.

16. Focus group in Haifa, March 23, 2017.

17. Personal interview with a prominent civic activist, Haifa, April 14, 2018.

18. Diaa Hadid, "Play Set in Israeli Prison Imperils Arab Theater," *The New York Times*, 13 June, 2015, retrieved from https://www.nytimes.com/2015/06/14/world/play-set-in-israeli-prison-imperils-arab-theater.html

19. Personal interview with a prominent civic activist, Haifa, May 18, 2018.

20. Personal interview with a prominent civic activist, Haifa, June 12, 2017.

21. Personal interview with a prominent civic activist, Haifa, April 14, 2018.

Chapter 10

1. It is important to note that the number of women working in CSOs is much larger than their percentage in society. That has to do with the fact that some of the CSOs are feminist organizations that mostly employ women and that many of the educated Arab elite are women, which translates into certain fields of the job market, such as education, nursing, and CSOs.

2. Personal interview with Sheikh Kamal Khatib, vice president of the Northern Branch of the Islamic movement, Kufar Kanna, July 31, 2008.

3. A factor analysis is a statistical analysis that reveals which variables are related to each other and which are not. In this analysis, we found that the ideological aspect explains 41.52% of the variance in the participants' answers, and the practical aspect further explains 31.55% of the variance. In total, then, these two aspects explain 73.07% of the variance in the responses. Therefore, we can safely assume that there is a relationship between the ideological motives—the desire to improve the PCI and the desire to shape its character—and that this relationship is different in nature from that which is between the practical motives—the lack of promotional opportunities in the Israeli job market and the desire to be independent of this market or of the state.

4. Land Day commemorates the killing of six Palestinian citizens by the Israeli police forces on March 30, 1976, during a demonstration that took place in the Sakhnin-Arrabeh area in the Galilee in which thousands of Palestinian citizens participated in protest for a governmental decision to confiscate thousand of acres of Arab land and provide them for Jewish use.

5. Nakba Day commemorates the loss of Palestine in the 1948 war and the total destruction of Palestinian society and the creation of the Palestinian refugee problem by the Israeli army.

6. These are organized marches which engage thousands of people marching to Palestinian villages destroyed by the Israeli government after 1948.

7. The October 2000 events are the demonstrations that took place in early October 2000 in sympathy with the Palestinian second intifada, in which 12 Palestinian citizens were assassinated by the police forces in the triangle area and in the Galilee.

8. We found no significant relationship between the various collaborations (both in the indexes and in the indexes' elements) and the associations' orientation (secular, neutral, or religious).

9. During the consultation meeting of March 18, 2016, the leaders of two feminist organizations attacked each other on this ground.

10. Personal interview with a prominent civic activist. Haifa, March 14, 2017.

11. No significant relationship was found between the internal democracy index (and its various components) and the organization's orientation (secular, religious, or neutral).

Chapter 11

1. The Israeli government had a permanent policy of separating the state's lands into different areas and prioritizing them. Areas that were graded as "A" received a larger portion of the resources compared to their size and population. Areas near the borders, especially the Northern Lebanon border, got special attention and many investments by the government. These prioritized areas were usually settled by Jews exclusively. Arab cities and villages were excluded systematically from them. For further details regarding this policy, see Yiftachel, 1998.

2. Menna Ekram, "In-Between: Your Palestinian Identity and your Israeli-Funded Film," retrieved from https://www.madamasr.com/en/2018/01/24/feature/culture/in-between-your-palestinian-identity-and-your-israeli-funded-film/

3. It is true that the 922 economic plan of the government enacted in 2017 devoted more resources to the PCI, the plan haven't come and couldn't have closed the gaps between the resources devoted to PCI compared with those allocated to Jewish society.

4. The Qa'adan Case involved an Arab family who demanded to move into a Jewish town next to their original village. Their request was denied by Israel Land Authority. The Supreme Court reversed their decision. For further information on this case, please refer to Jabareen (2002).

5. Personal interviews, Shefa'amr, March 20, 2007, and Haifa, March 14, 2017.

6. Personal interview with a prominent civic activist. Nazareth, April 13, 2017.

7. Personal interviews, Beer Sheva, September 20, 2012, and April 4, 2017.

8. http://www.cbs.gov.il/publications/mishke_bait_arabs06/pdf/t05a.pdf

9. Yaniv Ronen, "Crime Statistics among Arab Society in Israel" (Jerusalem: The Knesset's Research and Information Center, 2010).

10. http://www.cbs.gov.il/reader/newhodaot/hodaa_template.html?hodaa=201115219

11. https://www.latet.org.il/worlds/latet_food_security/

Bibliography

Abd Al-Malik, A. (1978). *Political thought in the struggle for progress*. Beirut: Dar Al-Aadab. [Arabic]

Abu Baker, Kh. (2003). "Career women" or "working women"? Change versus stability for young Palestinian women in Israel. *Journal of Israeli History, 21*(1–2), 85–109. [Hebrew]

Abu-Baker, Kh. (2007). *Arab society in Israel: Unit 5, the Palestinian family*. Ra'anana: Open University. [Hebrew]

Abu Baker, Kh. (2009). The impact of Arab women's image in women's magazines on the socialization for personal welfare. In F. Azayzeh, Kh. Abu Baker, R. Hertz-Lazarowitz, & A. Ghanem (Eds.), *Arab women in Israel* (pp. 71–90). Tel Aviv: Ramot Publications.

Abu-Baker, H., & Patir, D. (2000). *Project Shiluv Report: Regarding the integration of Arab citizens in civil service, in governmental companies and in the academy*. Jerusalem: Sikkuy. [Hebrew]

Abu-Habla, Z. (2012). We are not paying municipal taxes. *Ro'eh Hakheshbon, 28*, 98–104. [Hebrew]

Abu Zayd, N. (1994). *Naqd Al-Khitab Al-Dini [Critique of the religious discourse]*. Cairo: Sina Publishing.

Achcar, G. (2016). *Morbid symptoms: Relapse in the Arab uprising*. Stanford: Stanford University Press.

Adalbert, E. (2010). Observations on incivility: blind spots in third sector research and policy. Voluntary Sector Review, *1*(1), 113–117.

Agamben, G. (2005). *State of exception*. Chicago: University of Chicago Press.

Agbaria, A., & Mustafa, M. (2012). Arab civil society in Israel and the engagement in education: The politics of the difference between the civil-national and the communal-religious. *Mifgash Le'avoda Hinukhit-Sotzialit, 20*(35), 253–281.

Agbaria, A., & Mustafa, M. (2014). The case of Palestinian civil society in Israel: Islam civil society, and educational activism. *Critical Studies in Education, 55*(1), 44–57.

Ahmad, A. (1994). *On theory: Classes, nations, literatures*. New York: Verso.

Al-Azm, S. (1997). *Thehniyat Al-Tahrim* [Beyond the tabooing mentality]. Damascus: Al-Mada P.C. [Arabic]

Al-Azmeh, Aziz. (2008). *Secularism from a different perspective*. Beirut: Center for Arab Unity Studies. [Arabic]

Alexander, J. C. (1995). *Fin de siecle social theory: Relativism, reduction and the problem of reason*. London: Verso.

Alexander, J. C. (2006). *The civil sphere*. New York: Oxford University Press.

Al-Haj, M. (1988). The Arab internal refugees in Israel: The emergence of a minority within the minority. *Immigrants and Minorities, 2,* 149–165.

Al-Haj, M. (1995). *Education empowerment and control: The case of the Arabs in Israel*. Albany: State University of New York Press.

Al-Haj, M. (2003). Higher education among the Arabs in Israel: Formal policy between empowerment and control. *Higher Education Policy, 16,* 351–368.

Al-Haj, M., & Rosenfeld, H. (1988). *Arab local government in Israel*. Tel Aviv: International Center for Peace.

Al-Jabari, M. A. (2005). "Civil society: meaning and implications." In *Criticism of the Need for Reform* (pp. 171–190). Beirut: Center for Arab Unity Studies. [Arabic]

Al-Madani, T. (1997). *Civil society and the political state in the Arab homeland*. Damascus: Arab Writers Union. [Arabic]

Al-Maskini, F. (2011). *Al-Hawiya Wal-Hurriya* [Identity and liberty]. Beirut: Jadawel. [Arabic]

Almond, G., & Verba, S. 1963. *Civic culture: Political attitude and democracy in five nations*. Newbury Park, CA: Sage.

Al-Naqeeb, H. K. (1991). *The despotic state in the Arab east: a structural comparative study*. Beirut: Center for Arab Unity Studies. [Arabic]

Al-Omoush, K. S., Yaseen, S. G., & Alma'aitah, M. A. (2012). The impact of Arab cultural values on online social networking: The case of Facebook. *Computers in Human Behavior, 28*(6), 2387–2399.

Al-Sabihi, A. S. (2000). *The future of civil society in the Arab world*. Beirut: Center for Arab Unity Studies. [Arabic]

Alvarez, S., Rubin, J., Thayer M., Baiocchi, G., & Laó-Montes, A. (Eds.). (2017). *Beyond civil society: Activism, participation, and protest in Latin America*. Durham: Duke University Press.

Anthias, F. (2007). Ethnic ties: Social capital and the question of mobilisability. *The sociological review, 55*(4), 788–805.

Arendt, H. (1958). *The human condition*. Chicago: University of Chicago Press.

Arendt, H. (1968). *Men in dark times*. New York: A Harvest Book.

Aristotle. (1906). *Nicomachean ethics* [1893]. (Peters, F. T., Trans.). London: Kegan Paul Trench, Truebner and Co.

Arraf, S. (2007). *Lmsat Wfa'a* [Glimpses of Loyalty]. Mielya: Center for Rural Studies.

Asseburg, M. (2017). Shrinking spaces in Israel: Contraction of democratic space, consolidation of occupation, and ongoing human rights violations call for a paradigm shift in Europe's policies (SWP Comment, 36/2017). Berlin: Stiftung Wissenschaft und Politik-SWP-Deutsches Institut für Internationale Politik und Sicherheit. Retrieved from https://nbn-resolving.org/urn:nbn:de: 0168-ssoar-54348-3

Asseburg, M., & Wimmen, H. (2016). Dynamics of transformation, elite change and new social mobilization in the Arab world. *Mediterranean Politics, 21*(1), 1–22.

Azoulay, A., & Ophir, A. (2008). *This regime which is not one: Occupation and democracy between the sea and the river.* Tel Aviv: Resling. [Hebrew].

Balibar, A. (2002). Three concepts of the political. In E. Blibar (Ed.), *Politics and the other scene* (pp. 1–39). London: Verso.

Balibar, A. (2014). *Equaliberty: Political essays.* (Ingram, J., Trans.). Durham, NC: Duke University Press.

Barakat, H. (2005). The Arab family and the challenge of social transformation. In H. Moghissi (Ed.), *Women and Islam: Critical concepts in sociology—social conditions, obstacles and prospects* (pp. 145–165). London: Routledge.

Barak-Erez, D. (2012). *Citizen-subject-consumer: Law and government in a changing state.* Or Yehuda: Kineret-Zmora-Bitan. [Hebrew]

Barber, B. R. (2003). *Strong democracy: Participatory politics for a new age.* Berkeley: University of California Press.

Barely, S., & Tolbert, P. (1997). Institutionalization and structuration: Studying the links between action and institution. *Organization Studies, 18*(1), 93–117.

Barry, B., & Hardin, R. (1982). *Rational man and irrational society?* Beverly Hills, CA: Sage Publications.

Bar-Tal, D. (2005). In Teichman Y. (Ed.), *Stereotypes and prejudice in conflict: Representation of Arabs in Israeli Jewish society.* UK; New York: Cambridge University Press.

Bashir, N. (2006). *Land Day.* Haifa: Mada Al-Carmel.

Bäuml, Y. (2007). *A blue and white shadow: the Israeli establishment's policy and actions among its Arab citizens: The formative years: 1958–1968.* Haifa: Pardes. [Hebrew]

Bayart, J. F. (1986). Civil society in Africa. In P. Chabal (Ed.), *Political domination in Africa: Reflections on the limits of power* (pp. 109–125). Cambridge: Cambridge University Press.

Ben-Bassat, A., Momi, D., & Esteban K. (2009). *The political economics of the municipalities.* Jerusalem: The Israel Democracy Institution. [Hebrew]

Ben Beri, W. (2018). *Youth social movement among Indigenous peoples: The case of Bedouin society in the Negev.* (Unpublished master's thesis). Ben Gurion University.

Ben-Eliezer, U. (1998). *The making of Israeli militarism.* Bloomington: Indiana University Press.

Ben-Eliezer, U. (1999). Is there a formation process of a civil society in Israel? Politics and identity of new CSOs. *Israeli sociology: A journal for the study of society in Israel, 2*(1), 51–97. [Hebrew]

Ben Eliezer, U. (2003). New associations or new politics? The significance of Israeli style post-materialism. *Hagar, International Social Science Review, 4*(1), 5–34.

Ben Eliezer, U. (2012). *Old conflict, new war: Israel's politics toward the Palestinians.* New York: Palgrave MacMillan.

Ben Eliezer, U. (2015). The civil society, the uncivil society, and the difficulty Israel has making peace with the Palestinians. *Journal of Civil Society, 11*(2), 170–186.

Bennett, W. L. (2003). Communicating global activism: Strengths and vulnerabilities of networked politics. *Information, Communication & Society, 6*(2), 143–168.

Berger B. (2009). Political theory, political science, and the end of civic engagement. *Perspectives on Politics, 7*(2), 335–350.

Berman, S. (1997). Civil society and the collapse of the Weimar Republic. *World Politics, 49*(3), 401–429.

Bhabha, H. (1994). *The location of culture.* New York: Routledge.

Bimber, B., Flanagin, A., & Stohl, C. (2005). Reconceptualizing collective action in the contemporary media environment. *Communication Theory, 14*(4), 365–388.

Bishara, A. (1993). Regarding the issue of Israel's Palestinian minority. In U. Ram (Ed.), *Israeli society: Critical aspects* (pp. 203–221). Tel Aviv: Brerot. [Hebrew]

Bodo, B. (2016). Minority civil society. *European and Regional Studies, 10,* 51–64.

Bourdieu, P. (1985). The forms of capital. In J. Richardson (Ed.), *Handbook of theory and research for the sociology of education* (pp. 241–258). New York: Greenwood.

Bourdieu, P. (1991). *Language and symbolic power.* Cambridge: Harvard University Press.

Bourdieu, P., & Wacquant, L. (1996). *An invitation to reflective sociology.* Chicago: University of Chicago Press.

Boyatzis, R. E. (1998). *Transforming qualitative information: Thematic analysis and code development.* Thousand Oaks, CA: Sage Publications.

Boyd, R. (2004). Michael Oakeshott on civility, civil society and civil association. *Political Studies, 52,* 603–622.

Bratton, M. (1989). Beyond the state: Civil society and associational life in Africa. *World Politics, 41*(3), 407–30.

Braun, V., & Clarke, V. (2006). Using thematic analysis in psychology. *Qualitative Research in Psychology, 3*(2), 77–101.

Brosig, M. (2012). No space for constructivism? A critical appraisal of European compliance. *Research Perspectives on European Politics and Society, 13*(4), 390–407.

Brown, D. (1989). The state of ethnicity and the ethnicity of the state: Ethnic politics in Southeast Asia. *Ethnic and Racial Studies, 12*(1), 47–62.

Brownlee, J., Masoud, T., & Reynolds, A. (2015). *The Arab Spring: Pathways of repression and reform.* Oxford: Oxford University Press.

Brubaker, R. (1996). Nationalizing states in the old "new Europe"—and the new. *Ethnic and Racial Studies, 19*(2), 412–437.

Burnell P., & Calvert, P. (2004). *Civil society in democratization.* London: Frank Cass.

Campbell, D. T. (1975). "Degrees of freedom" and the case study. *Comparative Political Studies, 8*(2), 178–193.

Campbell, J. (1998). Dewey's conception of community. In L.A. Hickman (Ed.), *Reading Dewey: Interpretations for a postmodern generation* (pp. 23–42). Bloomington, IN: Indiana University Press.

Carpenter, J., & Myers, K. C. (2010). Why volunteer?—evidence on the role of altruism, image, and incentives. *Journal of Public Economics, 94*, 911–920.

Castells, M. (2009). *Communication power.* New York: Oxford University Press.

Cavatorta F. (2012). Arab Spring: The awakening of civil society: a general overview. Retrieved from http://www.iemed.org/observatori-en/arees-danalisi/arxius-adjunts/anuari/med.2012/Cavatorta_en.pdf

Cavatorta, F., & Durac, V. (2010). *Civil society and democratization in the Arab world: The dynamic of activism.* London: Routledge.

Chambers, S., & Kopstein, J. (2001). Bad civil society. *Political Theory, 29*(6), 837–865.

Chandhoke, N. (2001). The "civil" and the "political" in civil society. *Democratization, 8*(2), 1–24.

Charmaz, K. (2002). Grounded theory: Methodology and theory construction. In N. J. Smelser & P. B. Baltes (Eds.), *International encyclopedia of the social and behavioral sciences* (pp. 6396–6399). Amsterdam: Pergamon.

Chatterjee, P. (2001). On civil and political society in post-colonial democracies. In S. Kaviraj & S. Khilnani (Eds.), *Civil society: history and possibilities* (pp. 165–178). Cambridge: Cambridge University Press.

Chazan, N. (2012). Democratic recession and the changing contours of civil society in Israel. *Palestine-Israel Journal, 18*(2–3), 1–6.

Clarke, G. (1998). Non-governmental organizations and politics in the developing world. *Political Studies, 46*(1), 36–52.

Coffe, H., & Bolzendahl, C. (2011). Civil society and diversity. In M. Edward (Ed.), *The Oxford handbook on civil society.* Oxford: Oxford University Press.

Cohen, H. (2006). *Good Arabs.* Jerusalem: Keter. [Hebrew]

Cohen, J. L. (1982). *Class and civil society: The limits of Marxian critical theory.* Amherst, MA: University of Massachusetts Press.

Cohen, J. L. (1988). Discourse ethics and civil society. *Philosophy and Social Criticism, 14*, 315–337.

Cohen J. L., & Arato, A. (1992). *Civil society and political theory.* Cambridge, MA: MIT Press.

Colas, A. (2002). *International civil society: Social movements in world politics.* Cambridge, MA: Polity Press.

Colas, A. (2005). Global civil society: Analytical category or normative concept? In G. Baker & D. Chandler (Eds.), *Global civil society: Contested futures* (pp. 14–28). London: Routledge.

Conge, P. J. (1988). The concept of political participation: Toward a definition. *Comparative Politics, 20*(2), 241–249.

Connolly, W. E. (1973). Theoretical self-consciousness. *Polity, 6*(1), 5–35.

Daher, A. (1990). *Al-Akhlaq Wal-Akel* [Morality and the mind]. Amman: Dar Al-Shuruk.

Dahl, R. (1998). *On democracy.* New Haven: Yale University Press.

Dahl, R. (2005). What political institutions does large-scale democracy require? *Political Science Quarterly, 120*(2), 187–197.

Dahlberg, L., & Siapera, E. (Eds.). (2007). *Radical democracy and the internet: Interrogating theory and practice.* UK: Palgrave Macmillan.

Dallasheh, L. (2012). *Nazarenes in the turbulent tide of citizenships: Nazareth from 1940 to 1966.* (Unpublished PhD dissertation). New York University.

Dalton, R. (2008). Citizenship norms and the expansion of political participation. *Political Studies, 56,* 76–98.

Dalton, R. (2019). *Citizen politics: public opinion and political parties in advanced industrial democracies* (7th ed.). New York: CQ Press.

Delanty, G. (2000). *Citizenship in a global age: society, culture, politics.* Buckingham: Open University Press.

De Maggio P., & Anheier, H. (1990). The sociology of nonprofit organizations and sectors. *Annual Review of Sociology, 16,* 137–159.

de Tocqueville, A. (1961). *Democracy in America.* (Reeve, H., Trans.). New York: Schocken Books.

Deutsch, K. (1966). *Nationalism and social communication: An inquiry into the foundations of nationality.* Cambridge, MA: MIT Press.

Diamond, L. (1994). Rethinking civil society: Toward democratic consolidation. *Journal of Democracy, 5,* 4–18.

Doron, A. (2003). The welfare regime in Israel: The changes and their social implications. *Israeli Sociology, 5*(2), 417–434. [Hebrew]

Doron, G., Harris, M., Katz, Y., & Woodlief, A. (1997). Ideology and privatization policy in Israel. *Environment & Planning C: Politics & Space, 15*(3), 363–372.

Douzinas C., & Zizek, S. (2010). *The idea of communism.* London: Verso.

Dunn, J. (2001). The contemporary political significance of John Locke's concept of civil society. In S. Kaviraj & S. Khilnani (Eds.), *Civil society: History and possibilities* (pp. 39–57). Cambridge: Cambridge University Press.

Edwards, M. (1999). NGO performance—What breeds success new evidence from South Asia. *World Development, 27,* 361–374.

Edwards, M. (ed.). (2011). *The Oxford handbook of civil society.* Oxford: Oxford University Press.

Ehrenberg, J. (1999). *Civil society: The critical history of an idea.* New York: New York University Press.

Ekman, J., & Amnå, E. (2012). Political participation and civic engagement: Towards a new typology. *Human Affairs, 22*(3), 283–300.

Enjolras, B. (2008). Two hypothesis about the emergence of a post-national European model of citizenship. *Citizenship Studies, 12*(5), 495–505.

Farr, J. (2004). Social capital: A conceptual history. *Political theory, 32*(1), 6–33.

Feldman, S. (1997). CSOs and civil society: (Un)stated contradictions. *Annals of the American Academy of Political and Social Science, 554*, 46–65.

Feurstein, M. (2008). Epistemic democracy and the social character of knowledge. *Episteme, 5*(1), 74–93.

Filc, D., & Ram, U. (2004). *The power of capital: Israeli society in the global era.* Tel-Aviv: The Van Leer Institute and Hakibbutz Hameuchad. [Hebrew]

Fischer, E. (2007). Introduction: Indigenous peoples, neo-liberal regimes, and varieties of civil society in Latin America. *Social Analysis, 51*(2), 1–18.

Fischer, E. (Ed.). (2009). *Indigenous peoples, civil society and the neo-liberal state in Latin America.* New York: Berghahn Books.

Fisher, J. (1998). *Non-governments: CSOs and the political development of the Third World.* West Hartford: Kumarian Press.

Fishkin, J. (2009). *When the people speak: Deliberative democracy and public consultation.* Oxford: Oxford University Press.

Fleischmann, E. (2003). *The nation and its "new" women: The Palestinian women's movement, 1920–1948.* Oakland: University of California Press.

Flyvbjerg, B. (2001). *Making social science matter: Why social inquiry fails and how it can succeed again.* Cambridge: Cambridge University Press.

Foley, M., & Edwards, B. (1996). The paradoxes of civil society. *Journal of Democracy, 7*, 38–52.

Foucault, M. (1980). In C. Gordon (Ed.), *Power/knowledge: Selected interviews and other writings, 1972–1977.* Brighton, Sussex: Harvester Press.

Foucault, M. (1991). Governmentality. In G. Burchell, C. Gordon, & P. Miller (Eds.), *The Foucault effect: Studies in governmentality* (pp. 87–104). Hemel Hempstead: Harvester Wheatsheaf.

Foucault, M. (2003). Truth and power. In P. Rabinow & N. Rose (Eds.), *The Essential Foucault: Selections from essential works of Foucault 1954–1984* (pp. 300–318). London: The New Press.

Fox, J. (1996). How does civil society thicken? The political construction of social capital in rural Mexico. *World Development, 24*(6), 1089–1103.

Frisch, H. (2011). *Israel's security and its Arab citizens.* Cambridge: Cambridge University Press.

Gal, J. (2010). Is there an extended family of Mediterranean welfare states? *Journal of European Social Policy, 20*(4), 283–300.

Galion, B. (1992). *Igtiyal Al-Akal* [The assassination of the mind]. Beirut: Arab Institute for Research and Publishing.

Galnoor, I., & Blender, D. (2013). *The political system of Israel: Formative years, institutional structure, political behavior and unsolved problems.* Tel Aviv: Am Oved. [Hebrew]

Ghanem, A., & Azaiza F. (Eds.). (2008). *Is it possible to overcome the crisis? The Arab municipalities in Israel in the beginning of the 21st century.* Jerusalem: Carmel. [Hebrew]

Ghanem, A., & Mustafa, M. (2010). *Palestinians in Israel: The politics of indigenous minority in an ethnic state.* Ramalla: Madar. [Arabic]

Ghanim, H. (2005). *Attitudes towards the status of Palestinian women and their rights in Israel.* Nazareth: Women Against Violence Association.

Ghanim, H. (2009). *Reinventing the nation: Palestinian intellectuals in Israel.* Jerusalem: Magnes. [Hebrew]

Ghanim, H. (2017). The Communist Party in Israel: Between nationalism and the state. *Journal of Palestine Studies, 28*(112), 102–127. [Arabic]

Ghannūshī, R. (1994). *Fī al-Mabādiʿ al-Asāsīyah lil-Dīmuqrāṭīyah wa-Uṣūl al-Ḥukm al-Islāmī* (The Principles of democracy and the fundamentals of Islamic government). Al-Dar al-Baydaa: Dar Alfurqan.

Gharrah, R. (2016). *Arab society in Israel: Population, society, economy.* Jerusalem: Van Leer Institute Press. [Hebrew]

Gharrah, R. (2018). *Arab society in Israel: Population, society, economy.* Jerusalem: Van Leer Institute Press. [Hebrew]

Gidron, B., Bar, M., & Katz, H. (2003). *The third sector in Israel.* Tel Aviv: Hakibbutz Hameuhad. [Hebrew]

Glaser, B. (1992). *Basics of grounded theory analysis.* Mill Valley, CA: Sociology Press.

Gramsci, A. (1994). *Letters from prison.* F. Rosengarten (Ed.) & R. Raymond (Trans.). New York: Columbia University Press.

Grendstad, G., & Selle, P. (1995). Cultural theory and the new institutionalism. *Journal of Theoretical Politics, 7*(1), 5–27.

Griffiths, G. (1994). The myth of authenticity, representation, discourse and social practice. In C. Tiffin & A. Lawson (Eds.), *De-scribing empire: Postcolonialism and textuality* (pp. 70–86). London: Routledge.

Gurr, T. (2015). *Political rebellion: Causes outcomes and alternatives.* London: Routledge.

Gutmann, A. (Ed.). (1998). *Freedom of association.* Princeton, NJ: Princeton University Press.

Habermas, J. (1973). *Theory and practice* (J. Viertel, Trans.). Boston: Beacon Press.

Habermas, J. (1975). *Legitimation crisis.* (T. McCarthy, Trans.). Boston: Beacon Press.

Habermas, J. (1989). *The Philosophical discourse of modernity: Twelve lectures* (F. Lawerence, Trans.). Oxford: Polity Press.

Habermas, J. (1992). *The structural transformation of the public sphere: An inquiry into a category of bourgeois society.* Oxford: Polity Press.

Habermas, J. (2005). Concluding comments on empirical approaches to deliberative politics. *Acta Politica, 40,* 384–392.

Habib, A. (2005). State-civil society relations in post-Apartheid South Africa. *Social Research, 72*(3), 671–692.

Hadenius, A., Uggla, F. (1996). Making civil society work, promoting democratic development: What can states and donors do? *World Development, 24*(10), 1621–1639.

Haider, A. (2010). *The collapse of Arab local authorities: Suggestions for restructuring.* Jerusalem: The Van Leer Jerusalem Institute and Hakibbutz Hameuchad. [Hebrew]

Haider, H. (2017). *Political aspects in the life of Palestinians in Israel.* Jerusalem: Van Leer Institute.

Haider, A. (Ed.). (2018). *Political aspects in the lives of Arab citizens of Israel.* Jerusalem: Van Leer and Hakibbutz Hameuchad.

Haklai, O. (2004). Palestinian CSOs in Israel: A campaign for civic equality or "ethnic civil society"? *Israel Studies, 9*(3), 157–168.

Haklai, O. (2008). Helping the enemy? Why transnational Jewish philanthropic foundations donate to Palestinian CSOs in Israel? *Nations and Nationalism, 14*(3), 581–599.

Haklai, O. (2011). *Arab ethnonational in Israel.* Philadelphia: University of Pennsylvania Press.

Hall, S. (1996). When was "the post-colonial"? Thinking at the limit. In L. Chambers & L. Curti (Eds.), *The post-colonial question: Common skies, divided horizons.* London: Routledge.

Harb, A. (2014). *Mullak Al-Allah Wal-Awtan* [The owners of God and the homelands]. Beirut: Arab Scientific Publishers Inc. [Arabic]

Harding, S. (1993). Rethinking standpoint epistemology: What is "strong objectivity"? In L. Alcoff & P. Elizabeth (eds.), *Feminist epistemologies* (pp. 49–82). London: Routledge.

Harlap, I. (2017). *The "after" television: New Israeli drama.* Tel Aviv: Resling.

Harriss, J. (2006). Middle class activism and the politics of the informal working class. *Critical Asian Studies, 38*(4), 445–465.

Hart, V., Thompson, L., & Stedman, T. (2008). The indigenous experience of Australian civil society: Making sense of historic and contemporary institutions. *Social Alternatives, 27*(1), 52–57.

Hassan, M. (2006). Patriarchy, the state and the killing of women in the name of family honor. In D. Izraeli, A. Fredman, H. Dahan-Kalev, S. Fogiel-Bijaoui, H. Herzog, M. Hassan, & H. Naveh (Eds.), *Sex gender politics: Women in Israel* (pp. 267–305). Tel Aviv: Hakibbutz Hameuchad.

Hasson, S., & Abu-Asbah, K. (Eds.). (2004). *Jews and Arabs in Israel facing a changing reality—dilemmas, trends, scenarios and recommendations.* Jerusalem: Fluersheimer Studies, 3/32. [Hebrew]

Hasson, S., & Michael K. M. (2006). *Arabs in Israel: Barriers to equality.* Jerusalem: Fluersheimer Studies. [Hebrew]

Havel, V. (1985). The power of the powerless. In J. Keane (Ed.), *The power of the powerless* (pp. 78–79). Armonk: M. E. Sharpe.

Haveman, P. (1999). *Indigenous peoples' rights in Australia, Canada and New Zealand.* Oxford: Oxford University Press.

Haynes, J. (1996). *Democracy and civil society in the Third World: Politics and new political movements.* Cambridge: Polity Press.

Hegel, G. W. F. (1952). *The philosophy of right.* Oxford: Oxford University Press.

Herman, T. (1995). *From the bottom up: Social movements and political protest.* Tel-Aviv: Open University. [Hebrew]

Higgs, J. (2001). Charting stand-points in qualitative research. In H. Byrne-Armstrong, J. Higgs, & D. Horsfall (Eds.). *Critical moments in qualitative research* (pp. 44–67). Oxford, UK: Butterworth Heinemann.

Hofmann, M., & Jamal, A. (2012). The youth and the Arab Spring: Cohort differences and similarities. *Middle East Law and Governance, 4*(1), 168–188.

Hopkins, N., & Ibrahim, S. E. (Eds.). (2006). *Arab society: Class, gender, power and development.* Cairo: American University of Cairo Press.

Horowitz, D., & Moshe, L. (1977). *From a community to a state: The Jews of Palestine during the British Mandate as a political community.* Tel-Aviv: Am Oved. [Hebrew]

Hulme, D., & Edwards, M. (Eds.). (1997). *CSOs, states and donors: Too close for comfort?* London: Macmillan.

Huntington, S. (1991). *The third wave: Democratization in the late twentieth century.* Norman, OK: University of Oklahoma Press.

Ibrahim, H. (2004). Political parties, civil society and the transition into democracy. In G. S. Makdisi, R. Dabbas, G. Sa'adeh, F. Kiwan & M. R. Zalzal (Eds.), *Civil society in the Arab world and the challenge of democracy.* Beirut: Lebanese Association of Women Researchers and the Fridrich Ebert Association. [Arabic]

Israel, J. (2015). Capabilities, religionizing effects and contemporary Jewishness. In T. Stack, N. Goldenberg, & T. Fitzgerald (Eds.), *Religion as a category of governance and sovereignty* (pp. 197–227). Leiden: Brill.

Jabareen, H. (2002). The future of Arab citizenship in Israel: Jewish-Zionist time in a place with no Palestinian memory. In D. Levy & Y. Weiss (Eds), *Challenging ethnic citizenship* (pp. 196–220). New York: Berghahn Books.

Jabareen, H. (2001). Israeli spirit that predicts the future of Arabs according to a Jewish-Zionist time, in a space with no Palestinian time. *Mishpat U-Mimshal, 1*(1), 53–86. [Hebrew]

Jabareen, H. (2014). Hobbesian citizenship: How the Palestinians became a minority in Israel. In W. Kymlicka & E. Pföstl (Eds.), *Multiculturalism and minority rights in the Arab world* (pp. 189–218). Oxford: Oxford University Press.

Jacobson, A. (2018). The national liberation leagues in Mandatory Palestine: Between ideology and practice, between national liberation and national conflict. *Historia, 39–40,* 75–104. [Hebrew]

Jacobson, K., & Korolczuk, E. (Eds.). (2017). *Civil society revisited: Lessons from Poland.* New York: Berghahn Books.

Jamal, A. (2002). Abstention as participation: About the dilemmas of Arab politics in Israel. In A. Asher & M. Shamir (Eds.), *Israel elections—2001* (pp. 57–100). Jerusalem: The Israel Democracy Institution.

Jamal, A. (2003). Thoughts on the dilemma of under-representation and in-affectivity. *Eretz Acheret*, 20–24. [Hebrew]

Jamal, A. (2005). On the morality of Arab collective rights in Israel. *Adalah's Newsletter*, 12, Retrieved from www.adalah.org/newsletter/eng/apr05/ar1.pdf

Jamal, A. (2006a). Political participation and the lack of effective vote for Arabs in Israel. In Sh. Hasson & M. Karayani (Eds.), *Arabs in Israel: Barriers to equality* (pp. 125–140). Jerusalem: Floersheimer Institute for Policy Studies. [Hebrew]

Jamal, A. (2006b). The Arab leadership in Israel: Ascendance and fragmentation. *Journal of Palestine Studies, 35*(2), 6–22.

Jamal, A. (2006c). *The culture of media consumption among national minorities: The case of Arab society in Israel.* Nazareth: I'lam Center.

Jamal, A. (2007a). Nationalizing states and the constitution of "hollow citizenship": Israel and its Palestinian citizens. *Ethnopolitics, 6*(4), 471–493.

Jamal, A. (2007b). Strategies of minority struggle for equality in ethnic states: Arab politics in Israel. *Citizenship Studies, 11*(3), 263–282.

Jamal, A. (2008). Future visions and current dilemmas: On the political ethos of Palestinian citizens of Israel. *Israel Studies Forum, 23*(2), 3–28.

Jamal, A. (2009). Media culture as counter-hegemonic strategy: The communicative action of the Arab minority in Israel. *Media, Culture and Society, 31*(4), 1–19.

Jamal, A. (2010). *The dialectics of memory and forgetfulness: Israeli independence and Palestinian Nakba.* Tel Aviv: Walter Lebach Institute for Jewish-Arab Relations. [Hebrew]

Jamal, A. (2011). *Arab minority nationalism in Israel: The politics of indigeneity.* London: Routledge.

Jamal, A. (2014). Israels palästinensische Bürger: Status und Rolle einer separierten Bevölkerungsgruppe. In B. Schwarz-Boenneke (Ed.), *Israel im Auge des Sturms Gesellschaftlich gespalten – politisch gefordert* (pp. 54–71). Freiburg: Herder Verlag.

Jamal, A. (2016). Constitutionalizing sophisticated racism: Israel's proposed nationality law. *Journal of Palestine Studies, 45*(2), 40–51.

Jamal, A. (2017). *Arab civil society in Israel: New elites, social capital and challenging power structures.* Jerusalem: Hakibbutz Hameuchad [Hebrew].

Jamal, A. (2018). The hegemony of neo-Zionism and the nationalizing state in Israel: The meaning and implications of the Nation-State Law. In S. Rabinovitch (Ed.), *Defining Israel: The Jewish state democracy and the law* (pp. 159–182). Hebrew Union College Press.

Jamal, A. (2019). Ontological counter-securitization in asymmetric power relations: Lessons from Israel. *International Studies Review*, 1–25. Retrieved from https://doi.org/10.1093/isr/viz057

Jamal, A., & Bsoul, S. (2014). *The Palestinian Nakba in the Israeli Public Sphere: Formations of Denial and Responsibility.* Nazareth: I'lam Media Center. [Hebrew]

Jamal, A., & Kensicki, A. (2016). A theory of critical junctures of democratization: A comparative examination of constitution making in Egypt and Tunisia. *Law and Ethics of Human Rights, 10*(1), 185–222.

Jamal A. (2006). Reassessing support for Islam and democracy in the Arab world? Evidence from Egypt and Jordan. *World Affairs, 169*(2), 51–56.

Jamal, A. (2008). *Barriers to democracy: The other side of social capital in Palestine and the Arab world.* Princeton: Princeton University Press.

Jorgensen, M. W. (2010). The terms of debate: The negotiation of the legitimacy of marginalized perspective. *Social Epistemology: A Journal of Knowledge, Culture and Policy, 24*(4), 313–330.

Jessop, B. (2007). *State power: A strategic-relational approach.* Cambridge: Polity Press.

Jiryis, S. (1976). *The Arabs in Israel.* New York: Monthly Review Press.

Joseph, S. (Ed.). (1999). *Intimate selving in Arab families: Gender, self and identity.* Syracuse: Syracuse University Press.

Kaadan, T. (2019). Ande—The establishment and development of a women's organization. In A. Jamal (Ed.), *The conflict: Sociological, historical and geopolitical aspects* (pp. 71–92). Tel Aviv: Walter Lebach Institute.

Kaase, M., & Marsh, A. (1979). Political action: A theoretical perspective. In S. Barnes, K. R. Allerbeck, B. Farah, F. Heunks, R. Inglehart, K. Jennings, H. D. Klingemann, A. Marsh & L. Rosenmayr (Eds.), *Political action: Mass participation in five Western democracies* (pp. 27–56). London: Sage.

Kahwaji, H. (1972). *The Arabs in the shadow of Israeli occupation of 1948.* Beirut: PLO Reasearch Center.

Kanaaneh, R., & Nusair, I. (2010). *Displaced at home: Ethnicity and gender among Palestinians in Israel.* New York: State University of New York Press.

Kandiyoti, D. (Ed.). (1991). *Women, Islam and the state.* Philadelphia: Temple University Press.

Karkabi-Sabah, M. (2009). The organizational base of the Hamulah and the status of Arab women. In F. Azazyeh, K. Abu Baker, R. Hertz-Lazarowitz, & A. Ghanem (Eds.), *Arab women in Israel* (pp. 47–70). Tel Aviv: Ramot Publications.

Kaufman, I. (1997). *Arab national communism in the Jewish state.* Gainesville: University of Florida Press.

Kaufman, R. & Gidron, B. (2006). *The institutionalization and professionalization of protest?: Characteristics and trends in the establishment of organizations for social change in Israel.* Beer Sheva: Ben Gurion University, the Center for the Study of the Third Sector.

Kaviraj, S., and Khilnani, S. (Eds.). (2001). *Civil society: History and possibilities.* Cambridge: Cambridge University Press.

Keane, J. (1998). *Civil society and the state: New European perspectives.* London: University of Westminster Press.

Keane, J. (1998a). *Civil society: Old images, new visions.* Cambridge: Polity Press.

Keating, M., & McGarry, J. (2001). *Minority nationalism and the changing international order.* Oxford: Oxford University Press.

Kedar, A., Amara, A., & Yiftachel, O. (2018). *Emptied lands: Geography of Bedouin rights in the Negev.* Redwood City, CA: Stanford University Press.

Khadouri, M. (1970). *Political trends in the Arab World: The role of ideas and ideals in politics.* Baltimore: The Johns Hopkins University Press.

Khaldun, I. (1967). *An introduction to history: The Muqaddimah* (N. J. Dawood, F. Rosenthal, Eds.). Princeton, NJ: Princeton University Press.

Khilnani, S. (2001). The development of civil society. In S. Kaviraj. & S. Khilnani (Eds.), *Civil society: History and possibilities* (pp. 11–32). Cambridge: Cambridge University Press.

Kidar, S., & Yiftachel, O. (2006). Land regime and social relations in Israel. In H. de Soto & F. Cheneval (Eds.), *Realizing property rights.* Zurich: Ruffer and Rub Publishing House.

Kimmerling, B. (2004). *Immigrant, settlers, natives.* Tel Aviv: Am Oved. [Hebrew]

Kimmerling, B. (2001). *The Invention and decline of Israeliness.* Berkeley, CA: University of California Press.

Kopecky, P., & Mudde, C. (2003). Rethinking civil society. *Democratization, 10*(3), 1–14.

Korovkin, T. (2001). Reinventing the communal tradition: Indigenous people, civil society and democratization in Andean Ecuador. *Latin American Research Review, 36*(3), 37–67.

Korten, D. (1990). *Getting to the 21st century: Voluntary action and the global agenda.* West Hartford, CT: Kumanian Press.

Krueger, R. A. (1994). *Focus groups: A practical guide for applied research.* New York: Sage Publications.

Krueger, R. A. (1998). *Analyzing and reporting focus group results.* Thousand Oaks, CA: Sage.

Kymlicka, W. *Politics in the Vernacular: Nationalism, multiculturalism, and citizenship.* Oxford: Oxford University Press.

Langohr, V. (2004). Too much civil society, too little politics: Egypt and liberalizing Arab regimes. *Comparative Politics, 36*(2), 181–204.

Latour, B. (2005). *Reassembling the social.* Oxford: Oxford University Press.

Lavi, N., & Jamal, A. (2019). Constructing ethno-national differentiation on the set of the television series, Fauda. *Ethnicities, 9*(6), 1038–1061.

Lax, J., & Phillips, J. (2009). How should we estimate public opinion in the states? *American Journal of Political Science, 53*(1), 107–121.

Leontsini, E. (2013). The motive of society: Aristotle on civic friendship justice and concord. *Res Publica, 19*(1), 21–35.

Levy, Y. (2007). *Israel's materialist militarism.* Lanham: Lexington Books.

Lewin-Epstein, N., & Semyonov, M. (1993). *The Arab minority in Israel's economy.* Boulder: Westview.

Limor, N. (Ed.). (2010). *Regulation of not-for-profit organizations.* Be'er Sheva: The Israeli Center for Third-Sector Research and Hakibbutz Hameuchad. [Hebrew]

Limor, N. (2012). *Principles for legal organization of nongovernmental organizations' law.* Jerusalem: Van Leer Institute.

Linz, J., & Stepan, A. (1996). *Problems of democratic transition and consolidation: Southern Europe, South America, and post-communist Europe.* Baltimore: Johns Hopkins University Press.

Litoselliti, L. (2003). *Using focus groups in research.* London: Continuum.

Lowndes, V. (1996). Varieties of new institutionalism: A critical appraisal. *Public Administration, 74*(2), 181–197.

Lukes, S. (2005). *Power—a radical view* (2nd ed.). New York: Palgrave-Macmillan.

Lustick, I. (1980). *Arabs in the Jewish State: Israel's control of a national minority.* Austin: University of Texas Press.

Lutterbeck, D. (2012). Arab uprisings, armed forces, and civil-military relations. *Armed Forces & Society, 39*(1), 28–52.

Lynch, M. (2014). The Arab uprisings explained: New contentious politics in the Middle East. *Turkish Journal of Middle Eastern Studies, 3*(1), 197–201.

Macedo, S. (1999). *Deliberative politics: Essays on democracy and disagreement: essays on democracy and disagreement.* Oxford: Oxford University Press.

Mandelkern, R., & Shalev, M. (2010). Power and the ascendance of new economic policy ideas: Lessons from the 1980s crisis in Israel. *World Politics, 62*(3), 459–495.

Manna, A. (Ed.). (2008). *Arab society in Israel: Populations, society, economy (2).* Jerusalem: The Van Leer Jerusalem Institute and Hakibbutz Hameuchad. [Hebrew]

Manna, A. (2016). *Nakba and survival: The story of the Palestinians who remained in Haifa and the Galilee 1948–1956.* Beirut: Institute for Palestine Studies. [Arabic]

March, D., & Olsen, J. (1983). The new institutionalism: Organizational factors in political life. *American Political Science Review, 78*(3), 734–749.

Mari S. (1978). *Arab education in Israel.* Syracuse: Syracuse University Press.

Marshall, T. H. (1950). *Citizenship and social class and other essays.* London: Cambridge University Press.

Martinez, T., & McMullin, S. (2004). Factors affecting decisions to volunteer in nongovernmental organizations. *Environment and Behavior, 36*(1), 112–126.

Marx, K. (1906). *Capital: A critique of political economy* (1st American ed.). F. Engels, S. Moore, B. Aveling., & E. Untermann (Eds.). Chicago: C. H. Kerr.

Massalha, K., & Jamal, A. (2012). *The discourse of human rights in the Israeli Media.* Nazareth: I'lam Center.

Mautner, M. (2002). The 1980s—time of fear. *Iyuney Mishpat, 26*(2), 645–736. [Hebrew]

McAdam, D., Tarrow, S., & Tilly, C. (2001). *Dynamics of contention.* New York: Cambridge University Press.

Melucci, A. (1989). *The nomads of the present: Social movements and individual needs in contemporary society.* K. John. & M. Paul (Eds). Philadelphia: Temple University Press.

Mendelson, S., and Glenn, J. (Eds.). (2002). *The power and limits of CSOs: A critical look at building democracy in Eastern Europe and Eurasia.* New York, NY: Columbia University Press.

Menuhin, Y. (2011). The fundamentals of civil society. *Civil society and third sector in Israel, 3*(2), 7–28. [Hebrew]

Mercer, C. (2002). CSOs, civil society and democratization: A critical review of the literature. *Progress in the Development Studies, 2*(1), 5–22.

Mesch, G. (2006). Family characteristics and intergenerational conflicts over the internet. *Information, Communication & Society, 9*, 473–495.

Mill, J. S. (2001). *Considerations on representative government.* London: Electric Book Company.

Mitchell, T. (1991). The limits of the state: Beyond statist approaches and their critics. *American Political Science Review, 85*(1), 77–96.

Moghadam, V. (2004). Women and changing family in the Middle East. *Journal of Comparative Family Studies, 35*(2), 137–162.

Mundlak, G. (2007). *Fading corporatism: Israel's labor law and industrial relations in transition.* Ithaca, NY: ilr Press/Cornell University Press.

Murray, M. (2003). Narrative psychology and narrative analysis. In P. Camic, J. Rhodes & L. Yardley (Eds.), *Qualitative research in psychology: expanding perspectives in methodology and design* (pp. 95–112). Washington, DC: American Psychological Association.

Mutz, D. (1998). *Impersonal influence: How perceptions of mass collectives affect political attitudes.* Cambridge: Cambridge University Press.

Nassar, M. (2017). *Brothers apart: Palestinian citizens of Israel and the Arab World.* Stanford: Stanford University Press.

Neblo, M. (2005). Thinking through democracy: Deliberative politics in theory and practice. *Acta Politica, 40*(2), 169–181.

Neuberger, B. (2010). *Parties and elections, leadership and media.* Raanana: Open University. [Hebrew]

Nitzan, J., & Bichler, Sh. (2002). *The global political economy of Israel.* London: Pluto Press.

Oakeshott, M. (1990). *On human conduct.* Oxford: Clarendon.

O'Connell, B. (1999). *Civil society: The underpinnings of American democracy.* Hanover, NH: University Press of New England.

O'Donnell, G., & Schmitter, P. (1986). *Transitions from authoritarian rule: Tentative conclusions about uncertain democracies.* Baltimore: The John Hopkins University Press.

Offe, C. (1999). How can we trust our fellow citizens? In M. Warren (Ed.), *Democracy and trust* (pp. 42–87). Cambridge: Cambridge University Press.

Olson, M. (1965). *The logic of collective action: Public goods and the theory of groups.* (Revised ed.). Cambridge: Harvard University Press.

Ophir, A. (2010). State. *Mafte'akh: Lexical review of political thought, 1*(35–60). [Hebrew]

Ozacky-Lazar, S. (2002). The military government as a mechanism of controlling Arab citizens: The first decade, 1948–1958. *Ha-Mizrah Ha-Hadash, 33*, 103–132.

Palatnik, R., & Shechter, M. (2012). The Israeli economy and potential post-Kyoto targets. *Israel Economic Review, 8*(1), 21–43.

Pappe, I. (2006). *The ethnic cleansing of Palestine.* Oxford: One-World Publications.

Parekh, B. (1995). Liberalism and colonialism: A critique of Locke and Mill. In J. Pieterse & B. Parekh (Eds.), *The decolonization of imagination: Culture, knowledge and power* (pp. 81–98). London: Zed.

Parekh, B. (2004). Putting civil society in its place. In M. Glasius, D. Lewis, & H. Seckinelgin (Eds.), *Exploring civil society: Political and cultural contexts* (pp. 15–25). London: Routledge.

Parsons, J., & Harding, K. (2011). Post-colonial theory and action research. *Turkish Online Journal of Qualitative Inquiry, 2*(2), 1–6.

Pateman, C. (1970). *Political participation and democratic theory.* Cambridge: Cambridge University Press.

Pattie, C., & Seyd, P. (2003). Citizenship and civic engagement: Attitudes and behavior in Britain. *Political Studies, 5,* 443–468.

Payes, S. (2003). Palestinian CSOs in Israel: A campaign for civic equality in a non-civic state. *Israel Studies, 8*(1), 60–90.

Pedhazur, A. (2004). *The Israeli defensive democracy.* Jerusalem: Carmel. [Hebrew]

Pelcynski, Z. A. (1998). Solidarity and "the rebirth of civil society" in Poland. In J. Keane (Ed.), *Civil society and the state: New European perspectives* (pp. 361–380). London: Verso.

Peled, Y. (2005). The Or Commission and Palestinian citizenship in Israel. *Citizenship Studies, 9*(1), 89–105.

Peled, Y. (2005b). Civil society in Israel. *Palestine-Israel Journal, 12*(1), 1–4.

Peled, Y., & Peled, H. (2018). *The religionization of Israeli society.* London: Routledge.

Peled, Y., & Shafir, G. (2005). *Being Israeli: The dynamics of multiple citizenship.* Tel Aviv: Tel Aviv University Press. [Hebrew]

Platt, J. (1992). Cases of cases . . . of cases. In C. Ragin & B. Becker (Eds.), *What is a case?: Exploring the foundations of social inquiry* (pp. 21–52). Cambridge: Cambridge University Press.

Portes, A. (1998). Social capital: Its origins and applications in modern sociology. *Annual Review of Sociology, 24,* 1–24.

Potter, J. (1997). Discursive psychology and the study of naturally occurring talk. *Qualitative research: Theory, Method and Practice, 2,* 200–222.

Putnam, R. (2000). *Bowling alone: The collapse and revival of American community.* New York: Simon and Schuster.

Rabinovitch, S. (Ed.). (2018). *Defining Israel: The Jewish state, democracy and the law.* Cincinnati: Hebrew Union College Press.

Rabinowitz, D. (2001). De Tocqueville in Umm Al-Fahm. In Y. Peled. & O. Adi (Eds.). *Israel: from a recruited society to civil society?* (pp. 350–360). Jerusalem: The Van Leer Institute and Hakibbutz Hameuchad. [Hebrew]

Ragin, C., & Becker, H. (1992). *What is a case?: Exploring the foundations of social inquiry.* Cambridge: Cambridge University Press.

Ragnedda, M., & Muschert, G. (Eds.). (2013). *The digital divide: The internet and social inequality in international perspective.* Oxon: Routledge.

Ram, U. (1996). Memory and identity: sociology of the historians' debate in Israel. *Theory and Critique,* 8, 9–32. [Hebrew]

Ram, U. (2005). *The globalization of Israel: Mcworld in Tel Aviv, Jihad and Jerusalem.* Tel Aviv: Resling. [Hebrew]

Ranciere, J. (2004). *The politics of aesthetics: The distribution of the sensible.* (R. Gabriel, Trans.). London: Continuum International Publishing Group.

Ranciere, J. (2010). *Dissensus: On politics and aesthetics.* (S. Corcoran, Trans.). London: Continuum International Publishing Group.

Razin, E. (2000). *How to secure municipal amalgamation.* Jerusalem: Fluersheimer Studies, 1/51. [Hebrew]

Reiter, I. (Ed.). (2013). *Arab society in Israel-information collection.* Naveh Ilan: The Abraham Fund Initiative.

Reiter Y. (2009). *National majority, regional minority: Palestinian Arabs versus Jews in Israel.* Syracuse: Syracuse University Press.

Rekhess, E. (1993). *The Arab minority in Israel: Between communism and Arab nationalism.* Tel Aviv: Hakibbutz Hamiuchad.

Reynolds, D. (2015). *The Cambridge companion to modern Arab Culture.* Cambridge: Cambridge University Press.

Richmond, O. P. (2011). Critical agency, resistance and post-colonial civil society. *Co-operation and Conflict,* 46(4), 419–440.

Riessman, C. K. (1993). *Narrative analysis.* Newbury Park, CA: Sage.

Riker, W. (1982). *Liberalism against populism: A confrontation between the theory of democracy and the theory of social choice.* San Francisco: W.H. Freeman.

Rivlin, P. (2011). *The Israeli economy from the foundation of the state through the 21st century.* Cambridge: Cambridge University Press.

Robson, L. (2011). *Colonialism and Christianity in Mandate Palestine.* Austin: Texas University Press.

Rojas, H., Shah D., & Friedland, L. (2011). A communicative approach to social capital. *Journal of Communication,* 61, 689–712.

Rosenblum, N. (1998). *Membership and morals: the personal uses of pluralism in America.* Princeton: Princeton University Press.

Rosenblum, N., & Post, R. (Eds.). (2002). *Civil society and government.* Princeton: Princeton University Press, 1–25.

Rouhana, N. (Ed.). (2007). *Attitudes of Palestinians in Israel on key political and social issues: Survey research results.* Haifa: Mada Al-Carmel.

Rouhana, N., & Ghanem, A. (1998). The crisis of minorities in ethnic states: The case of the Palestinian citizens in Israel. *International Journal of Middle East Studies,* 30, 321–346.

Rouhana, N., & Huneidi, S. (2017). *Israel and its Palestinian citizens: Ethnic privileges in the Jewish state*. Cambridge: Cambridge University Press.

Rubin-Peled, A. (2001). *Debating Islam in the Jewish State*. New York: State University of New York Press.

Sa'di, A. H., & Abu-Lughod, L. (2007). *Nakba: Palestine, 1948, and the claims of memory*. New York, NY: Columbia University Press.

Sartori, G. (1970). Concept misformation in comparative politics. *American Political Science Review, 64*(4), 1033–1053.

Schmidt, V. (2008). Discursive institutionalism: The explanatory power of ideas and discourse. *Annual Review of Political Science, 11*(1), 303–326.

Schneider, C. L. (1995). *Shantytown protest in Pinochet's Chile*. Philadelphia: Temple University Press.

Schwarzberg, M. (2015). Epistemic democracy and its challenges. *Annual Review of Politics, 18*, 187–203.

Schwarzenbach, S. (1996). On civic friendship. *Ethics, 107*(1), 97–128.

Seale C. (1999). *The quality of qualitative research*. London: Sage Publishing.

Seligman, A. (1992). *The idea of civil society*. New York: Free Press.

Shafir, G., & Peled, Y. (2002). *Being Israeli: The dynamics of multiple citizenship*. Cambridge: Cambridge University Press.

Shalev, M. (1992). *Labour and the political economy in Israel*. Oxford: Oxford University Press.

Shalev, M. (2004). Have the globalization and liberalization normalized the political economy of Israel? In D. Filc & U. Ram (Eds.), *The rule of capital: Israeli society in the global age* (pp. 84–115). Tel Aviv: Hakkibutz Hameuchad and Van Leer Institute.

Shalhoun-Kevorkian, N. (Ed.). (2007). *Palestinian feminist writing: Between oppression and resistance*. Haifa: Mada Al-Carmel.

Shamir, J., & Shamir, M. (2000). *The anatomy of public opinion*. Ann Arbor: The University of Michigan Press.

Sharabi, H. (1988). *Neopatriarchy: A theory of distorted change in Arab society*. New York: Oxford University Press.

Shefer, G., Barak, O., & Oren, A. (Eds.). (2008). *An army that has a state?: A new view on Israel's security and the security sector*. Jerusalem: Carmel. [Hebrew]

Shen, K., & Shakir, M. (2009). Internet usage among Arab adolescents: Preliminary findings. *International Journal of Logistics Systems and Management, 11*(2), 147–159.

Shepsle, K. (1989). Studying institutions: Some lessons from rational choice approach. *Journal of Theoretical Politics, 1*(2), 131–147.

Shkedi, A. (2003). *Words that try to touch: A qualitative research—theory and practice*. Tel Aviv: Ramot. [Hebrew]

Shore, P., & Sabar Ben-Yehoshua, N. (2010). From report to a narrative: On searching for a meaning in research interviews. In R. Tuval-Massiah. &

G. Spector-Marzel (Eds.), *Narrative research: Theory, production and interpretation* (pp. 197–220). Jerusalem: Magnes Press and Mofet Institute.

Skocpol, T. (1979). *States and social revolutions: A comparative analysis of France, Russia and China.* Cambridge: Cambridge University Press.

Smith, R. (1997). *Civic ideals: Conflicting visions of citizenship in U.S. history.* New Heaven: Yale University Press.

Smooha, S. (1992). *Arabs and Jews in Israel. Change and continuity in mutual intolerance, 2.* Boulder and London: Westview Press.

Smooha, S. (2012). *Still playing by the rule: Index of Arab-Jewish relations in Israel 2012.* Jerusalem: Israeli Democracy Institute.

Sorek, T. (2015). *Palestinian commemoration in Israel: Calendars, monuments and martyrs.* Stanford: Stanford University Press.

Sosin, M. (2011). Social expectations, constraints, and their effect on nonprofit strategies. *Nonprofit and Voluntary Sector Quarterly, 41*(6), 1231–1250.

Steinberg, G. From Durban to the Goldstone Report: The centrality of human rights CSOs in the political dimension of the Arab-Israeli conflict. *Israel Affairs, 18*(3), 372–388.

Steinberg, G. (2013). False witness?: EU-funded CSOs and policymaking in the Arab-Israeli conflict. *The Israel Journal of Foreign Affairs, 2*(2), 59–72.

Sunstein, C. (2017). *#Republic: Divided democracy in the age of social media.* Princeton: Princeton University Press.

Tamimi, A. S. (2001). *Rachid Ghannouchi: A democrat within Islamism.* Oxford: Oxford University Press.

Tamir, Y. (1993). *Liberal nationalism.* Princeton: Princeton University Press.

Tarrow, S. (1994). *Power in movement: Social movements and contentious politics.* Cambridge: Cambridge University Press.

Tarrow, S. (1996). Making social science work across space and time: A critical reflection on Robert Putnam's "Making Democracy Work." *American Political Science Review, 90,* 389–397.

Tauben-Oberman, Y. (2014). *Protest as a mirror?: Organizations of social change and the social protest of summer 2011 in Israel* (Unpublished master's thesis). Tel Aviv University, Tel Aviv.

Toland, J. (Ed.). (2017). *Ethnicity and the state.* Abingdon: Routledge.

Touraine, A. (1983). *Solidarity: The analysis of a social movement: Poland, 1980–1981.* Cambridge: Cambridge University Press.

Tsao, R. (2002). Arendt against Athens: Rereading the human condition. *Political Theory, 30*(1), 97–123.

Tsosie, R. (2003). Tribalism, constitutionalism and cultural pluralism: Where do indigenous peoples fit within civil society. *Journal of Constitutional Law, 5*(2), 357–404.

Tsutsu, K. (2004). Global civil society and ethnic social movement in the world today. *Sociological Forum, 19*(1), 63–87.

Tufekci, Z., & Wilson, Ch. (2012). Social media and the decision to participate in political protest: Observations from Tahrir Square. *Journal of Communication, 62*(2), 1460–2466.

Van Deth, W. J. (2014). A conceptual map of political participation. *Acta Politica, 49*(3), 349–367.

Van Genugten, W., & Perez-Bustillo, C. (2004). The emerging international architecture of indigenous rights: The interaction between global, regional and local dimensions. *International Journal on Minority and Group Rights, 11*, 379–409.

Van Till, J. (2008). A paradigm shift in the third sector: Theory and practice: refreshing the wellsprings of democratic capacity. *American Behavioral Scientist, 52*(7), 1069–1081.

Verba, S. (1967). Democratic participation. *Annals of the Academy of Political and Social Sciences, 373*(1), 53–78.

Vertovec, S. (1999). Minority associations, networks and public policies: Reassessing the relationship. *Journal of Ethnic and Migration Studies, 25*(1), 21–42.

Vraga, E., Thorson, K., Kligler-Vilenchik, N., & Gee, E. (2015). How individual sensitivities to disagreement shape youth political expression on Facebook. *Computers in Human Behavior, 45*, 281–289.

Wada, T. (2005). Civil society in Mexico: Popular protest amid economic and political liberalization. *International Journal of Sociology and Social Policy, 25*(1/2), 87–117.

Walzer, M. (1992). The civil society argument. In M. Chantal (Ed.), *Dimensions of radical democracy: Pluralism, citizenship, community* (pp. 89–107). London: Verso.

Walzer, M. (1995). The civil society argument. In B. Ronald (Ed.), *Theorizing citizenship* (pp. 153–74). Albany: State University of New York Press.

Whittington, K. (1998). Revisiting Tocqueville's America: Society, politics and association in nineteenth century. *American Behavioral Scientist, 42*, 21–32.

Wiktorowicz, Q. (2000). Civil society as social control: State power in Jordan. *Comparative Politics, 33*(1), 43–61.

Willig, C. (2003). Discourse Analysis. In J. Smith (Ed.), *Qualitative psychology: a practical guide to research methods* (pp. 159–183). London: Sage.

Wilson, J., & Musick, M. (1997). Who cares? Toward an integrated theory of volunteer work. *American Sociological Review, 62*(5), 694–713.

Wolfsfeld, G., Abraham, E., & Abu-Raya, I. (2000). When prophesy always fails: Israeli press coverage of the Arab Minority Land Day protests. *Political Communication, 17*(2), 115–131.

Woods, D. (1992). Civil society in Europe and Africa: Limiting state power through a public sphere. *African Studies Review, 35*(2), 77–100.

Yadgar, Y. (2017). *Sovereign Jews: Israel, Zionism, Judaism*. London: Routledge.

Yazback, H. (2019). In the shadow of the military government: Transformations in the social class of the internally displaced Palestinian in Israel. In A. Jamal (Ed.), *the Conflict: Sociological, historical and geopolitical aspects* (pp. 49–70). Tel Aviv: Walter Lebach Institute.

Yiftachel, O. (1998). Construction of nation and space allocation in the Israeli ethnocracy: Land and communal gaps. *Iyoni Ha-Mishpat* (Law Review), *21*(3), 637–665.

Yiftachel, O. (2006). *Ethnocracy.* Philadelphia: University of Pennsylvania Press.

Yisachar, H. (2009). *Contrarians—sketches of the feminist left counterculture in Israel.* Tel-Aviv: Resling. [Hebrew]

Yishai, Y. (1997). *Between the flag and the banner: Women in Israeli politics.* Albany: State University of New York Press.

Yishai, Y. (1998). Civil society and political transition: Interest politics in Israel. *Annals of the American Academy of Political Science, 555,* 147–162.

Yishai, Y. (2003). *Civil society in Israel.* Jerusalem: Carmel. [Hebrew]

Yishai, Y. (2008). Civil society under deconstruction? A few notes on the current situation. *Civil Society and Third Sector in Israel, 2*(2), 7–27. [Hebrew]

Yona, Y., & Spivak, A. (Eds.). (2012). *To do things different: The model for a well-ordered society.* Tel Aviv: Hakibbutz Hameuchad.

Zertal, E., & Eldar A. (2007). *Lords of the land: The war over Israel's settlements in the occupied territories, 1967–2007.* New York: Nation Books.

Zuniga, H., Jung, N., & Valenzuela, S. (2012). Social media use for news and individuals' social capital, civic engagement and political participation. *Journal of Computer-Mediated Communication, 17*(3), 319–336.

Zureik, E. (1979). *The Palestinians in Israel: A study in internal colonialism, International Library of Sociology.* London: Routledge.

Zureik, E., Lyon, D., & Abu-Laban, Y. (2011). *Surveillance and control in Israel/ Palestine: Population, territory and power.* London: Routledge.

Reports and Documents

Abu-Bader, S., & Gottlieb, D. (2009). *Poverty, education and employment in the Arab-Bedouin society: A comparative view.* Jerusalem: National Insurance Institute and Van Leer Institute, working paper 98. [Hebrew]

Adva Center. (1999). Employment according to trade, continent of origin, group affiliation and gender. Retrieved from http://www.adva.org/ivrit/pearim/occupation-continents.htm [Hebrew]

Haider, A. (2012). Appointed committees for the Arab municipalities are not the solution. *De-Marker*, October 18th, 2012. [Hebrew]. Retrieved from https://www.themarker.com/opinion/1.1845000

Haifa Declaration. (2007). Haifa: Mada Al-Carmel. Retrieved from http://mada-research.org/wp-content/uploads/2007/09/watheeqat-haifa-english.pdf

Hasson, N. (2011, Nov, 15). Who funds Israel's right-wing organizations? *Haaretz.* Retrieved from https://www.haaretz.com/1.5209702

Ilan, S. (2017, April 12). End to transparency?—The number of CSOs asking for discretion rose by 130%. *Calcalist.* Retrieved from https://www.calcalist.co.il/local/articles/0,7340,L-3711307,00.html

Mada Al-Carmel. (2004). *Palestinians in Israel: Socio-Economic Survey 2004.* Haifa.

Mossawa Center. (2009*). Main findings of the 2009–2010 State Budget Proposal and the Needs of the Arab Citizens in Israel.* Retrieved from http://www.mossawa.org/files/files/File/Publications/Main%20findings%20of%20the%202009-2010%20State%20Budget%20Proposal%20and%20the%20needs%20of%20Arab%20Citizens[1].pdf

Mossawa Racism Report. (2009). Retrieved from http://www.mossawacenter.org/default.php?lng=1&dp=2&fl=13&pg=2

Rikaz Center. (2018). *The Palestinians in Israel: 5th Socio-Economic Survey.* Shafa'amr: The Galilee Society.

Sikkuy Report. (2010). *The Equality Index of Jewish and Arab Citizens in Israel.* Jerusalem: Sikkuy. Retrieved from http://www.sikkuy.org.il/wp-content/uploads/2010/12/sikkuy_eng09.pdf

Shizaf, I. (2015). *The sources of funding and transparency of nine CSOs identified with the Israeli right.* Retrieved from http://peacenow.org.il/wp-content/uploads/2015/12/december15.pdf

Swirski, S., Konor-Attias, E. & Lieberman, A. (2019). *Israel: A Social Report—2018.* Tel Aviv: Adva Center.

The Future Vision of the Palestinian Arabs in Israel. (2006). Nazareth: The National Committee for the heads of the Arab local authorities in Israel. Retrieved from https://www.adalah.org/uploads/oldfiles/newsletter/eng/dec06/tasawor-mostaqbali.pdf

The Israel Democracy Institute. (2011). *The Democracy Index 2011.* Jerusalem: The Israel Democracy Institute. Retrieved from https://en.idi.org.il/media/4275/democracy_english.pdf

The Israel Democracy Institute. (2015). *The Democracy Index 2015.* Jerusalem: The Israeli Democracy Institute. Retrieved from https://en.idi.org.il/media/3585/democracy_index_2015_eng.pdf

The Israel Democracy Institute. (2016). *The Democracy Index 2016.* Jerusalem: The Israeli Democracy Institute. Retrieved from https://en.idi.org.il/media/7811/democracy-index-2016-eng.pdf

The Israel Democracy Institute. (2017). *The Democracy Index 2017.* Jerusalem: The Israeli Democracy Institute. Retrieved from https://en.idi.org.il/media/10545/the-israeli-democracy-index-2017.pdf

The Israel Democracy Institute. (2018). *The Democracy Index 2018*. Jerusalem: The Israeli Democracy Institute. Retrieved from https://en.idi.org.il/media/12170/the-israeli-democracy-index-2018.pdf

Index